THE Blue Zones OF Happiness

THE
Blue
Zones
Happiness
OF

Lessons From the World's Happiest People

Dan Buettner

NATIONAL
GEOGRAPHIC

Washington, D.C.

Published by National Geographic Partners, LLC
1145 17th Street NW, Washington, DC 20036

ISBN: 978-1-4262-1848-4

Since 1888, the National Geographic Society has funded more than 12,000 research, exploration, and preservation projects around the world. National Geographic Partners distributes a portion of the funds it receives from your purchase to National Geographic Society to support programs including the conservation of animals and their habitats.

National Geographic Partners
1145 17th Street NW
Washington, DC 20036-4688 USA

Become a member of National Geographic and activate your benefits today at natgeo.com/jointoday.

For information about special discounts for bulk purchases, please contact National Geographic Books Special Sales: specialsales@natgeo.com

For rights or permissions inquiries, please contact National Geographic Books Subsidiary Rights: bookrights@natgeo.com

Interior design: Katie Olsen

Printed in the United States of America

17/QGF-LSCML/1

CONTENTS

Foreword

D AN BUETTNER BRINGS TOGETHER in this book a wonderful mix of inspiring stories and practical recommendations to help you understand happiness and how you might increase it in your own life and in those of people around you.

Unlike those found in many books on happiness, his recommendations are based not on hunches, opinions, or guesswork, but on scientific findings. I have been conducting scientific research on well-being for the past 35 years—on measuring it, determining what causes it, and learning what happens when people achieve it. It is exciting to see a world-class popular writer such as Dan use the findings from the research that I and others have been pursuing.

Some of these recommendations apply to pretty much everyone. Exercising and eating nutritiously are all-around good ideas, for example. Spending quality time with others is also essential for most of us to achieve happiness, no matter where you happen to live. (In a recent study, we found that every person in Costa Rica who was asked mentioned that their family was a source of happiness for them.) Sustainable happiness also requires pursuing our goals and values, developing supportive relationships with others, and engaging in other endeavors that matter.

At the same time, as Dan recognizes, when it comes to happiness, one size does not fit all. Each person must individualize his or her own happiness program. What works for Dan might not work for me. I work long hours and love it, and I have no need or desire to cut back, while Dan recommends that you find a job that allows you to work less than 40 hours a week in order to spend more time socializing. So you can pick and choose from Dan's recommendations to see which ones might work best for you, and then focus on those. Make them a permanent part of your life.

Another valuable aspect of Dan's book is that, besides offering personal suggestions for happier individuals, it also makes policy recommendations for happier communities—again, based on scientific findings. These include such ideas as providing more green space, more bike paths, and more opportunities for people to exercise in nature, as well as zoning that allows residents to shop and work closer to home, reducing the horrendous amount of commuting that many now must undertake. This book is chock-full of such ideas derived from research about things communities can do to make life more rewarding.

The fact is that those around us, including our leaders and our larger social spheres, have a lot to do with our feelings of well-being. Even in a nation such as the United States there are happy and unhappy places, and these have a lot to do with their circumstances and the policies that drive them. We might fool ourselves into thinking our happiness is entirely up to us, but in truth our friends, community, society, and even our nation can do a lot to help or hinder us. Societal and organizational policies complement and enhance people's own activities in determining how happy they are.

It might surprise you to learn that I occasionally come across leaders both in business and government who object to such policies on principle, because they believe that happiness is something that people need to pursue on their own. They view it as a luxury, or a hobby, and say that things such as work, values, and the welfare of society must come first. Some even see happiness as a hedonistic endeavor, concerned with individual pleasure rather than the well-being of others.

These ideas are 100 percent wrong, and they fly in the face of all the scientific evidence we have collected. We now know that happiness is an essential part of functioning well, and that it gives a boost in well-being not only to individuals, but also to those around them, their communities, and their societies. Rather than being a luxury to be pursued only after we take care of the more important things in life, happiness is beneficial to everything else we desire: It aids our health and helps us live longer; it aids our social functioning and makes us better citizens; it helps us perform better at work; and it builds up our resilience, which enables us to bounce back after setbacks and or when bad events occur in our lives. The happier we are, the better we are for our friends and family, our workplaces, our communities, and our society as a whole.

By contrast, angry and depressed people do not function as well as those who enjoy life and find it rewarding and meaningful. People who frequently experience negative emotions suffer from worse health, tend to be less cooperative, and are found to be less helpful to others on the job, while happy workers tend to be more creative, energetic, and productive. The happiest people are superstars of giving support to others, which makes everyone perform better. It is important for business leaders to understand that employees who enjoy their work are likely to outperform others, and that companies with many such employees are more likely to thrive.

There are many things I love about Dan Buettner, the author of this book. He is an adventurer who loves life. He has set world records by biking across Asia, North and South America, and down the length of Africa. He has prepared stories for *National Geographic* in remote and exotic locations. He traveled the world to find the places where people live the longest, and then, perhaps more important, he fashioned a health and wellness program that cities here in the United States can adopt to create healthier and happier lives for their own citizens. Now that work has extended across many cities, helping many more experience the benefits of living in a healthier society.

Let me say, finally, that Dan Buettner is a great guy. In reading his book, filled with both intriguing individual stories and valuable recommendations, one cannot help but go away happier. If you truly pursue and practice Dan's recommendations, you will have a more rewarding life, and you will create better lives for those around you.

Happy reading!

—Edward F. Diener
Professor of psychology at the University of Utah and the
University of Virginia
Senior Scientist for the Gallup Organization
Author of *Happiness: Unlocking the Mysteries of Psychological Wealth*

PART ONE

Blueprint for a Happier Life

W HEN I FIRST MET ARNETTE TRAVIS, my initial impulse
was to hug her. Her round face radiated warmth. We
sat down at an outdoor café in Redondo Beach, California. She was wearing a white smocklike blouse, long dangling
earrings, and Jackie-O sunglasses pushed up on her hair, which
made her look younger than her 61 years. She crossed her arms and
leaned in eagerly on her elbows.

"How can I help?" she asked.

"You just did," I said. "I feel happier already."

Travis had moved from Kentucky to Redondo Beach to pursue the
California dream of sunshine and a healthier life, she told me. She had
a good business working at home as an investment adviser, but she
was feeling increasingly isolated. When she did get out of the house—
to the store, to drop her daughter off at school, or to see a client—her
trips were always in the car, often in choking traffic. She wasn't getting
enough exercise, and she gained weight. Except for her husband, her
teenage daughter, her ailing mother for whom she cared, and a pair of
friends back in Kentucky, she didn't have any personal connections.

Then her life started to unravel. Within six months, she lost both
of her dear friends in Kentucky, her mother had a fatal heart attack,
and her beloved dog died. "I just imploded," she said. "I was sinking
into a very dark place, and I realized I didn't want to go there. But
I didn't see an exit."

Travis found a way out of her dark pace—but in a way that might
surprise you. She didn't attend a seminar, buy a self-help book, seek

counseling, or take an antidepressant. Instead, she found ways to reshape her surroundings to favor happiness. She made changes in her social network, her work environment, her house, and the way she spent her free time, all of which nudged her life toward greater health and well-being. It didn't take willpower so much as changes to the environment that she called her own. Arnette Travis had learned something powerful about finding happiness—and in the pages that follow, I'll show you how you can do that, too.

Like many happy people, Arnette Travis didn't set out to create the framework for a more satisfying life. She made a few life choices, one by one, and they all added up to big changes. She made friends with a group of healthy-minded women who got together several times a week to walk and talk about each other's lives. Then she took a fresh look at her house and set up various nudges to get her moving more and eating better (such as putting junk food in an out-of-the-way drawer in the kitchen). She attended a "purpose workshop" and realized that her true passion in life wasn't financial planning or selling insurance, but rather nurturing and bringing people together. As a result, she started volunteering, signing people up for exercise classes and fun runs.

Travis made a new best friend, Taylor, and together checked out a Zumba class, at first just watching from the sidelines. "Then at a certain point we looked at each other and said, 'Why not?'" Travis remembered. "Taylor gave me the courage to try it, and it stuck." Travis also began bike-riding with her husband.

Without really noticing it, Travis began to modify her old habits. Although she'd smoked for 42 years, she now found it inconvenient with her new lifestyle, and even embarrassing to smoke around her new acquaintances. Her new lifestyle gave her the helpful nudge she needed to quit.

"This may sound frou-frou but these new things I've been doing have made me happier than I've ever been in my life," Travis told me. And then she paused, looking up at an imaginary point on the ceiling. Her eyes welled with tears. "I'm not going to cry," she said, when she saw me looking at her. "It's just that it was so hard for so many years." And then tears rolled down her face.

Within a year of taking action, Travis had turned her life around. She had a clear focus for her life, had a half-dozen new friends, felt fitter, and was, as she put it, "seeing life without the dark glasses."

Arnette Travis is one of many people who have found the best way to redesign her life to make it happier. I've been fortunate enough to get to know many people on the same path, because that has been my focus now for more than 15 years—meeting the people throughout the world who are living the healthiest, happiest, most long-lasting lives and discovering what the rest of us can learn from them. I've traveled to the statistically happiest parts of the world, gotten to know the people who live there, and learned their lessons on happiness. I've convinced the scientists at Gallup and other big databases to run the numbers and discern what factors favor happiness. Finally, I've worked with more than 20 of the world's top experts to distill the most effective strategies to boost life satisfaction, both in society and in the lives of individuals. The suggestions that have emerged from these investigations are both simple and challenging, and they represent the basics of a blueprint for a better life.

This is a book about designing your life to make it happier. No matter where you live, what challenges you might be facing, or what aspirations you may hold for you and your family, this book can help. It offers simple, evidence-based steps you can take to improve your happiness for the long run. No one can guarantee you greater happiness. But I promise you that if you read this book and take action, you'll be stacking the deck in your favor.

CHAPTER I

 ❧

What Is Happiness?

WHO IS THE WORLD'S HAPPIEST PERSON? He may be a father over age 55 who lives in Cartago, a region south of San José in Costa Rica's Central Valley. He socializes at least six hours a day and has a handful of good friends he can turn to on a bad day. He sleeps between seven and nine hours per day, wakes to a big breakfast, walks to work, and eats at least six servings of vegetables per day. He's a soccer fan. He puts in fewer than 40 hours per week at a job with friends who are a bunch of jokesters. He watches no more than an hour of TV a day. He spends at least two hours every week volunteering, and he worships on the weekend. He makes enough money to put food on the table and a roof over his and his family's heads, to put his kids through school, and to pay for basic health care. He trusts the local police, the politicians governing his country, and his neighbors. We'll call him Alejandro.

Or she may be a young woman living near Aalborg, Denmark. The daughter of an educated mother, she lives with her husband and two young daughters in a tightly knit neighborhood with 21 other families who share a large garden, toolshed, and community kitchen.

She works as a development consultant in social psychology, a job that challenges her and allows her to put her strengths and passions to work every day. She's an extrovert who married an introvert, but she and her husband share values, and over the years they've negotiated a strong love for each other. She doesn't raise her children alone—the neighborhood does. Kids play together, run in and out of neighbors' houses, and sometimes stay overnight with one another. Most of her neighbors are friends with whom she socializes about six hours per day. All the families eat communal dinners together that they take turns preparing. She and her family bicycle to work, to the store, and to her children's school, which helps keep them fit. She pays high taxes on her modest salary, but in return she gets health care and education for her family, as well as a guaranteed income for a comfortable retirement in the years to come. We'll call her Sidse.

Or maybe the world's happiest person lives in the tiny nation of Singapore. He drives a $750,000 BMW and lives in a $10 million house. He has a beautiful wife and three well-behaved children who are "A" students. He grew up without a lot of money, but he put himself through school working four jobs and eventually started a company that grew into an $80 million multinational enterprise. He puts in about 60 hours per week, splitting his time between his business and philanthropic work. He's loved by his family, respected by his employees, honored by his country, and envied by his peers. Although he's succeeded largely because of his own hard work and ingenuity, he leads from behind, freely sharing the credit for his accomplishments. He's proud of his country, happily pays his taxes, and has given back millions of dollars over the years to his community. We'll call him Douglas.

Alejandro, Sidse, and Douglas are all real people. You'll meet each of them again later in this book. I'm profiling them here briefly because the details of their lives map out the three basic strands of well-being. I call them the "three P's" of happiness: pleasure, purpose, and pride. Although at first glance these strands may seem quite different from one another, we often find them braided together in the lives of the world's happiest people—and in the chapters that follow I'll show you how to identify these three strands in your own life and weave them together to boost your happiness.

Consider Alejandro's strand of happiness. He enjoys life from moment to moment, laughing and smiling in the company of people he likes. I call this strand of happiness "pleasure," representing the sum of moments in Alejandro's life that scientists would call his experienced happiness or positive affect. Researchers measure it by asking people how often they smiled, laughed, or felt joy during the past 24 hours (a period most people can remember accurately). They also typically ask if their day was free of negative feelings such as pain, anger, or worry.

Sidse represents what I call the "purpose" strand of happiness. It has to do with living out your values and passions in the service of a greater purpose. Academics refer to this as eudemonic happiness, a term that comes from the Greek word for "happy." The concept was made popular by Aristotle, who believed that true happiness came only from a life of meaning—of doing what was worth doing.

Douglas represents what I call the "pride" strand of happiness, which has to do with how satisfied people are with their accomplishments and positions in life. Researchers often measure this type of happiness with a tool called the Cantril Self-Anchoring Striving Scale, a technical name for a method of asking someone to rate his or her life overall on a scale of zero to 10. Scientists call this evaluative happiness, in that people offer an assessment of how satisfied they are with their life overall. It's an important measurement because it's all-encompassing.

But the people who live in the world's happiest places, as we'll see in the chapters that follow, manage to weave all three "P's" of happiness into their lives. They combine pleasure, purpose, and pride into a resilient form of well-being. They follow the interests of their heart with enthusiasm, but not at the expense of feeling joy and laughter, and they look with pride on what they are doing or what they have already accomplished. And they're able to do this, in many cases, because the places where they live—their nations, communities, neighborhoods, and family households—give them an invisible lift, constantly nudging them into behaviors that favor long-term well-being.

In writing this book, I've tapped the world's most credible scientific sources to help you set up your life to be happy for the long run. In reading it, I think you will gain a deeper understanding of what authentic happiness means and how you can get more of it. As proven by the people who live in the world's happiest places—from the rural villages of Costa Rica to the crowded skyscrapers of Singapore—lasting happiness isn't something just for privileged, suburban, latte-drinking, yoga-trained Americans. It's something that everyone can create for themselves and their families—whether they're farmers, suburbanites, or city folks. No matter where you live, this book will tell you how to arrange your house, curate your social network, manage your finances, optimize your work life, and ground yourself in meaning and purpose. It won't give you instant fixes, but it will tell you how to stack the proverbial deck in favor of the most joyful, fulfilling, and appropriate life for you. In the end, it will show you how to combine all three strands of happiness—pleasure, pride, and purpose—into a strong, durable rope.

DISCOVERING THE BLUE ZONES

This book distills the lessons of the world's happiest people. It builds on a methodology I developed for unraveling the secrets of the longest-lived people. In 2002, with a grant from the National Institutes of Aging, I commissioned a team to identify places where people lived the longest. Together with Michel Poulain, a Belgian demographer, and Dr. Gianni Pes, an Italian physician and medical statistician, we identified five areas that we called the world's Blue Zones.

We found that the longest-lived women resided in Okinawa, Japan; that the longest-lived men inhabited a cluster of mountain villages on the Italian island of Sardinia; and that middle-aged individuals with the longest and healthiest lives could be found in the Nicoya region of Costa Rica. Off the coast of Turkey, we discovered that people on the Greek island of Ikaria lived about eight years longer than most Americans and largely without dementia. And in Loma Linda, California, we found a population of Seventh-day Adventists who lived about a decade longer than their Californian neighbors.

Next, with a grant from National Geographic, I recruited teams of experts to help me tease out the characteristics of longevity in these Blue Zones. Remarkably, wherever we found long-lived populations, the same healthy practices seemed to be present. About five years into the project, I was struck with an epiphany: In a place like Okinawa, where I met a 100-year-old teaching karate, no one had ever set out to live forever. None of the spry centenarians that I encountered had resolved at age 50 to adopt a better diet, start exercising, or begin taking supplements. Longevity had just happened to them.

In other words, instead of seeing a long, healthy life as a goal that required discipline, effort, and a prescribed routine, people in the Blue Zones found that it occurred almost naturally; it flowed from their surroundings. In these places, it seemed, the healthy choice wasn't just the deliberate choice; it was the unavoidable choice. Grains, greens, and beans—which many studies have linked to healthy, long lives—were the least expensive and most accessible foods in these places. People used time-honored recipes to make food tasty, and their kitchens were set up to allow fast and easy preparation. When friends and neighbors got together, they often shared the same healthy meals as part of their regular social activities. Being lonely wasn't an option. And in all of the Blue Zones, people had a vocabulary for their purpose in life. People knew why they woke up in the morning. They were able to describe their responsibilities, and they pursued their passions into their 10th decade. They lived not only long lives but also rich, happy ones.

In my first book, *The Blue Zones: Lessons for Living Longer From the People Who've Lived the Longest*, I described the factors shared by the world's longevity champions as the "Power 9," a cross-cultural distillation of best practices. Since then, these recommendations have become a kind of shorthand for the Blue Zones approach to a better life. In a nutshell, here they are:

1. **Move Naturally.** *The world's longest-lived people don't pump iron, run marathons, or join gyms. Instead, they live in environments that constantly nudge them into moving. They grow gardens and don't have mechanical conveniences for house and yard work. Every trip to work, to a friend's house, or to church occasions a walk.*

2. **Purpose.** *The Okinawans call it* ikigai, *and the Nicoyans call it* plan de vida; *for both it translates to "why I wake up in the morning." In all the Blue Zones, people had something to live for beyond just work. Research has shown that knowing your sense of purpose is worth up to seven years of extra life expectancy.*

3. **Downshift.** *Even people in the Blue Zones experience stress, which leads to chronic inflammation, associated with every major age-related disease. The world's longest-lived people*

have routines to shed that stress: Okinawans take a few moments each day to remember their ancestors, Adventists pray, Ikarians take a nap, and Sardinians do happy hour.

4. **The 80 Percent Rule.** Hara hachi bu—*the 2,500-year-old Confucian mantra spoken before meals on Okinawa—reminds people to stop eating when their stomachs are 80 percent full. The 20 percent gap between not being hungry and feeling full could be the difference between losing weight and gaining it. People in the Blue Zones eat their smallest meal in the late afternoon or early evening, and then they don't eat any more the rest of the day.*

5. **Plant Slant.** *Beans, including fava, black, soy, and lentils, are the cornerstone of most Blue Zones diets. Meat—mostly pork— is eaten on average only five times per month, and in a serving of three to four ounces, about the size of a deck of cards.*

6. **Wine @ 5.** *People in all Blue Zones (even some Adventists) drink alcohol moderately and regularly. Moderate drinkers outlive nondrinkers. The trick is to drink one to two glasses per day with friends and/or with food. And no, you can't save up all week and have 14 drinks on Saturday.*

7. **Belong.** *All but 5 of the 263 centenarians we interviewed belonged to a faith-based community. Denomination doesn't seem to matter. Research shows that attending faith-based services four times per month will add 4 to 14 years of life expectancy.*

8. **Loved Ones First.** *Successful centenarians in the Blue Zones put their families first. They keep aging parents and grandparents nearby or in the home, which also lowers the disease and mortality rates of their children. They commit to a life partner (which can add up to three years of life expectancy), and they invest in their children with time and love, which makes the children more likely to be caretakers when the time comes.*

9. **Right Tribe.** *The world's longest-lived people choose, or were born into, social circles that support healthy behaviors. Okinawans create* moais—*groups of five friends that commit to each other for life. Research shows that smoking, obesity, happiness, and even loneliness are contagious. By contrast, the social networks of long-lived people favorably shape their health behaviors.*

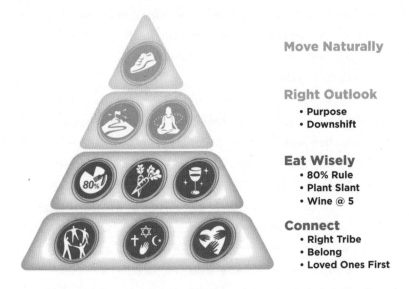

Move Naturally

Right Outlook
- Purpose
- Downshift

Eat Wisely
- 80% Rule
- Plant Slant
- Wine @ 5

Connect
- Right Tribe
- Belong
- Loved Ones First

Following these nine habits won't guarantee that you'll make it to age 100, of course. As I often like to say, you have to win the genetic lottery to become a centenarian. But if you use the Power 9 as daily guidelines, you'll stand an excellent chance of adding happy years to your life.

BUT COULD IT WORK IN AMERICA?

After writing a cover story for *National Geographic* magazine about the world's longest-lived peoples and publishing my first book on the subject, I wondered if we could take lessons from the Blue Zones and use them to transform an American community. Could we take a town looking for change and make it healthier and happier? I'd heard about a remote region in eastern Finland that had done just that. North Karelia was home to 170,000 hardy Scandinavians, most of them from dairy farming families. In the 1970s they were suffering from unusually high rates of cancer and cardiovascular disease—some of the highest in the world. Men were dropping dead at age 55. The Finnish Department of Health assigned a young epidemiologist, Pekka Puska, to investigate. He discovered that North Karelians were exceptionally fond of not only cigarettes but also a diet that included tons of sausage and other processed meats, cheese fried in butter, and almost no vegetables except potatoes. They were literally smoking and eating themselves into heart attacks. But instead of trying to change the behavior of individuals, Puska and his team took aim at the whole ecosystem.

Working with local women's organizations, Puska's team lobbied against smoking and introduced healthier versions of traditional recipes. They persuaded sausage manufacturers and bakeries to produce foods with less fat and salt. They developed a local market for canola oil. They encouraged farmers to grow and preserve greater quantities of berries, the only native fruits in the region. They recruited members of the community to serve as "ambassadors" of the new movement. And over time, these changes began to pay off. After five years, the heart attack rate among middle-aged men fell by 25 percent. Lung cancer dropped by 10 percent. They were on their way.

Inspired by Puska's success, but daunted by the obvious difficulty of such an endeavor, I began more seriously to investigate the idea of creating an American Blue Zone. In partnership with the University of Minnesota School of Public Health, I secured a grant from AARP (formerly the American Association of Retired Persons) to see if a pilot project using the tenets of the Blue Zones could transform an entire town. I knew that the average American spends most days within 10 miles or so of his or her home and workplace—what we called a Life Radius. So I reasoned that if we could embed nudges toward optimal habits throughout an American community, as Puska had done in North Karelia, we'd end up with a healthier, happier population by default.

We chose Albert Lea, Minnesota, a town of 18,500 people near the southern border with Iowa, for our pilot program. During the next two years, we put the plan into action. Every school in Albert Lea took part, making healthy changes, as did the big grocery store chains and most workplaces and restaurants. The city created four community gardens, made downtown more walkable, and built a path around a lake. Just as we hoped, 25 percent of the adult population took steps to optimize their homes, social networks, and sense of purpose. After all these changes, the average life expectancy in Albert Lea increased by three years, residents had shed at least two tons of weight, and health care costs for city workers fell by some 40 percent.

Since then, our Blue Zones Project teams have engaged with communities all across the country. We're now working in 31 cities, from Naples, Florida, to Fort Worth, Texas, to the Big Island of Hawaii. In 2001, we accepted a challenge from Governor Terry Branstad to help transform the entire state of Iowa into the healthiest in the nation. (At the time, it ranked 19th. It has since climbed five spots.) We launched projects in 15 Iowa communities, from small towns like Harlan to big cities like Cedar Rapids. In every community we've been invited into, we've found the dynamic: Longevity, health, and happiness happen simultaneously. Whether people try volunteering, community gardens, purpose workshops, bicycle lanes, walking groups, parks and green spaces, or some other initiative, they end up feeling better—and feeling better about their lives.

So, why has a project that focused on health turned its spotlight on happiness? Because our experience, echoed by recent studies, shows that the connection between health and happiness is a two-way street. People with positive attitudes tend to smoke less and exercise more, eat better foods, wear their seat belts more often, take their medicines more regularly, have stronger immune systems, and enjoy better cardiovascular health. There's also evidence that happier people recover from illnesses faster, that emotional vitality reduces the risk of strokes, and even that an optimistic spouse can improve a patient's outcome. Being happy actually helps you to become healthier.

LEARNING TO THRIVE

At the same time that Blue Zones Project teams were pushing ahead with community projects, it became obvious to me that the pursuit of happiness was worth its own investigation. So in addition to working on health and longevity, I began a parallel search for the root causes of happiness. If we could identify places around the world where people led happier lives, just as we had found the places where people lived the longest, perhaps we could learn and share their secrets, too.

I realized, of course, that getting my arms around happiness was going to be trickier than it had been with longevity. To determine a region's longevity, one needs only to gather reliable statistics on births and deaths. The rest is simple math. But determining a region's happiness was likely to be more complicated. What did we mean by happiness, anyway? Kathy's notion of a perfectly happy night might be reading a book in front of a fire, while Dan's might be a raging party with shots of tequila. Was it even possible to measure something as personal as happiness if people experienced it in such different ways?

The surprising answer was yes, as I quickly discovered from a review of the research. For decades, scientists around the world had been collecting a mountain of data on happiness, often using surveys to measure how happy people felt at a certain point in time and correlating those data with other information from their lives to figure out the likely causes of their happiness. One of these scientists, Ruut Veenhoven of Erasmus University in Rotterdam, the Netherlands, managed the World Database of Happiness, a collection of thousands of studies examining the "subjective enjoyment of life" from every angle. For Veenhoven, as for many other researchers, the best way to measure people's happiness was simply to ask them. If people say they are happy, then they are happy.

Many surveys of "subjective well-being," as this form of happiness was called, include the Cantril Self-Anchoring Striving Scale, mentioned earlier. Developed in 1965 by a public opinion expert named Hadley Cantril and his colleagues at Princeton University, this technique asked you to imagine a ladder with steps numbered from zero at the bottom to 10 at the top. If the top represented the best possible life for you and the bottom represented the worst, then on which step of the ladder would you say you were standing at that time? The idea was to quantify your sense of how well you were doing in your life.

The "Cantril ladder," as it's also known, turned out to be a reliable research tool, especially for measuring what researchers call the "evaluating self," akin to what we are calling the "pride" strand in this book. The Cantril ladder is now an important part of both Gallup's World Poll, which annually measures happiness levels in over 150 nations, and the Gallup-Sharecare Well-Being Index, which measures aspects of a life well lived by interviewing 500 Americans a day across the country. Like many other surveys, these polls also ask people a second type of question about how they felt the previous day: whether they laughed or smiled, were happy, were angry, or were worried. This question taps into what we are calling the "pleasure" strand of happiness, and what researchers call the "experiencing self." A third type of question on these types of polls addresses a person's sense of purpose, asking if they believed that the things they did in their lives were "worthwhile." Taken together, these categories of questions explore the important ways that people experience and interpret happiness, each of which must be measured to provide a full picture of well-being.

That partly explains why, when asked to rank countries by happiness levels, the big surveys don't always agree. In some polls, the wealthy nations of Europe, especially those in Scandinavia, seem to dominate the top positions. According to the *World Happiness Report* for 2017, for example, the happiest nations included Norway, Denmark, Iceland, Switzerland, and Finland. In other surveys, the top spots tend to go to Latin American nations, as in the 2014 Gallup-Sharecare Global Well-Being Index, which listed Panama, Costa Rica, Brazil, Uruguay, El Salvador, and Guatemala among the highest-ranking countries. The variation among these lists, I learned, was due in part to the differences in the metrics used to measure what I understood as the "pride" or "pleasure" strands of happiness.

No matter the poll, though, you'll always find the countries wracked by violence, poverty, or disease at the bottom of the rankings. People who are worried about their safety, livelihood, or health have no time for the kinds of activities that lead to satisfaction and joy, which is why nations such as the Central African Republic, Burundi, Tanzania, Syria, and Rwanda barely register on happiness scales. As a rule, income levels need to rise before happiness levels can. The tiny nation of Bhutan, for example, with a gross domestic product (GDP) per person of only $2,350, still ranks 84th in happiness surveys despite the fact that its leaders have famously made happiness a goal of their public policies.

Once a country's basic needs are covered, other factors become more important than income in determining its well-being. As the authors of the *World Happiness Report* write, a nation's happiness won't begin to soar until corruption levels are low, good health care is available, generosity is common, people feel free to make important decisions in their lives, they have friends they can count on during times of trouble, and they find more time in their day for laughter than for anger, worry, or sadness. Even though prosperity levels have a big impact on happiness levels, in other words, so do cultural and geographical factors. Which explains how a self-sufficient Latin American farmer with few possessions can describe himself as a happy man, while a wealthy European with few friends can admit he's miserable.

Surveys were useful starting points to drill down into the unique characteristics of each place's happiness. But I reasoned that the world's statistically happiest places could also offer insights. So in 2008 I set out to explore three of the nations commonly ranked among the happiest—Denmark, Singapore, and Mexico—selecting them, in part, to represent varieties of well-being on three different continents. (Later, I decided to add the California town of San Luis Obispo for a U.S. perspective.) In each of these locations, I interviewed economists, psychologists, political experts, journalists, writers, and others to understand that locale's particular formula for happiness. Others were kind enough to share their stories with me as well. What emerged was a more nuanced sense of how happiness and satisfaction could evolve from a mix of hardship and hope. The result of this fieldwork was *Thrive: Finding Happiness the Blue Zones Way,* my first book on the subject of happiness, which came out in 2010.

CHAPTER 2

❧

What We Now Know About Happiness

A LOT HAS HAPPENED in happiness research since 2010. During the past five years alone, more than 14,000 academic papers have been published on the subject, written by psychologists, economists, sociologists, and policy experts of all stripes. Among the most exciting developments has been a surprising new trend among world leaders to acknowledge that a population's happiness should be a legitimate goal of public policy—an idea that resonates with my own aspirations for Blue Zones Communities. Politicians such as Germany's Angela Merkel and the U.K.'s David Cameron have endorsed the idea that measurements of life satisfaction—and the factors that shape it, such as greater employment, adequate housing, health care, and a clean environment, among others—should be considered alternative ways of measuring social progress alongside purely economic ones such as the GDP. "We often don't prioritize what's important to people," Merkel said in 2012 at a conference on well-being. Cameron called improving our society's sense of happiness "the central political challenge of our time."

More and more, the recent science of happiness is informing individual strategies. For instance, researchers who have compared the lives of identical twins (who share nearly identical DNA) with those of siblings (who don't) estimate that our genetic makeup accounts for only about half of the differences that we all experience in our happiness levels. Life circumstances, such as our upbringing, account for only about 10 percent of the differences. The rest is shaped by our behavior, which includes how we think as well as what we do. What this means is that a lot of factors besides genetics can affect our happiness—many of which we are capable of changing.

Positive psychology offers several evidence-based strategies for improving our well-being, including mindfulness, meditation, cultivating gratitude, developing resilience, learning to savor experience, and so on. This is valid research: Cultivating such practices will almost certainly improve your happiness. The problem with most of this advice is that it requires you to learn something new and then apply it for a long time. When you stop this behavior—whether it's mindfulness, gratitude, savoring, or whatever—you risk losing the positive effect. That's why I tend to think about such strategies in the same way that I think about diet and exercise programs: They may work in the short run, but they almost always fail over time. They're quick fixes that may evaporate before you know it.

Another painful truth is that many of the things we believe will make us happy are just plain wrong. Like taking a new job because the pay is better, or spending more to buy a bigger house, or picking someone as your mate because he or she is better looking than the competition. All of these assumptions have been proved to be unreliable. What about getting married, for example? Does it really yield greater happiness in life? The answer is yes and no.

Most research shows that married people are happier than single ones. But happiness peaks just after marriage, and then it gradually decreases over time. Whom you marry also matters. Happy people do better if they marry other happy people. Unhappy people, on the other hand, fare better with an unhappy partner. (Maybe misery really does love company?) That said, tying the knot isn't for everyone, studies show. People who tend to shy away from conflict may be happier if they stay single, and committed couples who cohabit without tying the knot tend to enjoy happiness at levels comparable to those enjoyed by their married counterparts.

The questions keep rolling in. What about hobbies, sleep, and health? If happiness is your goal, what else should be your focus? And how do our communities, workplaces, and social networks affect our well-being?

BUILDING A CONSENSUS

Considering the blizzard of advice out there in the bookstores (Google lists more than 24,187 happiness titles) and the mounting pile of counterintuitive findings in academic libraries, I decided to do a metastudy of sorts to sift through all the findings and come up with something manageable, concrete, reliable, and practicable. Working with Toben Nelson of the University of Minnesota and Ruut Veenhoven, manager of the World Database of Happiness mentioned above, I enlisted a blue ribbon panel of the world's leading happiness experts—economists, psychologists, sociologists, and statisticians—to take part in the first experiment of its kind to gather and rank the best ideas about happiness, including practical recommendations, not only about how to promote it in our societies but also how to boost it in ourselves. I have come to call this enterprise the Blue Zones Happiness Consensus Project.

These experts included well-known authors such as Dan Ariely of Duke University, who wrote the *New York Times* best seller *Predictably Irrational*, and Sonja Lyubomirsky, who wrote the best-selling *The How of Happiness: A New Approach to Getting the Life You Want*, as well as influential policy makers such as Lord Richard Layard of the London School of Economics, David Halpern of the United Kingdom's Behavioural Insights Team, and Bruno Frey of the University of Basel. Carol Graham of the Brookings Institution, Ed Diener of the Universities of Virginia and Utah, and a dozen other luminaries in their fields also generously gave the project their time and advice. (Take a look at their credentials in the appendix to this book, pages 255-271.) Their initial effort produced more than 120 recommendations in 11 categories, such as financial, environment, and health, ranked according to effectiveness, feasibility, and cost. Over the course of eight months, through round after round of carefully structured deliberations, we winnowed their many ideas down to the Top Ten Policies to improve the happiness of the greatest number of citizens (see page 253), and the Top Ten Practices that an individual can adopt to boost her or his own happiness, which are integrated throughout the book and listed in full on page 254. More on those illuminating findings, and on the fascinating process for the Consensus Project, lie ahead.

YOUR PERSONAL BLUEPRINT FOR HAPPINESS

So what does all this mean for you? How can you set up your own life to favor greater happiness? In the long run, I hope that this book will show you how.

The first step is to figure out *How happy are you?* To do so, we invite you to take the short quiz that follows. It's a way to explore in your own life the most important happiness factors we have found in the places around the world where wellness thrives. It is not a scientifically validated set of questions, but it's patterned after the surveys that scientists use to measure happiness, and revised to be simpler, shorter, and easier for you to score yourself. The scoring is based on my intuitive sense of the elements of happiness, drawn from years of research, travel, and observation. Answer each question honestly, and then, as you tally up your scores, you'll get a better sense of where you fall on the happiness continuum. Once you have taken the quiz and seen what it reveals about you and your happiness quotient, we'll use these results to point you in the direction of the most effective things you can do for greater happiness.

THE BLUE ZONES HAPPINESS TEST

The chart on the following pages contains a list of factors that have an impact on one or more aspects of happiness. This test has been designed to help you evaluate how various factors in your life contribute to your experience of pleasure, purpose, and pride.

First, read through the list of statements on the left, considering whether each one is true for you, and place an *X* in the boxes on the left next to all the phrases that apply to you. Don't worry about the columns to the right at first.

Once you are done, return to the beginning. Wherever you marked an *X*, circle the corresponding numbers in each of the three columns on the right. Now add up each column to find your Pleasure, Purpose, and Pride quotients.

The Blue Zones of Happiness

X	Life factors	Pleasure	Purpose	Pride
	You live with a loving partner	1	3	1
	You have kids		3	2
	You don't have kids	1		
	You spend 30 minutes of quality time with your kids at least five times per week	1	1	
	You own a dog	1	3	2
	You volunteer at least one hour per week	1	3	1
	You work less than 40 hours a week	2		
	You spend less than one hour watching TV or playing video games per day	2		
	You spend at least three hours per day socializing with people whose company you enjoy	2	3	2
	You have people in your life you can confide in after a difficult day		3	2
	You earn at least $75,000 per year	1		1
	You get at least 30 minutes of physical activity daily	2		1
	You eat at least six servings of fruits or vegetables daily			1
	You have at least some college education		3	2
	You practice religion at least every month	1	3	1
	Your commute to work is less than 15 minutes	2		1
	You have adequate savings/insurance and feel financially secure	1		2
	You regularly treat yourself to new experiences	1		2
	You have a lot of freedom and control in the work that you do		2	2
	You meditate at least once per week	2	3	2
	You live in a place free of noise and traffic sounds	1		
	You regard yourself as being likable	1		1
	You visit the doctor and dentist at least once per year			1
	Your home has good natural light	1		
	You spend less than one hour per day on social media	1		1
	You spend more than one hour per day on social media	1		
	You have house plants, a fish tank, live near a park, or have a window to view nature	1		1

You have clear life goals and monitor your progress	1	3	2
You get at least 7.5 hours of sleep	2		1
You don't smoke	1		2
You have sex 1-4 times per week	2		1
You don't spend more time on housework than you want	2		
You can articulate your sense of purpose or life mission		3	
You care for loved ones (such as sick children or parents)		3	
You laughed today—either with friends or because of something on TV or social media	2		
You have time to keep up with hobbies you enjoy	2		2
Your Totals			

Each column total tells you something about that strand of happiness in your life:

0–10	Poor
11–19	Fair
20–30	Good
Above 30	Excellent

Ideally, your totals for all three columns are high. But just as a cake recipe calls for eggs, flour, sugar, and baking soda, you don't need just some of every ingredient—you also need each in the right amounts. So to learn where you can make a difference in creating your environment to optimize happiness, pay special attention to any of the three columns to the right where your score falls short of 20. These totals can guide you through the reading of this book as well. Throughout, as we visit people in the world's happiest places and as we consult with our team of happiness experts, we'll keep these three strands of happiness in view.

If your total for the *Pleasure* column is less than 20, that could mean that you need to look for more ways to add fun, awe, and joy to your daily routines. In that case, you might, just to name a couple of possibilities, arrange your living space so it's easier to entertain guests, or find a way to work closer to home. As you will learn, the people of Costa Rica are famous for enjoying life, which they describe as *pura vida,* and they practice this special version of happiness by socializing as much as possible, setting a helpful example for the rest of us. We can all learn from them, and from others, that making new friends can open up a world of possibilities for those of us who want more joy in our lives.

If your total for the *Purpose* column is less than 20, that could be a sign that you don't have enough opportunities in your daily life to use your gifts and talents in pursuit of a meaningful goal. In that case, we'll help you find ways to make an adjustment, from listening to meaningful podcasts during your daily commute to walking a dog, your own or someone else's, on a regular basis. The people of Denmark taught me a lot about living a purposeful life during the time I spent with them. In their view, as I discovered, the best pursuits in life are those that fuel your soul, rather than those that add to your bank account or build up your ego. That's reflected in the fact that Danes work an average of only about 37 hours a week, which gives them ample time to join clubs, play sports, or pursue fulfilling hobbies. Later on in this book, you'll also learn about the "purpose workshops" developed to help residents of our Blue Zones Project demonstration communities identify their passions and interests and then put them to work in their towns. These workshops were designed by Richard J. Leider, who explains in his book *The Power of Purpose* that purpose "requires a goal outside ourselves" and that "only when our focus—our purpose—is larger than ourselves can meaning be deeply savored and long lasting, not just a goal completed and then forgotten."

If your total for the *Pride* column is less than 20, that could mean you've let your life become too busy and you can't point to anything significant that gives you a rewarding sense of accomplishment. In that case you might, for example, look for ways to align your job with your personal interests, set up an automatic savings plan for retirement, or put healthy foods front and center in your kitchen to create a better environment for your health. We'll visit Singapore to see what a life of pride in accomplishment looks like. Success in that tiny island nation means following the rules by advancing your education, getting a good job, providing for your family, and generally meeting or exceeding the expectations of society. Although that might require sacrificing personal pleasure from time to time, it actually brings great satisfaction to Singaporeans, as the nation's founding father, Lee Kuan Yew, hoped it would. Not that the rest of us aren't driven to succeed. There are plenty of hardworking folks in Iowa, Texas, and Hawaii, as well. But Americans seem to be more prone to the trap of "keeping up with the Joneses." As you'll discover, one key to an upward spiral of positive emotion may be to set up our daily routines to increase satisfaction with what we have while avoiding negative comparisons with others.

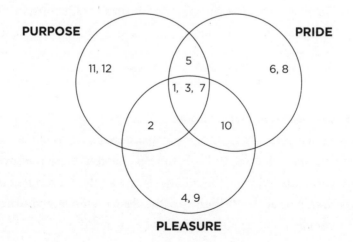

According to all I have learned, from the world's happiest people and the world's happiness experts, the formula for solid, long-lasting well-being weaves all three strands of happiness together. I've come to think of true happiness as overlapping zones of well-being that work like this:

1. You live with a loving partner
2. You spend 30 minutes of quality time with your kids at least five times a week
3. You own a dog
4. You spend less than one hour watching TV or playing video games per day
5. You have people in your life whom you can confide in after a difficult day
6. You eat at least six servings of fruits or vegetables daily
7. You meditate at least once a week
8. You visit the doctor and dentist at least once per year
9. Your home has good natural light
10. You live near nature, whether it's a park close by, houseplants or a fish tank inside, or a window through which you can clearly see outside.
11. You can articulate your sense of purpose or life mission
12. You care for loved ones, such as sick children or aging parents.

I've chosen just a few examples to fill in these circles, but they convey the idea well. Our environments and many of our life choices support one of the three strands of happiness. Some combine two of the strands. Those most likely to bring happiness are the environments and choices in the middle, where all three strands converge. It's up to you—with the help of the ideas, examples, and advice in this book—to find your way to that happy middle.

Taking the Blue Zones Happiness Test is a first step. Through it, you have learned something about the unique mix of ingredients in your own happiness recipe and have learned whether you are shortchanging yourself in one happiness dimension or another. With that knowledge about yourself, let's set out on a journey to three of the world's happiest places. They have a lot to teach us about achieving lives of pleasure, purpose, and pride.

Part Two takes you to the remarkable places all over the world where people live happier lives—so you can see for yourself what their type of well-being looks like. In the chapter about Denmark, you'll meet a young couple from eastern Europe who moved to the city of Aalborg, Denmark, because they were miserable in their home country, and you'll again see Sidse, whose happiness has deep roots in the country as well. You'll also revisit Douglas, from Singapore, who found happiness in amassing a fortune, as well as Alejandro in Costa Rica, who found happiness by giving a fortune away. Their stories portray different paths to experience happiness, and each chapter ends with actionable ideas on how you can put their lessons to work in your own life. As I mentioned earlier, environment plays a huge part in a person's and a community's happiness, so we'll conclude this part of the book by turning to the experts—those who participated in the Blue Zones Happiness Consensus Project—to hear their Top Ten Policies—the most important things that can be done at a national level to make life happier for all. It's fascinating to compare their consensus findings with what I've learned as I've traveled to visit the world's Blue Zones—but if these national recommendations don't interest you, feel free to skip to the following part about creating conditions for happiness in your immediate surroundings.

In Part Three, we'll dive more deeply into your own personal happiness, looking at the factors that have the greatest impact in shaping your sense of well-being. Imagine your world as a series of concentric circles that shape your environment: your community, your workplace, your friends and neighbors, your family, and your inner self. You'll find out why trust plays such an important part in well-being. As we move to the inner circles of your Life Radius, we'll look at evidence-based strategies to design your home, curate a social network, get the most out of your time at work, set up your finances, and reshape your emotional landscape so you're most likely to feel joy, pursue a life of purpose, and feel proud of what you've accomplished.

PART TWO

The World's Happiest Places

I N THIS SECTION, we'll visit three of the world's statistically happiest places and find out why people there are happy. In each case, I've gathered all the available research and statistical analyses to explain why these places are so happy—and happy in different ways. But instead of unleashing a tsunami of facts and figures, I'll introduce you to people who embody key characteristics of each place—and then tell you their stories. Through each person's story, I hope you'll get a richer sense of each strand of happiness—be it pleasure, purpose, or pride.

Notice, too, that none of these places is happy by chance or dumb luck. In each case, an enlightened individual—or group of individuals—set in motion one marquee project or policy that showed people they had control over their happiness. In all three places— the city of Aalborg in Denmark, the island nation of Singapore, and the Cartago region of Costa Rica—happiness had a genesis, a falling domino that set into motion a chain of events that first changed the environment to one that favored well-being and then changed the lives of everyone living there.

At the end of each chapter I'll offer clear, prescriptive takeaways, each one drawn from the lives of people who live in the Blue Zones of Happiness and translated into suggestions that you can put to work in your own life. Then, in the final chapter of this part of the book, I'll share some of the results from the Blue Zones Happiness Consensus Project, which I mentioned earlier. Here we'll take a look at what our panel of experts ultimately discovered to be the Top Ten

Policies that nations should adopt to create an environment conducive to the greatest happiness for all. It's interesting to see how many of those policies coincide with the practices we already see in place in the happiness hot spots of the world.

CHAPTER 3

❧

Happiness in Costa Rica

ALEJANDRO ZUNIGA, an avocado vendor, remembers the call with pristine clarity. It was 8:30 P.M. on July 18, 2014, when his flip phone rang. A friend he worked with at the central market in Cartago, a city just east of San José, had exciting news.

"You've won the lottery!" his friend shouted. He had purchased the winning ticket and was now about to receive 50 million colones (about U.S. $80,000) in the National Lottery.

Zuniga didn't believe him. His friend was a well-known practical joker. Besides, Zuniga wasn't in the mood. It had been a long day, and he hadn't sold all of his avocados. "I thought it was an ugly joke," he recalled. "I was down to my last eight dollars."

He hung up on his friend.

When Zuniga showed up for work the next day at the market, however, his fellow vendors erupted in applause. News of his winning had spread. Each week, he'd given his friend money to bet on the same number, and this time his number had indeed won. His friend could have probably kept his mouth shut and collected the money. Instead, he was there to greet him.

Giddy, Zuniga strode past the produce stalls with an alpha male's long-armed lope and high-fived his friends and colleagues. For decades, the husky 56-year-old had been a fixture at the market, showing up day after day to sell surplus avocados, socialize, and try out a new joke. Everyone knew him. Whenever any of the 60 or so other vendors fell ill or had a family emergency, it was Zuniga who passed a collection box to help. He organized weekend trips to cheer on the city's beloved but ever losing soccer team, C.S. Cartaginés. He was a charismatic friend and a natural leader. Now that he'd struck it rich, his fellow vendors assumed, they'd lose him to a new, more affluent life.

Zuniga had never had it easy. He'd grown up in shanty towns, quit school at 12 to earn a living, struggled with alcohol, and lost the love of his life at age 20. He credited his daughter and the Virgin of Los Angeles, Cartago's patron saint, with his beating the addiction. "I've found that, out of suffering, something positive grows," he said. "Sometimes a little sadness is beautiful."

In the weeks after his lottery win, though, Zuniga surprised his friends by returning to the market as usual, hawking his produce every day with the same zeal. Quietly though, he was giving away his fortune: a million to a friend who sold him the lottery ticket, another million to a food stall owner who fed him in lean times, and another million to a market beggar. The rest he gave to his mother and to the four mothers of his seven children. Within a year, he'd given it all away. He was back to being broke—a twist of fate that might have crushed another man's spirit.

And yet, he insisted, "I couldn't be happier."

How was that possible?

THE LATIN X FACTOR

The answer has to do with the complex calculus of happiness in Costa Rica, where an alchemy of geography and smart social policies has created a powerful blend of family bonds, universal health care, faith, peace, equality, and—a quality that Zuniga possesses in spades—generosity. This all culminates in an especially rich recipe for enjoying life day by day—the strand of happiness we call "pleasure."

Consider Zuniga's circumstances. He has no car, no expensive jewelry, no fine clothes or big electronics. But he doesn't need any of those things for happiness or a sense of self-esteem. His work life affords him an optimal six or more hours of social interaction with people he likes. And he lives in a country that, for most of the past century, has believed in supporting every citizen.

"Costa Rica's social system takes care of most people's needs," said Mariano Rojas, a Costa Rican economist and happiness expert at the Latin American Faculty of Social Sciences Institute in Mexico City. "It leaves them feeling safe, comparatively healthy, free of most of life's biggest worries, while providing an environment where most people can still make a living." In countries like Costa Rica, social connections, family gatherings, and an ability to create happy moments and laugh at adversity seem to make up for a lack of income, he said. People don't get into the trap of overworking, overspending, and undersocializing.

Indeed, Costa Ricans excel in the strand of happiness I described earlier as "pleasure." While Danes find deep "purpose" in their lives and Singaporeans seek to feel "pride" in theirs, Costa Ricans excel at getting the most joy out of their days. According to the *World Happiness Report*, which sums up 10 years of data from 156 countries, the happiness experienced in Costa Rica is driven primarily by high levels of social support from one's family, generosity and trust, a healthy life expectancy, and a sense of freedom to live out one's values.

Over the past six years the World Database of Happiness has consistently ranked Costa Rica first among the happiest Latin American countries. The nation's superlatives abound: It has Latin America's highest literacy rates and lowest corruption rates, is home to one of the world's longest-lived populations (on the Nicoya Peninsula), and is on its way to becoming the first carbon-neutral country on Earth. In short, Costa Rica produces longer, happier lives for less money than any other place in the world.

Generally speaking, the richer a country is, the happier it is. But this effect is most pronounced among nations that are struggling just to provide basic needs. Costa Rica goes beyond that, producing the highest day-to-day happiness, the largest number of happy life-years (the sum of life expectancy and life satisfaction), and one of the world's lowest rates of middle-age mortality. Here, a combination of strong religious beliefs, an extended sense of family, good health, peace, and a sense of equality, trust, and generosity—all statistically associated with well-being—delivers more happiness per GDP dollar than anywhere else.

"You walk around Costa Rica and everybody is saying *pura vida*," said Carol Graham, a happiness economics expert at the Brookings Institution who grew up in Latin America. She is using a term that's hard to translate into English. Literally it means "pure life," but it's commonly used to say "all good" and "take it easy." It epitomizes how much Costa Ricans appreciate life, Graham said. "It shows up in how they manage their country, shows up in how they manage their environment; nobody is walking around toting guns, shooting each other out."

The epicenter of Costa Rica's happiness lies in the 40-mile-long, 15-mile-wide Central Valley, a highland basin tufted with conifers and hemmed by verdant slopes rising to volcanic peaks. More than half of Costa Rica's five million people live here, most in cities such as San José, Heredia, and, most happily, Cartago. Blessed with eternal springlike weather, prosperity, and some of the world's finest coffee, the hardworking people of this valley have found a sweet spot between making a living and savoring it.

In most of Central America, land barons and the military-backed presidents who served their interests dominated the colonial period. Costa Rica was different. With rugged, ravine-etched mountain ranges and a lack of cheap indigenous labor, conditions here discouraged the rise of large haciendas. Instead, small property owners and independent-minded Central Valley farmers thrived, after discovering an international market for coffee. They elected teachers as presidents who, unencumbered by corrosive colonial institutions, introduced policies that launched an upward spiral of well-being.

As early as 1869, Costa Rica made primary school mandatory for every child, including, most notably, girls. By 1930, it boasted the lowest illiteracy rates in Latin America. At the same time, the nation invested in clean water for rural villages, stemming fatal childhood diseases such as cholera and diarrhea and better assuring that children's lives got off to a healthy start. The 1940s brought universal health care and social security. Even the most remote villages had a health outpost to serve pregnant mothers and infants.

And that tradition continues to this day. On a crisp winter morning, I followed a medical technician named Ileana Álvarez Chavez as she toted a backpack and a small cooler of vaccines on her rounds through the leafy Central Valley town of Paraíso. Part of the national program Equipos Básicos de Atención Integral en Salud (EBAIS), or Basic Comprehensive Health Care, the system was set up to support the health of every Costa Rican. Small teams including a doctor, a nurse, a record keeper, and several technicians are assigned the care of about 3,500 people. Ileana's quota called for her to visit 12 homes a day. At each one, she'd spend 30 minutes to update the medical history of residents, take blood pressure measurements, give vaccinations, dispense advice, and check for standing water (where Zika virus–bearing mosquitoes breed).

At the Hernandez-Torres home, Ileana counseled a young mother on a healthy diet for her two-year-old son and left behind vitamins and anti-parasite pills. As she walked through the house, she noted the white bread and milk on the kitchen table, advising to "try to eat more beans, fruits, and vegetables." At the home of 89-year-old Dora Astoria, Ileana inventoried medicines, took blood pressure readings, and set up an appointment for Astoria with her team's doctor. "I can often catch diseases before they erupt into full-blown diabetes or a heart attack," she said. "Many of my clients are lonely and they just appreciate someone who cares."

Since 1970, Costa Rica has seen life expectancy jump from 65 to 80 years and childhood mortality drop by a factor of seven. Cardiovascular mortality among middle-aged individuals is about half that of the United States, even though Costa Rica spends one-fifteenth as much on health care as the United States. The EBAIS program explains much of Costa Rica's extraordinary gains. As former president José María Figueres, who implemented the program, told me, the nation's health care system works so well because it aims to keep people healthy in the first place. "In the U.S. incentives are aligned to drive up costs," he said. "Here, for years, the emphasis has been on the preventive health system, because, quite frankly, the objective of a good health policy is for people not to get sick."

Costa Rica's current president, Luis Guillermo Solís, offered additional insights into Costa Rican happiness. "We abolished the army in 1949," the Tulane-educated historian told me when I met him at the Presidential Palace. "If you go to Honduras, the monuments in the square celebrate military heroes; here we celebrate peace." According to Solís, one monument in San José reads: "Blessed is the Costa Rican mother who never has to worry about her son going to war." He pointed out that almost everyone in Costa Rica gets a free education and that his newly instituted policies giving gays more rights enabled Costa Ricans to live largely without fear.

One afternoon we drove into downtown San José to see if Solís's policies were taking effect. It was late afternoon, and under sunset-lit magenta clouds we turned down a street of tin-roofed houses with caged windows and gated fences topped with razor wire. We pulled in front of one house painted bright orange. Natalia Lazaroni strutted out of the front door in four-inch heels, wearing a skintight leopard-print dress with jet-black shoulder-length hair and fuchsia lipstick. Only a husky voice betrayed her birth gender.

Born Byron Fuentes in Honduras, she switched sexes at 16 and endured years of jeers and abuse. She originally moved to Costa Rica, she said, because prostitution pays better there. But she stayed for the benefits: free health checkups, free psychologist visits, free condoms, a school scholarship, and even the right to draw social security when she retires. Mostly, though, she said that anywhere else in Central America, she'd be humiliated and beaten. I asked her to rate her happiness on a scale of 1 to 10.

"I'm a 9," she said. "Here I'm free to live a life that defines me."

Others reported similar levels of contentment. In Cartago, I talked to a Salvadoran immigrant who'd escaped the civil war of the 1980s and now parks cars, a mother who lives with her three daughters and runs a dress shop, a 104-year-old seamstress, a widow at 31 with six kids who now lives at the center of a huge family compound, and a Colombian refugee named Carlos who arrived in Costa Rica in 2002 with 200 pair of shoes to sell and now owns three businesses. Everyone I met described their happiness as a 9 or 10, and they credited Costa Rica for their well-being.

Designing Equality

He was waiting for me at a Denny's restaurant in Costa Rica's gritty, chaotic capital. It was dusk on a weeknight, and he sat alone at a table in the middle of the dining room, nursing a cup of Lipton tea. A short, energetic-looking man, he wore a white guayabera shirt and loafers. A fringe of brown hair covered his otherwise smooth head. When I stepped up to greet him, he shook my hand, gave my arm a squeeze, and welcomed me to his country.

We'd met by chance a few months before at a social event in another land. When he'd told me he was from Costa Rica, I'd launched us into a spirited discussion of the Nicoya Peninsula, a region of Costa Rica I'd gotten to know rather well during my reporting for *The Blue Zones,* my earlier book about longevity. My new acquaintance seemed to know all about Nicoya, including its complex network of health outposts and its low mortality rate. When I finally got around to asking him what he did for a living, he responded matter-of-factly, "I was the president"—as if he just told me he'd driven a bus.

His name was José María Figueres, and he led Costa Rica's government from 1994 to 1998. After our first encounter, he agreed to meet me again in San José in 2016, where he was still a highly popular public figure. During my interview with him at the restaurant, men and women kept coming up to the table to thank him for his service to the country. I asked the former president about his nation's remarkable success. What was Costa Rica's formula?

"That's not a simple question," he said. "But I would say, first of all, that we've created a very egalitarian society in terms of our social behavior. Everybody talks to everybody else in this country. There is no shyness because this person may have a higher standing in society and this person may have a lower standing. There are none of those barriers. So that's one reason.

"Another reason, I think, is that, over decades, a culture of peace has found its way into our DNA. In some countries that have gone through internal strife, civil warfare, or external warfare, when they have an argument, they chop off their heads. Here our DNA tells us if we have a disagreement, we talk about it.

"A third component, of course, is the very important investment we made in education, which again goes in the same direction of, shall we say, good manners, good social manners."

The former president spoke with pride of his nation's social progress. Costa Rica had overcome many challenges in its recent history. His father, José Figueres Ferrer, had led the revolution in 1948 that had resulted in the founding of modern Costa Rica. Known as "Don Pepe" to the people, his father was a social democrat who disbanded the army, granted full citizenship to women and blacks, nationalized the banks, taxed the wealthy, and strengthened the nation's health care and education systems. And then, after passing more than 800 decrees in 18 months, he'd stepped down, handing over power to a political rival. It was an impressive demonstration of his commitment to the democratic system.

"What was your father's biggest contribution to Costa Rica's happiness?" I asked, wondering if the senior Figueres had well-being in mind when he ruled the country.

"Without a doubt, it was the abolishment of the army, which gave us a culture of peace, civility, and very strong democracy," he said. "My father was a self-taught man, imbued with socialist (in the good sense) thinking and a lot of reading. He wanted to create government programs that would, in a way, level the playing field and open up opportunities for everybody."

Back at the central market in Cartago, Saturday morning shoppers were weaving through the stalls of peppers, onions, beets, yucca, cilantro, plantains, papayas, and greens, dickering over prices with vendors and filling their grocery bags. Amid the din of cheerful commerce and street traffic, the vendors, mostly middle-aged men with nicknames like Fang, Cracker, and Pancake, wearing smudged tank tops or slightly ragged T-shirts, attended to their sales—but mostly they interacted with one another. They operated under an unspoken oath: trust one another, never undercut prices, always lend a hand, and never miss an opportunity to mock one of their own.

At the edge of the market, a palpable wave of excitement rippled through the crowd. It was Zuniga, moving through the stalls in the foyer of the building, where his friends all worked. The vendors clapped and cheered, calling out his sobriquet, "Chambers, Chambers, Chambers," in mocking admiration. (His nickname, which loosely meant "kicking a curveball," referred to his obsession with soccer.) There was something about his presence, his height, his luminescent silver hair, his kinetic motion, that amped up the market's energy level. As he passed by in his blue polo shirt, pressed blue jeans, and hiking shoes, he bumped fists, engaged in dollops of conversation, exchanged market gossip, and dispensed jokes. His afternoon unfolded more like a frat party than a series of business transactions.

Presiding over 200 avocados in neat rows, Zuniga never rested. He whistled a greeting to a passing taxi, helped a delivery boy hoist a dolly up a curve, and shouted "I love you" to a friend across the street, the whole time bagging produce for customers. By late afternoon, as the other vendors began to cover their stalls for the evening, Zuniga still had 50 avocados to unload. I asked him what he planned to do if couldn't sell his inventory. "I'll give them away," he said with a wave. "A giving hand is never empty."

LESSONS: HOW TO LIVE LIKE A TICO

Much of the happiness experienced by Ticos, as Costa Ricans affectionately call one another, may be explained by three factors: extraordinary social support, freedom to make their own life choices, and a culture of generosity. The pura vida mentality of optimism and gratitude suffuses every aspect of life there, from the way people interact with each other to appreciation for the land, which is itself a source of enjoyment and pride.

Costa Rica has adopted innovative measures to protect its natural environment and extraordinary biodiversity. Since 1996, 3.5 percent of the nation's gas tax has been used to support its forests, which have nearly doubled in extent during the past 30 years. Besides contributing to the well-being of Costa Ricans, these policies have also boosted tourism, which has become a leading source of national income. In 2015, Costa Rica became the world's first country to produce 99 percent of its electricity from hydroelectric, geothermal, wind, biomass, and solar sources.

Here, with input from the aforementioned happiness experts Mariano Rojas and Carol Graham and happiness expert Nicole Fuentes of the University of Monterrey, Mexico City, are some tips for setting up your own life to live as cheerfully as a Costa Rican.

1. **Develop daily social rituals.** Costa Ricans are good at creating happy moments every day, with no need for special occasions. Friends get together to watch soccer, play music, prepare carne asada—barbecue—with family or neighbors, drink beer, and tell lots of jokes.

   Lessons: Live close to your friends or make friends of your neighbors. Organize impromptu happy hours, pot lucks, or backyard cookouts. Remember, people are happiest on the days when they socialize five to six hours. Being with others also enhances or prioritizes other activities, such as work, eating, watching TV, or doing housework.

2. **Enjoy special "little" days.** Women get together with girl-friends once a week to bond, laugh, and gossip on what they call *martesitos, miercolitos,* or *juevecitos*—little Tuesdays, little Wednesdays, or little Thursdays. For working women, it's usually in the early evening. For stay-at-home moms, it's often midday. Considered "their time," such get-togethers keep relationships healthy and vibrant.

   Lessons: Join a book club, walking club, or Bible study club—or create one. Set up one time a week when you invite over your best, most committed friends. Make it a ritual. Most of us don't socialize enough to optimize our happiness.

3. **Establish a weekly family ritual.** Costa Rican families tra-ditionally gather for meals on Saturdays or Sundays. They might get together for a late lunch, after which the kids will peel off to play while adults loll around the table for conver-sation. Or people might come early for Sunday dinner and stay late. The key is that they include grandparents, parents, sons, daughters, in-laws, cousins, and close family friends—so the conversations are intergenerational, lively, and often laced with humor.

   Lessons: Set up a weekly family dinner and invite your extended family. If you don't have many relatives nearby or if your family is boring, invite friends who will make the dinner interesting. Cook good food, be a good host, and make it fun so people will come back. A strongly connected family can serve as not only a social network but also a safety net for when times get tough.

4. **Eat together at work.** At the Cartago Market, vendors close their stands at noon to gather around La Marisquería, a seafood restaurant, to enjoy the famous fish soup, rice, and beans. There they blend shop talk, family news, soccer stories, and jokes. These guys are not only refueling their bodies but also their souls.

    Lessons: Resist the temptation to eat at your desk. Invite your co-workers out to lunch or organize a brown bag group. Talk to your employer about a company policy that favors co-workers eating together.

5. **Try a daily dose of humor.** Although Costa Ricans suffer the same hardships as the rest of us, they use humor to get by. When news about a corrupt politician makes people angry, social media erupts in jokes within minutes.

    Lessons: Read the comics as well as the op-ed pages. Watch a funny video on Facebook or YouTube. It can reduce stress as effectively as 20 minutes on a treadmill—and lift your spirits.

6. **Practice your faith.** The vast majority of Costa Ricans are Roman Catholics, especially in Cartago, which is home to the Virgen de los Angeles, the country's patron saint. Locals will tell you that their faith provides them with a sense of purpose and helps to ease the impact of life's hardships. For many, weekly mass is a chance to downshift and shed stress. Their best friends are church friends.

    Lessons: If you have a religion, practice it. If you don't, try out a few places of worship to see if any resonate with you.

7. **Eat six servings of fruits and vegetables a day.** The Cartago market glistens with fruits and vegetables, from papayas and mangoes to beets, cabbage, and yucca. Produce is fresh,

cheap, delicious, and accessible year-round—a daily source of nutrition and pleasure.

Lessons: Eat at least six servings of fruits and vegetables daily. Not only will this improve your health, it will also boost your happiness. Research shows that people who go from no fruit or produce in their diets to eight servings a day experienced a bump in their well-being equivalent to getting a new job.

8. **Shop for groceries daily.** People don't sit around in Cartago, waiting for Amazon to deliver their groceries. Most people walk to the market daily, where they exchange gossip and pleasantries with their favorite vendors and friends, returning home with the freshest foods possible.

   Lessons: Get your daily fix of social interaction, physical activity, and fresh produce by walking to your local grocery store. All three of these are ingredients for day-by-day happiness.

9. **Embrace generosity.** Costa Ricans have a saying, *Dios se lo paga,* which means that what you give in this life, God will pay back in the next. Studies show that generosity pays off, no matter where you live. (Case in point: Researchers at the University of Oregon found that when they gave people $100, participants were happier when they gave it away than when they spent it on themselves.)

   Lessons: Most of us will die with money, so share it now. Be the first to pick up the check at meals, give to charity, and overtip.

10. **Boost happiness in the workplace: the Cartago Code.** The 120 or so vendors at the central produce market in Cartago

observe an unspoken code of conduct that makes for not only good business but also a happy workplace. These men and women spend their careers selling specialty produce— often right next to a stall selling the exact same thing, and they all abide by these implicit rules:

- Start every day with a greeting. No one comes into work without a hello.
- Use nicknames. All have an endearing nickname that reflects their personality. Nicknames serve to create an atmosphere of lighthearted conviviality and familiarity.
- Turn competition into cooperation. Though technically all vendors are competitors, they look for ways to cooperate—Never undercut another's prices, be sure to cover each other's stalls during lunches and breaks, and refer customers to one another.
- Create a community. The vendors share a special bond: more than associates but not quite friends. When one of them gets sick or suffers a death in the family, the others collect money or cover the individual's stand during his or her absence.
- Never pass up a joke. Humor is a more important currency than cash. The vendors compete with one another to share a new joke or poke good-humored fun at a colleague. This creates a low-stress atmosphere of fun.
- Trust "with your eyes closed." This is how the Cartago Carrot Cartel describes their relationship with each other. Vendors do not lock up their money or inventory; and they do not steal one another's clients.

Lessons: Apply these rules to your own circumstances, wherever appropriate.

CHAPTER 4

❧

Happiness in Denmark

E RVINS TRANS MAY SEEM an unlikely poster boy for Danish happiness. A bearded, pony-tailed, self-described nerd who favors coiled scarves and Converse tennis shoes, the 29-year-old spent his first 25 years in Latvia. There, he said, he lived in a corrupt, inefficient society where police took bribes, doctors were overworked, and "firefighters slept drunk while buildings burned," as he put it. He watched his unemployed, spiritually broken father drink himself to death. On a meager stipend from his grandmother, he enrolled in law school while living in dorm rooms he described as "worse than sleeping on a mattress under a bridge." When he realized that a law degree in Latvia would earn him either a poorly paid civil servant job or a career "protecting bad people," he abandoned his studies.

To save money, Ervins moved to a sketchy part of Riga, the capital of Latvia, where he regularly witnessed muggings outside his door. His true passion was computer programming, but he couldn't afford the classes. "I spent a lot of time sitting alone in my room, and I always felt tired," he recalled. "I'd wake up each morning thinking *I have no certainty that I won't kill myself today. And tomorrow might be worse.* In fact, I couldn't see any tomorrow."

In 2012 he met Valerija Trane, a red-haired dynamo with an appetite for elsewhere. She shared Ervins's passion for web design and 3-D computer games. Like him, she'd had enough of Latvia and was feeling miserable. She'd grown up in a school system that required her parents to pay off teachers to teach, and fellow students teased her avant-garde dress and sculpted hair. "I was into the arts—and the arts are considered a silly profession there," she said. Ever since she was young, she'd endured catcalls from men. She didn't feel safe on the streets. She persuaded Ervins to join her in applying to foreign universities. When Denmark's University of Aalborg accepted them, their lives changed forever.

Aalborg is an odd little place located on a placid fjord that smells vaguely like smoked herring. For most of the past century, it was an industrial city—known for cement, pig's feed, and aquavit. Somehow though, when the European Union recently surveyed 83 of Europe's biggest cities, Aalborg topped the list in almost every category that portends a happy life. Aalborg University deserves much of the credit. In 1970, when it shifted its focus from vocational training to the sciences, it seeded a knowledge economy. Wind power, telecommunication, and microchip companies sprouted and thrived, along with a Tetris-like sprawl of blocky buildings designed by architects who apparently enjoyed playing with Legos as children. In August 2012, Ervins and Valerija moved into one of those buildings on the outskirts of Aalborg and started classes.

Their student visas permitted them to hold only part-time jobs. Working 15 hours a week left them worrying about how to make ends meet but like Danish students, Ervins and Valerija paid no tuition or health care costs. A housing stipend enabled them to rent an apartment on the edge of town, and though they couldn't afford a car, Aalborg's neatly gridded bike paths and public transport made it easy for them to travel anywhere in town in minutes. Then the kicker: They discovered that Danish students are typically paid about $900 a month to go to school.

"My upbringing taught me to trust no one," recalled Valerija when I met her at the "Love Café," a meeting place where immigrants from around the world share a potluck meal every Sunday night. "But over time, we've made many friends here. At one point, I actually gave a friend a spare key to my house."

"We're freakishly happy now," Ervins added, telling me that on a 1-to-10 scale, his happiness jumped—from a 4 in Latvia to an 8 in Denmark.

Here were two healthy, intelligent people who only a few years earlier had been miserable, with grim outlooks on life and on the verge of depression. They didn't get rich, cure themselves of a terrible disease, experience great fame or recognition, see a psychologist, take a happiness class, or try any tips or tricks they found in magazines. And yet they were both significantly and enduringly happier.

All they did was move to Aalborg.

HARNESSING HUMILITY

I met Ervins and Valerija on my third trip to Denmark to explore that nation's unique brand of happiness—one that seems to enable people to live a purposeful life better than anywhere else. For the past 40 years, Denmark has most dependably topped the rankings of the world's happiest countries. According to the World Database of Happiness, when people in Denmark are asked how much they enjoy their lives on a 1-to-10 scale, their answers average 8.4. And that happiness is more evenly distributed throughout Danish society than anywhere else on the globe.

Pocket Utopia

If Danish trust comes from a system that takes care of you from cradle to grave, then the young woman I met in the city of Aalborg was the perfect person to tell me what it felt like. I met Sidse Clemmensen in her kitchen, where she was sipping tea. A 35-year-old working mother, she had short brown hair and wore a sleeveless blouse and Moroccan slippers. Apart from the diamond stud in her nose, she looked like a soccer mom.

Clemmensen, her domestic partner, and two daughters (with a third child on the way) were one of 22 families living together in a cohousing complex—a *bofaellesskap,* or "shared home." Each family owned a small Lego-like house, but together all shared a huge garden, laundry, workshop, storage area, parking facility, and dining hall, where they could opt in to communal meals. (Each of the families cooks one or two meals a month for the whole community and then eats the rest of their meals free.) Perched on a low hill overlooking rolling pastures, the complex was conveniently located within biking distance of the neighborhood elementary school and the local university, where Clemmensen works as a researcher.

Of the current families in the co-op, Clemmensen said, two were original owners (former 1970s hippies whose homes were now equipped with laptop computers and espresso machines), four were single, and the rest were young parents. Kids roamed the grounds and surrounding woods on their own, as likely to end up at a friend's house as their own. It was a convenient arrangement for parents, who could find free child care at a moment's notice.

Residents called one another *bofaellas*—something more than neighbors but not quite friends, Clemmensen said. The cohousing design allowed for privacy but also provided nudges to socialize. Step outside and you were likely to bump into neighbors in the garden or at the washing machines.

"Danish cohouses are a nice in-between arrangement, providing a friendship network in an individualist context," said Ruut Veenhoven. In perfectly Scandinavian fashion, they offered an elegant mix of private and public. They also seemed to be an apt metaphor for Danish society as a whole, with its emphasis on trust and social support.

"The state provides me with everything I need," Clemmensen said. "My children are happy. I have a great partner. And I love my job."

As she talked about her life, Clemmensen offered me more tea and a plate of watermelon. She was interrupted only by her two young daughters, who leaped into her lap for a hug and a slice of melon for themselves. It occurred to me that this manufactured community struck the perfect balance between the need for privacy and our instinctual desire for human interaction, support, and trust.

Denmark's happiness, according to Peter Gundelach, a sociologist at Copenhagen University, may be traced to the Second War of Schleswig in 1864, when Denmark lost 40 percent of its territory and population to Prussia. "With that defeat, we lost our ambition to be a world superpower," he said. "It humbled us. Our government began to strengthen our national identity and build inwardly instead."

During the past century and a half, the Danish government has plowed funds into generous social programs, creating a prosperous welfare state with the world's highest gross national product per capita, the highest percentage of the national budget spent on child care, the lowest levels of corruption, and the highest levels of trust in one another—all factors closely linked to happiness. Danes grow up believing they have the right to health care, education, and life-long incomes. University students, as Ervins and Valerija discovered, draw a government stipend in addition to free tuition. It takes the average university student a leisurely 6.6 years to graduate in Denmark, which gives students the time they need to find the vocations and hobbies that will truly satisfy them for the long term. New parents can take a yearlong government-paid parental leave at nearly full salary; this includes gay and lesbian parents, who've been free to marry since 1986. People work hard in Denmark, but they rarely put in more than 37 hours a week or skip vacations. The price for such lavish benefits is the world's highest income tax rate, which starts at 42 percent and tops out at 68 percent for the biggest earners—a field leveler that makes it possible for garbage men to earn more than doctors.

"Danish happiness is closely tied to their notion of *tryghed*, the snuggled, tucked-in feeling that begins with a mother's love and extends to the relationship Danes have with their government," says Jonathan Swartz, an American anthropologist based in Copenhagen. "The system doesn't so much assure happiness as it keeps people from doing what will make them unhappy."

It may also have something to do with the Danish disdain for showiness, a throwback to village life expressed by the *Janteloven*, a list of dos and don'ts set forth in the 1933 novel *A Fugitive Crosses His Tracks* by Aksel Sandemose. You're no smarter than the rest of us, the Janteloven says, so don't even try. Ambition is a character flaw in Denmark; you're more likely to garner respect by riding a bicycle than a BMW. But in the counterintuitive world of Danish happiness, that's also a blessing. In a land where, as the joke goes, the extroverted man is the one looking down at your shoes instead of his own, there's little pressure to show off. The result: a nation in which there is little upside to working too hard at a job you don't like for income that won't buy status. So people are more likely to pursue jobs that they love doing, work that fuels their passions. Denmark produces some of the world's greatest architects, furniture makers, and chefs.

Given their high taxes and modest salaries, Danes aren't filling their houses with designer furniture and eating at Michelin three-star restaurants every week. But they do enjoy homegrown quality. "Danes will plan a purchase for months, researching it carefully and savoring the anticipation," Anders Weber, a Copenhagen journalist told me. "The centerpiece of our home is an expensive table that took a month's salary and a year of planning to purchase."

As Denmark's third largest city, Aalborg trails Copenhagen and Aarhus in size, arts, and, some would say, ostentation—but that only makes it more perfectly Danish. It is Denmark's northernmost regional capital, and here people endure long, dark winters but gather around candlelit tables and engage in conversations or play games—a much-hyped drama-free quality time known locally as *hygge*. Then, from May through October, they migrate outside to some 62,000 summerhouse gardens, where they grow vegetables and talk to neighbors over the hedge. Or they stroll along the Limfjord wharf in sensible shoes and subtly acknowledge each other with restrained nods—the standard greeting between these stoic Danes.

Aalborg possesses the additional advantage of being a medium-size city (about 200,000 people), big enough so you can find a job and a mate that suit you but not so big that it wears you down. That size tends to be the ideal setting for happiness worldwide, according to those who have studied the situation. "In cities of more than 200,000 people we see the biggest drop-off of happiness," says

Adam Okulicz-Kozaryn, an assistant professor of public policy at Rutgers University–Camden. "There's too much crowding, noise, and light pollution. It's not a social environment optimized for humans. In smaller cities, you're more likely to forge meaningful relationships." Research shows well-being is highest in places near water, with easy access to recreation, or where you're likely to bump into friends and acquaintances throughout the day to get what Gallup-Sharecare surveys suggest is the optimal six hours of social interaction daily. In other words, you're more likely to be happy in a city like Aalborg.

Which brings us back to Ervins and Valerija. They moved from a miserable life in eastern Europe to a satisfying one in Aalborg. Like a vast majority of those we surveyed who live in Denmark, they said they feel safe, trust their fellow citizens, and think local government is efficient and helpful. Almost all of the people in Aalborg were satisfied with their financial situation as well as their life overall. Is it any wonder Ervins and Valerija describe their own happiness as "freakish" compared with what they knew in Latvia?

LOCATION, LOCATION, LOCATION

To find out if the simple act of moving to a happier place could really make someone happier, I tracked down John Helliwell, a Canadian economist. John is an interesting man, someone for whom a career of studying happiness has rubbed off. He spends his summers living off the grid in a cottage on British Columbia's Hornby Island next to Helliwell Provincial Park—land his family donated to the park system. He also co-edits the annual *World Happiness Report,* the world's largest roundup of happiness data. A few years ago, he set out to explore the widely held belief among academics that we are all born with a "set point" of happiness and that life events can only temporarily affect our happiness. Famous studies in the past have suggested that people who experience extreme life events (like winning the lottery or becoming paralyzed) largely return to their inborn happiness levels within a year or so. In other words, the argument went, both good things—like a raise, a promotion, or getting married—and bad things—like getting fired, getting divorced, or losing a loved one—tend to have only temporary effects on our happiness. But in examining 400,000 life satisfaction responses in Canada, John and his colleagues noticed something different.

Canada is a pretty happy place, landing sixth overall in 2016 world rankings. (On a scale of 1 to 10, Canadians give themselves an 8.1.) Over the past 40 years, surveys have followed immigrants from more than 100 countries who have moved to Canada. They included people from Africa, Asia, Latin America, and eastern Europe—places where people reported much lower levels of happiness than people in Canada do. Remarkably, John and his colleagues discovered that no matter where they came from, within just a few years of arriving in Canada, they began to report the happiness levels close to those of their newly adopted home—no matter their class, gender, age, or profession.

All they did was move to Canada.

It's a study that tells us a lot about what happened to the friends I made in Denmark. I recently phoned Ervins from my home in Minneapolis. It was early evening in Aalborg, and they had just finished dinner. In the months that had passed since I'd last seen him, Ervins had secured a long-term contract to write computer code.

"Now that you have that job," I asked, "how happy are you?"

"Remember how I told you that in Latvia, I could not even see tomorrow?" he replied. "Now I can see a week of Sundays."

LESSONS FROM DENMARK: THE HAPPINESS TRIFECTA

Denmark excels in almost every facet of happiness, not only embodying a culture of purpose, but also consistently ranking at or near the top of every major list for the other two strands, both pleasure (experienced happiness) and pride (evaluative happiness). Here the government has cleared a life path for its citizens: They, by and large, don't have to worry about paying for health care, education, or retirement, so they're free to pursue jobs they love and to enjoy plenty of recreation time. It's a place where people can discover their passions and put them to work every day, so Danes not only do well and feel good, they also live deeply fulfilling lives.

They've achieved this happiness trifecta largely because as a nation they got a jump on the rest of the world in terms of happiness fundamentals. Denmark was the first country to educate farmers daughters (1860s) and give women voting rights (1915). Their Folk schools were the world's first to give peasants a liberal arts education. Their labor unions were among the first to assure workers a living wage. (In fact, Denmark's free education, health care, and retirement policies largely flow from this innovation.)

Denmark's purposeful flavor of happiness teaches us that, once our basic needs (food, shelter, health care, education, mobility) are covered, we should focus on pursuits that fuel the soul rather than fill our bank accounts or flatter our egos. Here are a few ideas on how to make that happen.

1. **Avoid the status trap**. Danes are famously egalitarian. Their Janteloven ethos assures that the tallest tree gets cut down; ambition is not admired; wearing designer labels is frowned upon. "Few have too much and even fewer have too little,"

as the writer N. S. F. Grundvig expressed it. As a result, Danes are not as tempted by status-rich jobs as they are by those that engage their interests and talents—those that ultimately drive satisfaction and encourage flow. So someone who loves to build furniture might not be as tempted by the prestige of lawyering. Danes are more likely to spend their extra money on a vacation or a piece of art rather than on designer dresses or luxury cars. Their neighbors occupy the same social class as they do, so they're less likely to be stressed about "keeping up with the Joneses."

Lessons: Contrary to what your real estate agent might tell you, don't buy the cheapest house on the block—or, on the other hand, the biggest McMansion you can find. Rather, consider purchasing an average home relative to your financial situation and lifestyle needs. Curate a group of friends who are at roughly the same class and income level as you. Avoid luxury malls, mailing lists, websites, and any other places where you're subtly reminded of material goods that you're "missing." Don't linger on Facebook where temptation to compare yourself with idealized profiles abounds. Consider volunteering your time to help people who have less than you. You'll feel better about your own lot in life.

2. **Favor handlebars over the steering wheel.** Perhaps more than anyone else in the world, Danes have embraced a culture of cycling. Ever since urban architect Jan Gehl started redesigning Copenhagen in the 1970s to favor bicycles, people have been riding them to work, to their favorite restaurants, or to the homes of their friends. Bicycles are the primary mode of transportation for most people under 30. Each day, 50 percent of Copenhagen citizens collectively

cycle some 932,000 miles. That means they're staying in better shape, avoiding obesity, and shedding stress—all on their commute to work. Meanwhile, they're saving money they'd otherwise spend on cars. Fewer people are dying in auto accidents. And their air quality is better. All of this contributes to their happiness.

Lessons: Buy a bike that thrills you and you'll be more excited about riding it. Get a map of local bike trails and try a few routes for weekend recreation. Most important, see if you can bicycle to work—or bus and bike. Nobel Prize-winning psychologist Daniel Kahneman found that one of the things we most hate on a day-to-day basis is commuting to and from our jobs in our cars.

3. **Join a club.** By some estimates, more than 90 percent of Danish adults belong to a club or association, among the highest rates in the world. Often subsidized by the government, membership in clubs—everything from model trains and cold-water swimming to competitive rabbit jumping—provides a nonwork outlet for people to pursue their passions. It also provides a means for these famously reserved people to boost their social interaction.

    Lessons: Take an internal inventory of your interests and passions, and then make an effort to join a relevant club, sports team, or service organization. Give priority to organizations whose members are like you in age, values, and interests and you'll create new friendships to boot.

4. **Empower your children.** Danish children are often full-fledged members of the family from about age five. They have a say in what the family eats and where they go on vacation and in the distribution of chores. At school, they call their

teachers by their first names; the curriculum focuses on teamwork, building consensus, and empathy (as opposed to rote memory and test scores).

Lessons: Treat your children like little adults. Eat meals together, give them a say when planning vacations, and give honest answers to their hard questions. Make them do chores, but let them decide which ones. Ask them to help you cook. Avoid ultimatums, but rather give them choices with consequences.

5. **Focus on trust.** Trust is a stronger predictor of a nation's happiness than any other factor except GDP, and Danes have a lot of it. Denmark routinely tops the list of the world's most trustworthy countries. People there trust politicians, the police, and their neighbors. They have the lowest corruption rates in the world (and, not coincidentally, Forbes rated Denmark the number one place to do business in 2015).

   Lessons: When choosing a job and a place to live, favor trustworthy people (bosses, co-workers, neighbors) over other factors. In building your own social network, remember that trustworthy people attract trustworthy people. So make it a point to be trustworthy yourself—show up on time, keep your word, and act with integrity.

6. **Eat quality, not quantity**. Denmark has more Michelin star restaurants than any other Scandinavian country. Breakfast is rye bread, cheese, jam, and coffee; lunch is a simple open-faced sandwich. Dinner used to be fish (pickled herring was a favorite), but in recent years Danish cuisine has evolved to include organic, locally sourced foods, exquisitely prepared. So dining out becomes more of an epicurean adventure than a belly-filling exercise. (In contrast, when Americans eat out,

they tend to consume about 200 extra calories than they would if they stayed home.)

Lessons: Design your menu based on the quality of the food you are eating. Choose fresh and local, fruits and vegetables. Eat out less often, but when you do, make it special.

7. **Take your time in school**. Danes don't start school until age six and often don't end their academic careers until they're 30. Along the way, they may travel, take a year off to try a profession, and switch majors. By the time they graduate, they're likely to have found a career that they love, not just one that pays. They've had a variety of life experiences and a rich liberal arts education. Indeed, among the happiest Danes are those in their late 20s and early 30s who are in the marriage market and transitioning from school to their first job.

   Lessons: Go to a school you can afford, take liberal arts classes, take a year off to travel before graduating. Don't rush into a job, mortgage, and debt.

8. **Take six weeks of vacation.** The Danes take at least four weeks a year to travel and often take two months. They'll summer in southern Europe or spend weeks at a time at the sea. A researcher in the Danish statistics office told me that the more Danes vacation, the more value they gain. After six weeks of vacation, they actually feel more satisfied to get back to work and become productive again.

   Lessons: Don't be lured by the notion that you'll take your dream vacation later in life. Use all your vacation time and negotiate for more until you're getting about six weeks off. No one on her deathbed wishes she had worked more.

9. **Consider cohousing.** Denmark is home to more than 100 cohousing projects, or *bofaellesskap*. In each case, about 30 families live in connected homes that form a long row or a circle around a common area. As a rule, you can walk into any house and announce yourself. Usually you are greeted by friends, but if no one answers, you don't stay. Kids are completely free-range—they end up at each other's houses and roam the grounds and surrounding woods freely. The cohousing arrangement strikes the perfect balance between private and public, as residents can be as social as they want, although circumstances nudge them into a minimum threshold of socialization. (Even introverts are happier, studies have shown, when they're around people rather than alone.)

   Lessons: Make a point of moving into a friendly neighborhood with people who share your stage in life. Get to know your neighbors, organize a potluck, help start a communal garden. If you have children, make a deal with other parents to take turns taking care of each other's kids. If you're interested in finding cohousing in the United States, investigate the Cohousing Association (*cohousing.org*).

10. **Plan purchases, savor shopping.** The Danish government provides all citizens with health care, education, and an adequate retirement. On the other hand, people in Denmark pay some of the highest tax rates in the world. This leaves them secure but not flush. When they do have disposable income, they tend to carefully shop for months or even years, savoring the process. Their homes tend to be small by American standards, uncluttered, and punctuated with a few, beautiful things—an elegant light fixture, a piece of furniture, a picture. They derive happiness both from the

selection process and from enjoying a few high-quality things for years.

Lessons: Avoid the big-box stores and cheap merchandise. Clean out your house and minimize clutter. Make fewer purchases, preferring high-quality purchases from craftsmen over low-cost, commercial stuff.

11. **Carpe retirement.** The happiest Danes are retirees. But retirement in Denmark doesn't mean repose. They tend to stay active: They travel, belong to clubs and organizations, and spend their summers at garden cottages, where they socialize with their neighbors.

    Lessons: Maximize savings now to plan for an early, long, satisfying retirement. Think of it as your next career.

12. **Work fewer than 40 hours per week.** Danes tend to show up at their jobs, get their work done, and go home as soon as they can. They work an average of 37 hours a week, which leaves them time to participate in club activities, cook with their families, exercise, or do other things more gratifying than just doing more work.

    Lessons: Choose a job that will cover your basic needs but allow you to work fewer than 40 hours per week. This can often be accomplished with job-flex plans, combining part-time jobs, working for yourself, or negotiating with your boss. (In the Blue Zones offices, employees struck a deal that lets them go home at noon on Fridays during the summer.)

13. **Create a hygge room.** *Hygge* roughly translates to "coziness," and traditionally this very Danish word describes the feeling you get when you tuck in around a candlelit table

with good drinks, friends, and conversation. I've also been with families who achieve a daily sense of hygge by designating one electronics-free room where the family can sit together, pursue hobbies, play games, read, play an instrument, or study.

Lessons: Create your own hygge room: Remove TVs, electronic games, and clocks. Line the room with books or shelves holding pictures and objects that inspire you to pursue your passions. Put a table in the middle that will accommodate your entire family. At the very least, have one room in your house where you can turn off any electronic devices, light a few candles, and focus on fellowship and conversation.

CHAPTER 5

⁓

Happiness in Singapore

DOUGLAS FOO'S CLAIM TO HAPPINESS is neither his expensive sports car nor his trophy case of business awards nor his multimillion-dollar company. It's his laugh: a wide-mouthed, back-tilted howl of joy.

Foo runs Sakae Sushi, Singapore's largest chain of quick-service sushi restaurants, but he still finds time to volunteer for 22 organizations. During his 14-hour workdays, wearing tailored blue suits, he presides over a dozen meetings with a mix of unctuous ceremony, careful consideration, baritone decisiveness, and pandemic humor. His gift for defusing stress—both his own and others'—with spontaneous laughter coupled with a herculean work capacity has earned him all the trappings of Singapore success. And while Foo will tell you he's happy, he still feels he hasn't yet arrived.

"In the scope of things, I'm just an insect," he says with a grave expression on his round face. Then, sensing his own hyperbole, he cracks up.

I first met Foo when I visited Singapore in 2008. My contacts told me he was the perfect emblem of Singaporean happiness: hugely successful, community-minded, consummately principled, and irrepressibly affable. But as I was to learn, he also felt somehow unfulfilled. Now 48, Foo is at an age that straddles the desperate-to-survive generation that founded Singapore in the 1960s and the twentysomethings who will marshal in a new future. So when I returned to the island nation to find an emblematic Singaporean, I asked if I could shadow him for a day.

Foo begins his day at 6 a.m. by convening a 15-minute meeting with his four young boys around bowls of oatmeal to review their schoolwork. We got together two hours later, at 8:00 a.m., when he picked me up and we zipped off to meetings he had planned with foreign ambassadors in his role as volunteer chairman of the Singapore Manufacturing Association. At noon, we lunched with four of Foo's protégés at one of his restaurants. He listened carefully to their questions and dispensed occasional advice—punctuated with bursts of his iconic laugh—as small plates of Japanese food moved past us on a conveyor belt. We spent the afternoon at his corporate headquarters, where Foo took me to his meetings with suppliers and with his managers. At 7 p.m. his wife, bejeweled, high-heeled, and pretty, joined him in a meeting with financial strategists to maximize returns for their family's philanthropic foundation.

"What drives you?" I asked him between meetings.

"Singapore has given me so much, and I don't do enough to give back," he said.

And I'm like, "Huh?"

WORK, SHOP, EAT, AND DO HAIR

Singapore itself is an enigma, a 31-mile-long nation dominated by highly educated, energetic, duty-fueled ethnic Chinese who are scared as hell they'll be "eaten for lunch" by their bigger Pacific Rim neighbors. In just over a half a century, Singapore has transformed itself from a large fishing village to a country of 5.4 million people living amid thousands of high-rises and more than 150 shopping malls, a metropolis graced by clean, tree-lined streets. On Orchard Road, the old colonial district's main thoroughfare, street vendors have been corralled into hawker centers to make way for shops such as Gucci and Hermes and for a Four Seasons Hotel. Kumar, Singapore's most popular drag queen comedian, told me a few years ago, "All we do is work, shop, eat, and do hair."

Over the years, people in Singapore have created one of the cleanest, healthiest, longest-lived, wealthiest, least corrupt, and happiest countries in Asia. The Gallup World Poll has consistently ranked Singapore the highest in Asia for "life satisfaction"—a measurement that captures how well you do, as opposed to how good you feel. "Singapore has done several things to virtual perfection," said psychologist Ed Diener. People there are mostly satisfied with their work and families, but they don't enjoy it as much as people in some other countries.

In Singapore, success lies at the end of a well-defined path: Follow the rules, get into the right school, win the right job, and happiness is yours. (It's traditionally summed up as the 5 C's: car, condominium, cash, credit card, and club membership.) In a system that aspires to be a meritocracy, talent and performance are rewarded, at least in theory. A good education and a good job are available to all. And while you'll hear Singaporeans complain about rising prices and their overworked lives, almost all of them say they feel safe, trust one another and the white-gloved police force, live in a nice home—and they brag about the best food in Southeast Asia (with 29 Michelin star restaurants and food stands).

The architect behind this social experiment was the late, Cambridge-educated founding father, Lee Kuan Yew, who led Singapore's independence movement in 1965. Overwhelmingly loved by

Singaporeans—some of whom still regard him as a patrician auto-crat—he famously endorsed strict laws and corporal punishment for violent crimes. When I met him in 2009, he wore a pink shirt and a Mister Rogers sweater. He didn't believe me when I told him that Singapore ranked highest in Asia for happiness. "All I hear are the complaints," he deadpanned. Lee died in 2015, at the age of 91.

With a keen understanding of Asian values, Lee had set out to build a society based on harmony, respect, and hard work. He favored jobs over welfare. Anyone who made an effort to work, no matter how lowly the job, was guaranteed a livable wage. His "workfare" program supplemented low salaries with housing, and health care subsidies that ensured basic necessities were covered for all. Able-bodied people who chose not to work were "out of luck," he said.

Lee wanted to keep families together, offering tax breaks to the young to live near their aging parents (and thus tapping an army of no-cost health workers). Sensing the Sisyphean nature of material-ism, he also led the charge to tax consumption. "We'll make sure you're clothed and fed, but if you want Swiss chocolate and fancy electronics, you're on your own," he said.

High taxes also helped curb tobacco use and decrease traffic, both of which, studies show, make us unhappy. A pack of cigarettes will set you back $15 in Singapore, and the $40,000 permit you must pay to operate a car in Singapore has kept traffic flowing and com-mute times short. "We like a short commute even more than we like frequent sex," said Donald Low of Lee Kuan Yew School of Public Policy, who helped set tax policy in Singapore.

Harmony also came by design. Though the population is largely composed of Chinese (75 percent), Malays (15 percent), and Indi-ans (7.5 percent), Lee's government retained English as the country's lingua franca to help assure that no ethnicity would have the upper hand. He assured religious freedom and equal education for all and provided a way for the majority of Singaporeans to own a flat in public housing, usually a high-rise unit. By law, such buildings must reflect the ethnic diversity of the country—so Singapore has no racial or ethnic ghettos.

Twenty-eight high-rise communities checker the country, each home to about 200,000 people. Holland Chase is a typical example. There I met Hilda Chaung, 37, who gave me a tour of her home, a tiny one-bedroom flat she shares with her husband, Alvin, a third-generation Indian. As in Singapore itself, size limitations beget innovation in home design: The Chaungs' living room serves as an office, a music room, and, by way of a ceiling-mounted projector, a screening room. Outside, 30 or more other high-rises towered above us, but the Holland Chase grounds evoked a botanical garden, with hedge-lined walkways, flower beds, and majestically tufted rain trees. No graffiti, ground litter, or broken windows sullied the environment—all more evidence that homeowners take better care of property than renters.

In an adjacent food court, families of all three ethnicities tucked in for Sunday night dinner around large round tables. For about $5 an entrée, diners could choose between glistening scoops of chili chicken rice, Malaysian curry, or tandoori fish served from stalls that ring the dining area. Within a 10-minute walk were dozens of shopping outlets, coffee shops, a community center offering everything from yoga to belly dancing, a stadium-size health club, dentists, beauty shops, and access to a clean, efficient subway that could take Hilda anywhere in the country inside of an hour. "We don't have to waste much time on the details of everyday living," she told me. "So we have more time to work."

Herein lies the conundrum of Singapore's happiness: It emphasizes the strand of pride, mostly enjoyed in a rearview mirror—satisfaction in what has been accomplished. This brand of happiness appeals to collective-minded people who like a firmly drawn line between right and wrong, people who like a neatly paved path to success, material rewards, and an upward-ratcheting of status. Follow the rules, work hard, and success is yours! Although this brand of happiness worked well for the nation-building generation in Singapore, some worry it might not be as effective in the future. A few years ago, the government hosted a series of focus groups branded "Our Singapore Conversation." What emerged was a realization that the emerging generation wanted lives with more individual expression and more creative jobs.

To see if Singapore could evolve with shifting values, I called on the current prime minister, Lee Hsien Loong, who also happened to be Lee Kuan Yew's son. He received me at Istana, Singapore's presidential residence, a 106-acre oasis of bucolic gardens hemmed by skyscrapers. In his large, fluorescent-lit office there, we sat on adjacent sofas. He had just come from Parliament, where the ministers were lamenting the slowing job market and the nation's anemic 1.5 percent economic growth.

Lee possessed his father's high-octane charm but with a softer demeanor, his face settling into a pleasant smile. "We do not know whether our grandchildren can quite pull off the same trick," he said. "Not that they are brighter or dimmer than us, but can they pull together in the same way with the same attitudes and values, and do they want to achieve the same goals?" Outlooks and perspectives can change over time, he said, including the way that younger people think about jobs, careers, and family relationships. "If you look at our children, they are very different," he said.

One criticism in recent years has been that Singapore's school system puts too much pressure on students. At the end of grade school, for example, every student must take a high-stakes exam that determines their next step in life, including which school or educational stream they're put in. Some have argued that the school system should put less emphasis on testing and more on teaching.

The New 5 C's

For Singapore's first generation of pioneers, the men and women who built the country beginning in the 1960s, success was often measured by the 5 C's: a car, condominium, cash, credit card, and club membership. But as a new generation emerges, the nation's values are shifting, leaving some wondering: Will its "pride"-driven style of happiness evolve too?

David Chan, a professor of psychology at Singapore Management University, has outlined a different set of 5 C's that provides some clues. In an article titled "Find Your Own Meaning in Life," published in Singapore's leading newspaper, *The Straits Times*, in 2016, Chan recommends a greater focus on the purpose side of happiness—a message more in tune with a self-actualizing youth than hard-charging overachievers.

Finding "meaning" in life provides lots of benefits, writes Chan, who directs the university's Behavioral Sciences Institute. Research shows that people who live with meaning—what we're calling "purpose" in this book—are happier and more satisfied with their lives, suffer less depression and anxiety, and bounce back quicker from adversity. They're also more likely to be healthy, to live longer, and to contribute more to their communities. For the future, Chan proposes the following components for a fulfilling life:

1. **Complementarity.** Find a good match between the challenges you take on and your skills and interests, Chan advises. You're more likely to find meaning in life if you follow your passions, rather than conforming to the expectations of others.
2. **Congruence.** Be your authentic self. Speak up and behave

in a way that is true to who you are, not what others think you should be.

3. **Commitment.** Set concrete goals and stick to them in pursuit of higher goals. Be realistic about what you can achieve.

4. **Contribution.** Do things to benefit others. Make a positive difference to society. Dedicate yourself to a cause, rather than for your self-interest like personal glory.

5. **Community.** Join a group or community that shares your interests and values, whether these are religious, social, or professional.

Wherever you look to find meaning in your life—whether in your family, friendship, religion, public service, volunteerism, skill mastering, or personal accomplishments—you should define it for yourself, rather than letting others define it for you, Chan says. In his view, life inherently involves some unpleasant responsibilities and people who are difficult to deal with, but a sense of meaning can help us better navigate such challenges. "Sometimes we need to say and do things that we do not enjoy but are necessary for good business, social, and political reasons," Chan explains. Nonetheless, he cautions against letting obligations and burdens we feel we "should" shoulder sap all of our energy or waste our time.

If Singapore were to replace the old 5 C's with these new, more introspective and purpose-focused ones, it might become an even happier place in which to live.

"I think we are evolving," Lee said. "Whether you like it or not, you have to evolve because you cannot be preserved in aspic. It is not possible. The world changes and you have to change." That may mean that Singaporeans will want to ease up bit on their national drive to succeed. But it won't mean that their government can stop worrying about economic progress, he said. "There is still a substantial number for whom life is not so easy. You have a house here, food and jobs. But you wish for better, and I think for better, it means that you must have a way and the economy must grow to do that."

For a tiny nation in an unpredictable world, the challenge for Singapore's leaders remains the same, he said. "Somehow you have to give people confidence, trust, faith, and hope."

HAPPINESS IN THE REARVIEW MIRROR

At the end of my day with Douglas Foo, we set out on an adventure. After a seal's feast of sushi and fine sake at one of Foo's restaurants, we commandeered bikes and struck off into the Singapore night. We followed a maze of bike paths and canals that threaded through high-rises and pocket parks. Though it was well after 11 p.m., kids still frolicked in playgrounds and single women strolled serenely down the streets. Warm breezes wafted off the South Pacific. "I'm taking you to Gardens by the Bay," he said, pointing to the blue aura that hovered above a pair of giant glass-domed terrariums in the distance. "My wife and I do this ride several times a week."

We pedaled side by side, making casual conversation. "Nine years ago, you told me that your goal was to spend Sundays with your children," I reminded him. "Have you succeeded?"

He fell silent for several long moments, looking straight ahead. Finally, he turned to me. "I've failed at that," he replied in a rare moment of wistfulness. Tears glistened in his eyes.

Not wanting to disrupt the evening's revelry, I changed the subject. "What do you and your wife usually talk about when you do this bike ride?"

"We talk about our kids, our relationship, and our positions," he replied, still uncharacteristically serious.

"Positions?" I asked, raising my eyebrows. Foo meant stock positions. And when he realized that I was thinking of marital positions, he threw back his head and bellowed laughter into the night.

We kept on riding for another half hour, pedaling through East Coast Park and past the National Stadium. In five short hours, Foo would have to be up again to catch a flight to Los Angeles. He'd be gone for another week, building his empire. But for a couple hours on this blissful night, Foo was in the moment.

We made another turn and pedaled along the Kallang River, always following the blue aura in the distant sky. But Gardens by the Bay was still a long way off. Like Singaporean happiness, it lay just beyond view, on an ever receding horizon.

LESSONS FROM SINGAPORE— MAXIMIZING LIFE SATISFACTION

The people of Singapore exemplify the third strand of happiness— what experts call life satisfaction and what we're calling pride. Researchers measure this type of happiness by asking you to look back on your life as a whole and rank it on a 1-to-10 scale. You score high on this survey when you like what you see. You're proud of your position in life and what you've accomplished. You're living your values. You've done what was expected of you. You are financially secure, have a high degree of status, and feel a sense of belonging. To achieve this type of happiness often takes years, and it often comes at the expense of enjoying moment-to-moment daily pleasures.

This type of happiness might appeal to you if, like many Singaporeans, you prefer a clear path to success and don't want to take financial risks when it comes to career choices. You feel comfortable being part of a tribe—belonging to a religion, an extended family, or a sports team. You don't mind following the rules and, in fact, find comfort in a clearly defined sense of right and wrong.

Like all types of happiness, this one requires for its foundation that your basic needs are already covered, that you have food, shelter, health care, some education, and a degree of mobility. Notwithstanding Singapore's strict rules, harsh punishments, and penchant for hard work, residents of the island currently have the world's lowest "negative affect," which means that those who live there experience low levels of anger, stress, and worry.

Singapore's flavor of happiness is not for everyone, but it does suggest some provocative ideas. If it feels right to you, here are some ways you might bring this sort of happiness into your own life.

1. **Favor security over unlimited freedom.** The citizens of Singapore live with hundreds of rules limiting their freedoms—from where they can walk on the sidewalk, to where they can smoke (only in yellow boxes painted on the sidewalk), to where they can put their hand on an escalator. They're not free to buy pornography or smoke pot, and even small crimes carry heavy penalties. The result, they believe, is that their nation enjoys one of the lowest crime rates in the world, which makes them feel a comfortable—if somewhat antiseptic—sense of order and cleanliness.

   Lessons: Choose a safe neighborhood in a safe city. Neighborhood Scout (*neighborhoodscout.com*) publishes an online list of the safest cities. They tend to be smaller or midsize cities like Winona, Minnesota, or Ridgefield, Connecticut. Pick a neighborhood with well-lighted streets, free of graffiti. Join a neighborhood watch group and make it a point to know your neighbors at least three doors down on each side of your house.

2. **Live your values.** Most Singaporeans subscribe to Confucian values, which tend to favor the welfare of the group over that of the individual—of social harmony over self-actualization. As Singapore's founder, Lee Kuan Yew, told me, "It comes with mother's milk that you must work hard"—a belief especially central to the nation's ethnic Chinese citizens. Making the family proud, respecting elders and authority, and achieving a certain level of status was important to the pioneer generation. Even today, residents report high levels of life satisfaction, perhaps due largely to the fact that it's easy for them to find a job where they can work hard and make enough money to provide secure housing and health care for their extended families.

   Lessons: Take time to know your values, and let them guide you in choosing a place to live, a social network, and a job. For instance, if your family is a priority, try to live near them. If you love to work with your hands, don't get a job in an office.

3. **Find your tribe.** For most Singaporeans, their tribe is their family, and it almost always includes aging parents and in-laws. Research suggests that we're all genetically hardwired to cluster into groups of familiar people who share our values, who will take care of us, and whom we, in turn, will care for.

   Lessons: Join a club, get involved at church, double down on your family, be the best sports fan you can. Likely you will feel more secure—and enjoy the camaraderie.

4. **Look for an environment of trust.** Singapore has one of the world's lowest rates of corruption, which is a measure of social trust. While citizens may not always agree with their politicians, they trust that they'll follow through on their promises (for good and for bad). The Singapore police force

is rigorously trained, and while citizens can count on them to be tough on crime, they can also trust them to be helpful in time of need.

Lessons: Move to a place where you trust your neighbors and local officials, work at a place where you trust your boss and co-workers, and seek out trustworthy friends. The *World Happiness Report* found that trust is one of the five factors that determine 90 percent of human happiness. At a certain level, trust is more important than income.

5. **Buy good health care.** Singapore has one of the best health care systems in the world—but unlike Denmark's, it's not free. Most residents have to pay into a system to get basic care. They can pay more to get more flexibility with doctors and better rooms in hospitals.

   Lessons: Make sure you're covered adequately by health insurance. It's hard to be happy if you're not healthy. Knowing that you'll get good care if you get sick removes one of the main stressors that can erode your happiness.

6. **Get rich.** Singaporeans believe in working hard, saving money, investing wisely, and building wealth. That may sound a little crass, but money does breed a certain type of happiness. We know that among the nations of the world, high GDP is one of the most important predictors of happiness. And Singapore has one of the highest GDPs in the world; 1 in 30 adults there is a millionaire. While wealth may work as a national indicator for happiness, however, the situation at the individual level is slightly different, in that wealth tends to increase evaluative happiness, or pride (billionaires report higher life satisfaction than millionaires), but it has a limited impact on pleasure, or experienced, day-to-day happiness.

Lessons: If status, financial security, and a sense of accomplishment are important to you, you might be happier if you put most of your life's focus on making as much money as you can. For someone like you, by and large, the richer you get, the more satisfied you'll be with your life. If, however, day-to-day joy and getting the most of your day is most important, making between $80,000 and $120,000 per year (less if you live in Iowa, more if you live in Manhattan) will probably be more than adequate. The rest of your time and energy should be spent on less material pursuits.

CHAPTER 6

❧

Lessons for Leaders

"The happiness and prosperity of our citizens . . .
is the only legitimate object of government."
                                        —*Thomas Jefferson, 1811*

A S INSPIRATIONAL AS THESE STORIES ARE from Costa
Rica, Denmark, and Singapore—from the Blue Zones
of Happiness, the homes of the happiest people in the
world—there are ways in which the solutions they represent do
not translate easily into solutions for the United States. What
works for Denmark, a social democracy of five million people,
for instance, might not necessarily work for a sprawling, diverse,
argumentative, freedom-loving nation like our own. Unlike Denmark's wealthy, well-educated, relatively homogeneous society of
consensus seekers, the United States is a crazy quilt of races,
religions, and ethnic groups more accustomed to settling issues
through competition than cooperation. Likewise, could we really
emulate the tolerance of Costa Rica? Or the values-driven security
of Singapore?

I think so. Each of these nations has in a sense manufactured happiness by adopting policies that favor quality of life, and that's something we in the United States can do, too.

What do these three statistically happiest nations show us about the capabilities and limitations of governments in promoting well-being among their citizens? And how can we apply these lessons right here in the United States and elsewhere? The answer goes back to the simple Blue Zones strategy laid out in the introduction. If we want to feel more joy in our lives, pursue our purpose, and find satisfaction in achieving our goals, we need to set up our surroundings to constantly nudge us in the right direction—beginning with those broad influences that only a nation can provide.

MOVE OVER, GDP

One of the most surprising—and encouraging—trends during the past decade has been the growing number of world leaders who have endorsed the idea that the pursuit of happiness should be an important goal of national governments, as Thomas Jefferson insisted two centuries ago.

"It's time we admitted that there's more to life than money," said David Cameron, former prime minister of the United Kingdom, when he announced in 2010 the creation of a government program to track his nation's well-being. "Well-being can't be measured by money or traded in markets," he said. "It's about the beauty of our surroundings, the quality of our culture and, above all, the strength of our relationships. Improving our society's sense of well-being is, I believe, the central political challenge of our times."

Angela Merkel stated much the same thing in 2013, following a two-year study of nationwide growth, prosperity, and quality of life that the German government conducted. "We look at the stock exchange index or currencies on the news each morning and talk a lot about growth in terms of gross domestic product, but we often don't prioritize what is really most important to people," the German chancellor said.

As former French president Nicolas Sarkozy said in 2009, there has been a troubling disconnect in recent years between what government statistics are saying about the economy and what most people are feeling. While production and profits may be rising, people may not be feeling any better about their lives. "The world over, citizens think we are lying to them, that the figures are wrong, that they are manipulated," he said. "And they have reasons to think like that." A year after the near collapse of the global financial system, Sarkozy commissioned a study to look into better methods of measuring societal progress, including surveys of well-being.

Until now, the most widely used indicator of progress has been gross domestic product (GDP), the total value of all goods and services produced in a nation divided by its population. When the GDP is rising, it generally means that an economy is growing, people are buying houses, and there are plenty of good jobs. When the GDP is falling, the opposite is likely to be true. But as most economists will readily tell you, the GDP doesn't measure everything important to a society, such as who is doing well, in a larger sense, and who isn't.

"GDP in the U.S. has gone up every year except 2009, but most Americans are worse off than they were a third of a century ago," said economist Joseph Stiglitz, who won a Nobel Prize in economics in 2001. "The benefits have gone to the very top. At the bottom, real wages adjusted for today are lower than they were 60 years ago. So this is an economic system that is not working for most people."

Apart from such questions of fairness, economists say there's a tricky relationship between money and happiness. Although it's true that wealthy nations in general are happier than poor ones, it's not true that additional wealth will continue to boost a nation's happiness indefinitely. Japan is a good example of that. Between 1958 and 1991, per capita income in Japan shot up sixfold but happiness levels in that nation didn't budge at all. Something similar happened in the United States. Between 1972 and 1996, average income levels went up 19 percent but happiness failed to keep pace. In fact, it even went down slightly, according to the General Social Survey.

The lesson from this, as leaders such as Cameron, Merkel, and Sarkozy have suggested, is that economic growth by itself doesn't guarantee a higher quality of life. The GDP doesn't measure all the factors that lead to greater well-being for a people. It was never meant to do that.

That's why many happiness experts today are gratified to see a growing number of policy makers coming around to the idea that governments should not only invest in measuring well-being and publicize the results—they should also apply insights from this research to their own decision-making. The idea, as David Cameron said, would come with policies "focused not just on the bottom line, but on all those things that make life worthwhile."

WHAT THE EXPERTS RECOMMEND

It has happened successfully in places around the world. As we've seen, political leaders in Denmark, Costa Rica, and Singapore stacked the deck in favor of well-being in their countries. Through a series of long-term policies, they've optimized their nation's environments to promote trust, security, good health, social support, greater opportunity, and generosity—conditions that separate happy peoples from unhappy ones.

How can we apply these lessons in our own country? It turns out that the United States, like most governments, continues to focus on economic growth as an indicator of success. And while the wealth of a nation is important, it's less than half of the story, especially for most of Europe and America. If maximizing well-being for all is truly the goal, what else could and should governments be doing?

To answer that question, we conducted the complex study that I have come to call the Blue Zones Happiness Consensus Project. I teamed up with Toben Nelson of the University of Minnesota School of Public Health and Ruut Veenhoven of Erasmus University to recruit 18 of the world's top happiness experts—economists, sociologists, psychologists, and statisticians—people who have spent much of their academic careers studying various facets of happiness. (See page 255 for more information about each of them.) Over a course of nine months, we challenged them to come to a consensus about which policies are mostly likely to produce happiness. Should our leaders be focused on guaranteeing good health, as in Costa Rica, generating trust, as in Denmark, or security, as in Singapore? Should we be increasing taxes or giving every citizen $10,000, as a Finnish community recently did? Should we embrace diversity or limit immigration? Should we be getting tough on crime and investing in prisons or investing in education? As you can see, questions about how to create the best environment for happiness touch on many of the controversial subjects in the political forum today.

We wanted to be sure that we took an approach that went well beyond simply brainstorming—throwing out ideas, then narrowing the field through discussion. A recent MIT study shows that the best thinking comes when we are doing it in *isolation* and *defending* our ideas. So we went looking for a systematic approach to the discussion, and we finally chose the Delphi method for our consensus process. Originally pioneered by the U.S. Department of Defense to forecast the future of weaponry, Delphi is the same technique used by the National Institutes of Health to decide how to allocate its research budget. Here's how it works:

1. Ask an expert panel to suggest their best ideas.
2. Digest the ideas into a master list.
3. Send the list back to experts to be ranked for effectiveness and feasibility.
4. Send the results to experts for debate.
5. Re-rank the ideas a second time.

The end product is a manageable list of ideas ranked in order of importance and developed through consensus.

In our Delphi study of happiness, we began by asking our experts to suggest evidence-based policies known to produce life satisfaction. They gave us more than 120 ideas, which we returned to them asking them to rate them all for effectiveness and feasibility. After considerable discussion of those results and a final re-ranking of the most effective and feasible (reflected in the order of the list below), our panel of experts came up with their recommendation for Top Ten Happiness Policies—what governments can do, in the spirit of Thomas Jefferson, to make "the happiness and prosperity" of citizens their top priority.

1. **Promote volunteering and national service.** It seems that everyone benefits when more people volunteer. Philanthropic organizations get free labor and the underserved get served. Worldwide, volunteers report higher life satisfaction, better health, and even lower health care costs. John Helliwell of the University of British Columbia examined survey data that represents 90 percent of the world population and found that countries with the most generous people also tend to be the happiest.

Lessons: Provide incentives or tax breaks for volunteer work. Promote civil service. Create scaled opportunities for people to volunteer, such as the U.K.'s National Citizen Service, which enables hundreds of thousands of young people in England and Northern Ireland to experience volunteering and community service, mixing young people from very different walks of life in a collective community task. In the United States, AmeriCorps and Volunteers of America offer good examples of public programs encouraging good will.

2. **Measure national well-being.** If you can't measure it, as the adage goes, you can't manage it. Since Bhutan developed the first Gross National Happiness measure, England, Canada, and France have all started to develop happiness measurements as well. The annual Gallup-Sharecare Well-Being Index measures 55 facets of well-being. By instituting well-being measurements, governments gain a tool to observe the effect of policies on people's life satisfaction or daily experience, thus grounding efforts to try new policies or eliminate old ones.

   Lessons: Invest in ever better tools to measure happiness—the ones we have are far from perfect—and make well-being the North Star measurement for annual performance of the government. (Imagine if our president got an annual score for how well he or she improved our lives!)

3. **Focus on the least happy.** One of our Consensus panel experts, Richard Layard, led the team that discovered that about one-third of the lack of happiness in a nation is driven by the 15 percent or so of people with depression, anxiety, or more severe mental illness. So the greatest "happiness

return" will come from investments that make those people's lives better. And since mentally ill people drive about half of the costs associated with crime, public assistance, and medical costs, investments to benefit this sector of the population also provide a tremendous financial return.

Lessons: Run public information campaigns to destigmatize depression. (Norway's president, for example, recently revealed his own depression very publicly—a brave and effective way to change social attitudes.) Pass health care legislation that requires providers to cover mental illness as if it were a chronic disease. Provide free or subsidized cognitive behavioral therapy, such as Britain's Improving Access to Psychological Therapies, which has cured up to half of all cases of depression and anxiety treated within the program.

4. **Combat discrimination.** Most of us instinctively know that discrimination—whether with respect to race, gender, age, religion, or sexual preference—is wrong. It breeds hatred among the discriminators and misery among the discriminated. As Ruut Veenhoven's worldwide studies have clearly shown, tolerance—the absence of discrimination—is one of the top factors associated with life satisfaction in nations.

Lessons: Investing in tolerance may even be a better investment than growing the economy. Toughening laws against discrimination may help, but positive initiatives may work better. The idea is to incentivize the mixing of different types of people. Singapore's policies that require all races to inhabit public housing and go to the same school eliminate segregation. Require government agencies to encourage a workforce mix that represents the general population; likewise, require agencies to give business to those companies that do the same.

5. **Allow freedom to make life decisions.** Maximizing freedom doesn't necessarily produce maximum happiness. For instance, you don't want to give people complete freedom to commit crimes or to act in a way that hurts others. But assuring people the freedom to choose the life that is right for them and to make their own lifestyle choices is one of the six most statistically important factors for a happy nation.

    Lessons: Find programs that free young people to explore possibilities before settling. Denmark's policies of free education and health care, for example, enable young people to try several jobs before deciding on a career (as opposed to getting sucked into the student debt–health insurance vortex that traps so many young Americans today). While the Danish example might be extreme, and not feasible in American society today, providing health insurance and subsidies for workers in transition would help. Reducing discrimination will also better empower people to live out their preferences and values.

6. **Invest in education.** A long-term investment in education—especially for women and the poor—was one foundational policy that put both Denmark and Costa Rica on their upward spiral toward happiness. Educated kids make for healthier, more productive adults who are much less likely to commit crimes, suffer depression, or require social assistance. They become a fully educated citizenry and elect better, more accountable leaders.

    Lessons: Increase investments in schools. Raise the pay for teachers to attract better talent. Offer free or heavily subsidized after-school and summer school programs. Emulate Singapore to create more public recognition of students who excel, elevating their social status in the eyes of their peers to that of professional athletes and celebrities.

7. **Teach life skills in schools.** American schools tend to focus on metrics and testing for academic abilities such as language arts, science, and math. While these topics are important, the ability to think creatively and solve life's problems, get along with other people, and engage in civic life are just as important, perhaps even more so, for the happiness of the public. Schools almost completely ignore life skills, such as choosing the right job or the right mate— decisions that will determine your happiness as an adult more than anything else. *How we feel* is just as important as *how we do* in life, and that message can be conveyed through the school experience.

   Lessons: Integrate life skills into schools. Denmark's Folk schools provide a great template for other school systems, teaching art appreciation, civics, and consensus skills to children. The U.K.'s experimental Healthy Minds Curriculum, taught in grades 7–10 in nearly three dozen English schools, provides lessons in resilience, relationship smarts, and parenting skills.

8. **Support families.** Happy families are the building blocks of happy societies. Spouses and children are happier in stable relationships. Married people are happier than nonmarried people, children who live in a two-parent home are better off in almost every metric, and aging parents who live with or near their children live longer and pass the benefits down the generations, making for healthier grandchildren. (Aca-

demics call this the "Grandmother Effect.") In other words, the family unit is worth protecting and nurturing.

Lessons: Find ways that government can support family life. Singapore offers a tax incentive for adult children who live near their aging parents, knowing that they'll be more likely to support each other. Likewise, it offers increased tax incentives for domestic partners to stay together and divorced parents to live in close proximity to their children. Leaders should consider laws that require parents with young children to explore staying together or at least co-parent closely together.

9. **Prioritize prevention in health care.** Treating disease costs an estimated 16 times more than preventing it. More than 85 percent of the annual two-trillion-dollar health care expenditure in the United States goes to treat preventable disease. Since health and happiness are interlaced, working to increase awareness of healthy lifestyles as well as to prevent disease will reduce suffering. People who knowledgeably care for themselves find more satisfaction in their health and the health of others.

   Lessons: Shift economic incentives away from treating sick people and in the direction of keeping them healthy in the first place. Increase budgets for public health and increase funding for prevention research. Costa Rica's EBAIS program, for example, gives every citizen access to an annual health care visit, and caregivers catch many diseases like diabetes, high blood pressure, and infections before they lead to costlier, often irreversible problems. Redirect Medicaid and Medicare reimbursements for outcomes rather than just treatment.

10. **Provide free health care.** We tend to think of happiness as joy or life satisfaction, but happiness is also the absence of

everyday worries. Being able to depend on regular, reliable, and inexpensive—even free—health care is a key to improving happiness in our country. Currently as many as 29 million people in the United States have no health insurance, which causes daily stress and can cause disaster, since if a medical catastrophe occurs, they have little or no safety net. They're likely to get inadequate care, to have to endure unnecessary suffering, to become disabled, or even to die owing to lack of appropriate medical attention.

Lessons: Work toward a universal health care system such as those in place in Singapore, Denmark, and Costa Rica. As a first step, shift subsidies away from the most expensive procedures and drugs and over to basic health care, to provide the most good for the most people. At the population level, this move is likely to reduce suffering and more likely to raise healthy life expectancy.

We often hear our politicians referring to their jobs in government as "public service" or promising to make our country great again. If leaders want to serve us, their job should be to listen to the emerging wealth of data that tells us how to manufacture happiness in nations. As a voter, you can choose to support leaders who value policies based on research that are designed to support well-being. Your happiness and the happiness of your community can only thrive when public policies are designed to nudge toward well-being—and endorsing change in this direction can help everyone.

PART THREE

Happier by Design

"I arise in the morning," E. B. White famously said, "torn between a desire to improve (or save) the world and a desire to enjoy (or savor) the world. This makes it hard to plan the day." The key is to find that sweet spot between savoring life now and doing things that lead to a richer, more meaningful outcome in the future. As we've seen in Costa Rica, Denmark, and Singapore, people in those places aren't happier because they try harder to be happy—they enjoy good lives because their surroundings nudge them into behaviors *more likely* to produce happiness. In this section, we turn to you. How can you set up your life so your circumstances nudge you into behaviors that make you happier?

To define your "surroundings," we'll consider the area where most of us spend most of our lives—the area 10 miles or so in all directions from home. We'll call this your Life Radius. Within that radius, we've identified six domains, represented as six concentric circles moving from outward (your larger social circles) to inward (your personal habits and choices). Moving inward, one by one, we'll explore how the lessons we have learned from the world's happiest people can help you design each domain to invite more pleasure, purpose, and pride into your life.

The two outermost domains—those of your community and workplace—determine how easy it is for you to flourish in your current environment. Though we have only limited power to shape these environments, we do have the ability to choose where we live and work. According to the U.S. Census Bureau, Americans move about 10 times in our adult lives, although not always to enhance our happiness. When you hear the statistic that 69 percent of Americans don't like their work, you recognize that many of us should—and all of us can—change jobs for the sake of increased happiness. And in fact, we can verifiably show the characteristics of cities and workplaces that produce greater happiness for the people who inhabit and work in them.

While you may not be able to change your hometown or work environment immediately, the innermost domains—your friends and family, finances, home, and personal emotions—are much more within your power. There are ways that you can take charge and start making changes right away that are sure to stack the deck in each of these realms in favor of greater happiness. With the help of our friends from the happiest places in the world, together with the panel of experts convened for our Blue Zones Happiness Consensus Project, we'll look at what works and what doesn't work, and we'll make practical suggestions so you can begin to make changes today that will last a lifetime.

CHAPTER 7

❧

Designing Happy Communities

O N A CHILLY SPRING AFTERNOON in Boulder, Colorado, 88-year-old Ruth Wright scooted down Pearl Street, the city's main pedestrian mall, past a lot of people going nowhere in a hurry. It was two o'clock on a workday, and a hard mountain sun was beating down on the brick pavement. Men in puffy down jackets huddled in conversation, dreadlocked students tapped on computers in outdoor cafés, and only a few people in office-friendly plaids seemed to be moving with a destination in mind.

Wright passed several buildings in the historic part of downtown, including Trident Booksellers and Café, the legendary Boulder hangout where Jack Kerouac used to write. Down the block, she frowned at a new glass and brick structure, occupied by eco-chic outdoor clothing boutiques and organic foodie emporiums, whose presence she found jarring. At the next intersection she stopped suddenly and gestured toward the end of the street. "My life's work has been in preserving that," she said, peering at me through dark sunglasses. She pointed to the end of Pearl Street, where the pine-dotted Rocky Mountains soared upward and towered majestically over the rooftops.

I'd come to Boulder to meet Wright because she played an important role in shaping the city's celebrated quality of life—one that now seems ready-made to produce happy citizens. But it didn't get that way without a struggle. Decades ago, when rapid growth threatened to overwhelm her community, Wright led a successful campaign against powerful developers. It was the beginning of a career of public service that led her to the state legislature, where she represented Boulder for 14 years, with a stint as minority leader. And through it all, she kept a protective eye on her hometown and its enviable natural beauty.

Surrounded by protected forests, Boulder is a place that draws you outdoors. The mile-high altitude makes for mild summers and winters, with sunshine in the weather forecast 300 days a year or more. As you approach Boulder from the highway, a line of tasteful, short buildings front a theatrical spread of Rocky Mountain foothills—no billboards or gated communities or fast-food restaurants. After you pass the leafy university on "the Hill," you encounter well-kept neighborhoods running down to the park-lined river and enter Boulder's vibrant, pedestrian-friendly downtown—all in the shadow of the mountains. Here, an office worker can take a nature hike on a lunch break.

But Boulder's appeal is more than skin-deep. Besides being a college town, adventure destination, and haven for artists, the city has also evolved over the decades into a happiness incubator. Having succeeded at doing a lot of things right, Boulder checks off many of the boxes for a community with high well-being, as Dan Witters, a senior scientist at Gallup, explained to me. Witters has spent much of his professional career thinking about the highly nuanced science of happiness. He's the research director of the Gallup-Sharecare Well-Being Index, which has conducted more than 2.5 million surveys in American communities since 2008. If you're looking for a happy city, he said, "you can't go wrong with Boulder."

I'd asked Witters for help in identifying the happiest place in the United States. He ticked off the many ways in which Boulder excels: It has one of the nation's lowest smoking rates, one of the lowest obesity rates, and one of the highest rates of exercise. Boulder residents report high life satisfaction and feel more safe and secure than residents of any other American community. Probably most important, they feel that they accomplish meaningful things every day. When asked if, during the past seven days, they've felt "active and productive every day," Boulder residents overwhelmingly responded in the affirmative. Pleasure, purpose, pride: Boulder provides the context for all.

Many other university towns also have high levels of education and good incomes, Witters pointed out. And they also score well in such surveys. But he reminded me that authentic happiness doesn't spring from one or two factors but rather emerges from a cluster of interconnected ones that almost always appear in a pack. He identified 15 of these factors—what he called "cowbell" metrics—that signal true happiness. They included:

- You manage your money well and live within your means. (You have enough money to do everything you want to do.)
- You set and reach goals on an ongoing basis.
- You always make time for trips or vacations with family and/ or friends.
- You use your strengths to do what you do best every day.
- You feel safe and secure in your community.
- You learn something new or interesting every day.
- You have someone in your life who encourages you to be healthy.
- You eat healthy every day.

- You eat five servings of fruits and vegetables at least four days every week.
- You get to the dentist at least once per year.
- In the last 12 months you have received recognition for helping to improve the city or area where you live.
- You exercise at least 30 minutes at least three days per week.
- You are active and productive every day.
- You don't smoke.
- You are normal weight.

When you consider all of these factors, Witters said, Boulder rises to the top of the heap.

COMMUNITY: THE OUTER RING OF YOUR LIFE RADIUS

As in Costa Rica, Denmark, and Singapore, happiness in Boulder began with a handful of people who had a clear vision of what they wanted for their community, and who then set in motion a chain of the right policies. In Boulder's case, those people were two university professors, Al Bartlett, a physicist, and Robert McKelvey, a mathematician.

Like many others in Boulder, Bartlett and McKelvey treasured the city's mountain views. But as housing developments started creeping up the hillsides on the edge of town during the 1950s, a time when the population of Boulder was booming, they feared that they were losing their view. So they went to work. With no real budget or political experience, but with a penchant for research, they discovered that the city's infrastructure could only pump water to an elevation of 5,750 feet, which was the height of the city's reservoir. Above that "Blue Line," as they dubbed it, more development would require an investment from taxpayers. With that discovery, they galvanized like-minded citizens to approve a referendum to the city charter restricting building above the Blue Line. Their success emboldened others and led to a culture of civic-led quality-of-life innovations. In one of the most ambitious moves, in 1967 Boulder became the first city in America to pass a sales tax to buy open space around the city to serve as a greenbelt, permanently preserving access to nature, beauty, and outdoor recreation for all. Today the city owns 45,000 acres of forests that surround it.

By the late 1960s the developers were back. This time they had a plan to build as many as 40 14-story high-rises in downtown Boulder. Ruth Wright had recently moved to town with her husband, Ken, and their two children. Although she'd earned a bachelor's degree in philosophy and had lived abroad, she described herself as a housewife. When she heard about the high-rise plan, she instantly knew that it would destroy the character of the town, and she decided to get involved. In 1971, Wright started a petition to put a referendum initiative on the ballot that would limit building heights to five stories. She soon found herself leading the movement and engaging the same civic apparatus that passed the Blue Line measurement. She was a second-year law student when the referendum narrowly passed that same year, thanks to the support of university students.

"Had I lost, Boulder would be a forest of high-rises crisscrossed by traffic-jammed streets," she said, pounding the air with a Kennedyesque fist.

Thanks to Wright, you can still see mountains instead of behemoth buildings when you look down Pearl Street today. More important, a culture that values quality of life has flourished. "We actually question the largely unquestioned virtue of growth," Wright told me during the first of three days we spent together. Looking like a robust version of Nancy Reagan, she wore a snow-white ski jacket, black sneakers, and a digital watch. "Growth usually just benefits special interests and rarely pays for itself," she said. "Here in Boulder, we had a jewel to preserve."

Boulder's active civic culture has begotten a like-minded city government, one that listens to citizens before taking action. "Government officials from a city this size often like to think they know what's best for the community," said Susan Richstone, a city planner. "I learned a long time ago that Boulder's citizens know what's best for them, so it's better to listen to them."

Accordingly, the city has developed a multistep process to decide on everything from designing a single bike path to the Transportation Master Plan. The municipal government has the biggest Twitter following of any Colorado city, and city officials answer every one of the 1,500 emails received annually. City Hall meetings are packed. Every meeting includes an "open mic" time when attendees can have two minutes to talk about whatever is on their mind.

Despite a population of 107,000 that's still growing, Boulder traffic hasn't gotten any worse since 1985. You can still drive across town in only 18 minutes. There's a reason, and it is not just traffic engineering. Boulder taxpayers have voted for 300 miles of bike paths that web the city, and yellow lights blink at crosswalks, reminding motorists that pedestrians have the right-of-way. As a result, more people per capita walk to work in Boulder than in any other city in the United States, and the convenient Hop, Skip, and Jump bus lines (as well as the Bound, Dash, and Stampede lines) assure that no one waits more than a few minutes for a ride. This all makes for cleaner air, less stress, fewer accidents, and fewer overweight people.

A progressive food policy also helps. The city's lack of free-standing billboards was no coincidence—researchers have found a correlation between the preponderance of billboards advertising junk food and the obesity rate of the adjacent population—and the city matches the federal Supplemental Nutrition Assistance Program (SNAP) dollar for dollar to encourage fruit and vegetable consumption. Last year Boulder became one of the nation's first cities to approve a soda tax aimed at reducing consumption of sugar-sweetened beverages. They plan to use the revenue from the soda tax to fund health programs for children. All of these measures shape an environment conducive to health and longevity—and, we have found, happiness.

Smart policies have also been designed to support a feeling of safety and security in Boulder. Walkable streets with buildings that face outward discourage nefarious activity that might occur in back alleys or outside of privacy fences.

Then there's Boulder's tradition of fitness. Beginning in the 1970s with the arrival of elite athletes like Olympic medalists Frank Shorter, Connie Carpenter, and Davis Phinney, a culture of fitness grew up in the city. You can climb, hike, ski, or go to a world-class gym all in the same day, said Sasha DiGiulian, at 24 years old one of the world's top-ranked female climbers and a recent Boulder arrival. "A pro moves into town and tells his friends," she said. "A gym follows. Then more climbers arrive, and more gyms pop up. Fitness is self-augmenting here."

Still, change continues to threaten Boulder's way of life. Since the 1960s Boulder's population has grown tenfold, and demand has driven the median price for a house up to $756,000. The civic-minded hippie generation that spawned companies such as Celestial Seasonings herbal tea company and White Wave tofu company are now giving way to Google and tech venture capital firms. A highly paid, more driven culture is replacing the laid-back outdoorsy one. For all of its list-topping well-being scores, Boulder comes through with curiously high levels of stress. "It's not Zen Boulder anymore," Dan Witters said. On any given day, 49 percent of people surveyed in Boulder report feeling stress. "But it's productive stress," he added.

Finding Your Happy Place

Dan Witters, a senior scientist at Gallup, agreed to help create a National Geographic Gallup Special Index of the happiest cities in the United States. He identified the 15 cowbell metrics, listed on pages 115-116 (which you can use to measure the well-being of your community, too), and then he applied a statistical technique to see where people responded "yes" to most of them. And voila, Boulder came in first. Here's a list of the other cities found to be the happiest according to this research.

Metropolitan Area	2015 Population (Estimated)	Sample Size (Unweighted)	National Geographic Index Score
Boulder, CO	319,372	361	64.7
Santa Cruz-Watsonville, CA	274,146	322	64.6
Charlottesville, VA	229,514	347	64.3
Fort Collins, CO	333,577	472	64.0
San Luis Obispo-Paso Robles-Arroyo Grande, CA	281,401	353	63.8
San Jose-Sunnyvale-Santa Clara, CA	1,976,836	1,394	63.6
Provo-Orem, UT	585,799	664	63.3
Bridgeport-Stamford-Norwalk, CT	948,053	900	63.1
Barnstable Town, MA	214,333	346	63.1
Anchorage, AK	399,790	571	63.1
Naples-Immokalee-Marco Island, FL	357,305	366	62.8
Santa Maria-Santa Barbara, CA	444,769	447	62.7
Salinas, CA	433,898	359	62.7
North Port-Sarasota-Bradenton, FL	768,918	970	62.7
Urban Honolulu, HI	998,714	654	62.6

Ann Arbor, MI	358,880	342	62.5
San Francisco-Oak-land-Hayward, CA	4,656,132	3,909	62.5
Colorado Springs, CO	697,856	867	62.3
Manchester-Nashua, NH	406,678	410	62.2
Oxnard-Thousand Oaks-Ventura, CA	850,536	786	62.2
Washington-Arlington-Alexandria, DC-VA-MD-WV	6,097,684	6,347	62.0
Minneapolis-St. Paul-Bloomington, MN-WI	3,524,583	3,879	61.9
San Diego-Carlsbad, CA	3,299,521	3,148	61.8
Portland-South Portland, ME	526,295	770	61.5
Austin-Round Rock, TX	2,000,860	1,958	61.5

If moving is in your future, your happiness is in the balance as well. You can preview a community by investigating where it falls on the Gallup-Sharecare Well-Being Index. To do that, check *www.gallup.com* and search for "well-being." You can also learn a lot by searching the website *walkscore.com,* which evaluates the walkability of communities across the country.

As you conduct your search for a new place to move to, here are key metrics to look for to maximize your well-being:

- Trust—trustworthy politicians, police, and neighbors
- Walkability—sidewalks and safe streets to facilitate physical activity and socializing
- Access to nature—proximity to parks, open spaces, and trees
- Civic engagement—people actively contribute to a willing city government on maintaining and improving quality of life

- Clean environment—clean water, air, and land
- Nice teeth—access to affordable and regular dental care
- People-friendly streets—quiet, safe streets that favor humans over cars
- Healthful food—farmers markets, local restaurants, plant-based food that's easier to find than fast foods from chain restaurants
- Healthy behaviors—local restrictions on smoking, less obesity, and less drug abuse

Ruth Wright has also been feeling stress, but in a good way. On the last day we met, she arrived brandishing a newspaper with the headline "Boulder Extends Height Limit." Two nights earlier, she'd testified at a six-hour city council meeting to fend off developers—and prevailed yet again.

"I'm a 10," she proclaimed, when I asked her to rate her happiness at that moment. "I've had a fabulous life." As a child she'd learned resilience, hard work, and compassion, she said. Her father had died young, forcing her mother to take in elderly boarders. Two years of living in Heidelberg, Germany, broadened her thinking and taught her independence. "I'm a feminist but not a typical one," she said. "There are some women who feel that they can't do things because they're repressed. I've never had that feeling. I have a husband who loves me, and we raised two wonderful children. I ended up serving 14 years in the state legislature." When I pointed out that her life didn't seem to include much day-to-day joy or celebration, she corrected me. "For me, fun is getting things done," she said. And there, in a nutshell, was the Boulder brand of happiness: a community of fit, successful, and mission-driven people with a clear vision of the good life, even if they don't completely live it yet. Pleasure, purpose, pride.

DESIGNING NEIGHBORHOODS

Boulder's high quality of life has been 60 years in the making and, as the table on pages 120-121 shows, other communities are following suit. In a grassroots movement taking shape across the country, many thousands of people are adopting evidence-based designs and policies to nudge themselves into eating better, moving more, volunteering, and connecting socially—which has already paid off in lower health care costs, less chronic disease, higher productivity, and greater well-being. As Ruth Wright recognized in Boulder, designing a happier city takes a concerted effort by many dedicated citizens to create an environment of well-being. It can be done—in your town, too—and the rest of this chapter will give you some examples taken from our years of experience at bringing the Blue Zones way of life to communities across the United States. We'll give you some real-life stories of people who changed their environments for the better, each one chosen to represent some important aspect of the practices we have found essential to boosting happiness and well-being. At the end of this chapter, we'll put together a checklist of key practices, every one of them based on years of research into how to support the happiest lives.

First of all, it takes commitment to the community or neighborhood. Consider what's been going on in Fort Worth, Texas, for example, where dedicated local leaders are striving to keep neighborhood spirit alive.

In White Lake Hills, a neighborhood in northwest Fort Worth, the Fourth of July parade was about to start. It was a patriotic scene worthy of a Norman Rockwell painting, with children sitting on the curb waiting for the procession to begin. As always, the local fire truck took its place in the lead. "They have to be at the very front in case they need to take a call," Linda Fulmer, the chair of the neighborhood planning committee, explained. Mounted police officers followed, along with classic cars carrying military veterans and a float with residents portraying George Washington, Thomas Jefferson, and soldiers of the Continental Army. Then came boys and girls on bicycles decorated with crepe paper and streamers; a Boy Scout troop; a Volkswagen Beetle dressed up like a mouse with whiskers, ears, and a tail; and a Mrs. Baird's Bread truck, driven by a resident who delivered baked goods for a living.

White Lake Hills had something special to celebrate this year. At a ceremony following the parade, the neighborhood association was named a Blue Zones Project participating organization. Like dozens of other organizations, churches, schools, worksites, grocery stores, and restaurants in Fort Worth, residents of the 580-home subdivision had completed a checklist of recommended activities. One of these was to organize moais of a half-dozen or so people to get together on a regular basis and share a potluck meal or go walking. As we have found in many Blue Zones locations, this Japanese social tradition helps to strengthen relationships among neighbors who might not otherwise interact. It was especially helpful in White Lake Hills, which had a long history of neighborhood activities, Fulmer said, but also an aging population with an increasing sense of isolation.

"The day we moved in, an older guy across the street told us he wasn't too sure about all the new people in the neighborhood," said Fulmer, who had lived in White Lake Hills for four and a half years. "So we knew that we needed to build some bridges between the generations. After hearing about the Blue Zones Project, I thought, well, that's a good way to expand the neighbor-to-neighbor connections."

Fort Worth's mayor, Betsy Price, had helped kick off the citywide Blue Zones Project in February 2015. The initiative promised to bring healthier choices to restaurants, cooking demonstrations to grocery stores, more exercise to kids, purpose workshops to adults, and improvements to neighborhoods to make them more walkable and bike friendly. By reducing obesity and smoking rates, among other things, the project was projected to save Fort Worth residents and businesses millions in medical costs over five years, increase worker productivity, and raise overall well-being.

Mayor Price had visited the White Lake Hills neighborhood that year to lead a walking group through the streets. "That created some excitement," Fulmer said. As Price was well aware, researchers from Gallup-Sharecare had recently measured her city's quality of life—and the results had been illuminating. Although Fort Worth scored on a par with other American cities with respect to financial security, physical well-being, sense of purpose, and pride of community, it lagged behind when it came to the quality of social relationships—a key contributor to happiness.

People in White Lake Hills apparently felt the same way. As the Blue Zones Project moais were getting started, Kathlynn Stone, a member of Linda Fulmer's walking group, came up with a plan to reach out to their neighborhood's most isolated and vulnerable residents. Stone was a caregiver for her 94-year-old mother. Her idea was to identify all the other seniors in the neighborhood who were either living alone or with a family member who might need help during a weather emergency. "We had a power outage a couple of years ago that lasted for five days," Fulmer said. "Kathlynn wanted to make sure everyone would be OK."

So Stone created a neighborhood committee to address the problem. That meant poring over old neighborhood directories, cross-referencing names with social media, and knocking on doors to get the word out about developing a city registry of citizens who depended on oxygen or otherwise needed help. "We're in the process of doing that now," Fulmer said. "We thought it might be a reason to invite our older neighbors to a tea, as a way to break the ice."

"I love living here," Fulmer said. "Whenever a bunch of us gets together, we're always talking about how happy we are to be living here. But this neighborhood spirit is hard won. You have to create that sense of community where you are. And it can be elusive."

DESIGNING A HEALTHY FOOD ENVIRONMENT

Although Hawaii has a well-deserved image as a tropical paradise—the state has ranked number one in well-being for several years now—many Hawaiians are, in fact, struggling to maintain a decent quality of life. One of those Hawaiians was Theresa Zendejas, a woman in her 80s. From the tiny town of Pahoa, she was heading for trouble with her health until she made some changes to her personal environment. Her story is a helpful reminder that well-being often starts with healthy food.

Zendejas happened to be interviewed by a TV crew in October 2014, when a stream of lava flowing from the east side of Kilauea Volcano took an unexpected turn and headed straight toward her hometown. Hissing and popping as it burned through nearby forests, the pillowy black lava was moving slowly enough to give people plenty of time to consider evacuating before it reached the outskirts of the community. "We don't know what we're going to do," Zendejas told the crew at the time. "It's really scary."

Fortunately for Pahoa, the flow stalled just before entering town. After melting through a chain-link fence, burying a barn, and blocking a local road, the lava stopped just short of the community's recycling and transfer station. Afterward, residents were relieved but philosophical about what had happened. "It's good that Pele is not coming here," one man told a reporter, referring to the Hawaiian goddess of fire. "But she might turn around and come back."

As Zendejas, a native Hawaiian, watched a replay of her TV interview not long ago, she shook her head in amusement. It wasn't the lava's unpredictable behavior that made her smile, but the dramatic change in her own appearance. During the past year or so, she'd lost 44 pounds.

"Oh, my gosh, I couldn't believe what I was seeing," she said, after watching the footage again. "I couldn't believe how fat I was. Let's be honest, I was F-A-T, fat."

At the time of the lava flow, Zendejas, who is five feet three inches tall, had weighed 207 pounds. "I was getting heavier and heavier, and I couldn't really walk that much," she said. "I mean, if I walked from my living room to my kitchen, I'd be looking for the closest chair so I could sit down." Her lack of mobility was affecting her happiness.

When her doctor's office called in the fall of 2015, saying they wanted to talk about her blood work, Zendejas was alarmed. "I said, uh oh, I bet it has something to do with diabetes," she said.

Zendejas's twin sister had died of complications from diabetes more than two decades before. In the years before her death, the disease had cost her sister both of her legs, as well as her eyesight. "Everything that could happen to a person with diabetes happened to my twin sister," Zendejas said. Now she knew she had to make changes in her own life.

Healthy eating, staying active, and good sleeping habits have all been associated with greater well-being. As it happened, the Blue Zones Project had recently come to the Big Island. Two communities on the island of Hawaii and one on Oahu had been named demonstration sites, sponsored by the Hawaii Medical Service Association (HMSA), a nonprofit health insurer in the Blue Cross Blue Shield system. As in other Blue Zones demonstration communities, a small team of professional health activists were now working with residents, businesses, faith-based organizations, and public officials to put evidence-based practices in action to nudge folks into eating better, moving more, and connecting socially—to boost their health and happiness.

"I started it right after I went to the Blue Zones Project Kick-Off last October, that big one they had in Hilo," Zendejas said of her personal campaign. She changed her diet, adding fruits and vegetables to her meals. She also started walking with a group of five other residents. "Us local people, we like to eat," she said. "But that first Blue Zones Project event really opened my eyes."

Although Hawaii, as a whole, still has the lowest rate of obesity in the nation—only 22 percent, compared with 36 percent in Louisiana, the state with the highest rate—the problem is getting worse. If the current trend continues, Hawaii's Department of Health has warned, more than half of Hawaii's adults will be obese by 2030. The problem is most serious among native Hawaiians and Pacific Islanders; among native Hawaiians, the obesity rate tops 40 percent. And along with obesity come many health problems, such as diabetes. Compared with the state's population as a whole, native Hawaiians have a 60 percent greater chance of developing diabetes.

"I'm a local girl, born in Honolulu," Zendejas said. "I read a lot, and I know we have the highest rate of diabetes here on the islands." She is proud of the changes she has made to her own eating habits, and she hopes to influence more of her friends and family in doing the same. "If I could do it," she says, "anybody could do it."

The Blue Zones Project in Hawaii made it a top priority to help islanders get access to healthy foods. They organized cooking classes, gardening demonstrations, and potluck moais. They signed up grocery stores to highlight nutritious products, sponsored tours of farms growing organic fruits and vegetables, and encouraged restaurants to offer more good-for-you dishes, such as coconut corn chowder, garden hummus wraps, and cacao tea. They also advised employers on how to add healthy food to vending machines, improve cafeteria options, and even create gardens at worksites.

To make fresh foods even easier to find on Oahu, the HMSA set up a farmers market next to its headquarters in Honolulu. From 11 a.m. to 2 p.m. every Friday, the company invited members of the public as well as employees to browse the tables of vendors selling papayas, coconuts, bananas, peppers, lemons, tomatoes, limes, mangoes, and avocados, as well as grilled corn, chicken masala, ahi poke (a local fish salad), and other healthy foods.

It was a good start for the Blue Zones Project team in Hawaii. But they knew that it was going to take time to change attitudes and behaviors on the islands. Meanwhile, they could take encouragement from other Blue Zones Project efforts around the country, places that were already showing measurable progress and had found a variety of ways to bring healthier food to their communities.

In Marion, Iowa, for example—one of 15 Blue Zones Communities in that state—in just two years residents had achieved a nearly 22 percent increase in the number of people eating healthy foods. They used a variety of strategies, among the most innovative a new town ordinance that allowed residents to keep bees, raise chickens, cultivate rooftop gardens, establish farmers markets, and build vertical gardens on buildings to bring fresh foods closer to home.

In Cedar Rapids, Iowa, the city's largest employer—the aerospace and defense firm Rockwell Collins—gave fresh foods a huge boost by approving a vegetable garden, run by company workers, using an empty piece of property the company owned. The food raised there by company volunteers—enough for thousands of meals—was donated to a Meals on Wheels charity that delivered ready-to-eat dishes to seniors and people with disabilities, thus combining the purposefulness of volunteerism with the production of fresh local produce.

In Southern California, the Beach Cities Health District has been so successful in making healthy foods available in schools and in homes that childhood obesity in Redondo Beach has dropped by 50 percent. Restaurant menus, school meals, and home eating habits have all changed. When Dr. Vivek Murthy, the then surgeon general of the United States, brought members of his staff there to see what the Blue Zones Project team had accomplished, he was impressed. "We tend to believe that our health problems are too big and intractable," he said. "But you have shown that communities can take charge and reverse the trend."

Back in Pahoa, Theresa Zendejas is facing a new problem—but one that she welcomes. Now that she's lost so much weight, she needs new clothes! "I went through every drawer in my bedroom, I went through my closet, and got rid of my big clothes," she said. Because she's walking more and eating better, she feels more energetic, and her tests for blood sugar levels have also improved. "People ask me, 'How are you doing it? What are you taking?' and I say to them, 'What do I take? Fruits and vegetables! I watch my carbs, I quit milk—and I've got a garden!'" Zendejas shows that anyone, even in a tight neighborhood, can grow his or her own fresh food. With help from her husband, she bought several black square plastic tubs, drilled holes in the bottoms, filled them with compost, and planted kale, okra, and string beans. Now she enjoys fresh vegetables from her own backyard.

"I wish I would've done this 20 years ago!" she said. "I've completely changed my way of living. I'm telling you, honey, this is the best thing that has ever happened to me."

DESIGNING AN ACTIVE CITY

For generations Albert Lea, Minnesota, a small town 90 miles south of Minneapolis, had been known as a hardworking meatpacking town. Over the decades the meat industry had declined, and Albert Lea faced the challenge of redefining itself, after shedding its blue-collar reputation. When the biggest packing plant in town burned to the ground in 2001, residents weren't sure where Albert Lea was headed. Businesses downtown withered. It was not a happy place.

But in 2009 we selected Albert Lea as the first demonstration community for what would later become the Blue Zones Project. The project began with a visit from Dan Burden, a leading expert on making towns more walkable, bikeable, and generally livable. Burden co-founded the nonprofit Walkable and Livable Communities Institute, and by that time he had helped more than 3,500 towns across the country. Dan possesses a certain genius for how a town's built environment affects everything that happens inside it. Much of it boils down to one question: Are the streets built for cars or for humans? If it's the former, as one might expect, you'll have more traffic, noise, air pollution, pavement, and accidents. If it's the latter, you'll have more sidewalks, trees, open spaces, areas to interact, safe ways for kids to get to school—and healthier, happier people. But was it too late for Albert Lea?

"When we came in, the downtown was virtually dead," Burden recalled. "A few businesses were still in operation, but many others were boarded over. I thought, oh, my gosh, can we even help this town?"

As it happened, that same year the town was preparing to dig up three downtown blocks to fix water and sewer lines and other aging infrastructure. As part of the project, the town planned to repave North Broadway Avenue, the main downtown thoroughfare, to widen vehicle lanes and speed up traffic by removing several stop lights. When Burden heard what they were planning to do, he suggested otherwise. "I said, wait a minute, if you've got the money, let's do it the right way," he told them. "Instead of widening the road, let's widen the sidewalks. Let's make it easier for pedestrians to get around, instead of speeding up cars."

Bike-Friendly Cities in Denmark

People who commute on their bikes are happier than those who drive cars or ride buses or trains to get to work, research shows. "We found that people are in the best mood while they are bicycling compared to any other mode of transportation," said Eric Morris, an assistant professor in Clemson University's city planning and real estate development department, who was the lead author of a 2015 study published in the journal *Transportation*. Biking not only makes you healthier, Morris said, but also it gives you a satisfying sense of accomplishment that you don't get from driving or riding.

From what I've seen in Copenhagen, most Danes feel the same way, whether they're college students with backpacks or business people in suits and ties. The bike lanes in that city always seem to be packed. During the past 20 years, bicycle traffic in the city has increased by 70 percent, and in fact cyclists in Copenhagen set a new record in November 2016, when for the first time the number of bikes in the heart of the city (265,700) outnumbered the number of cars (252,600). Danish officials estimate that more than one in three commuters in the capital get to work on bikes, using a network of lanes separated from vehicles.

To keep biking safe and convenient, the city spends about a fifth of its road budget each year on maintaining the network. As of 2015, it had 74,000 bike parking spaces available. An active population is a happy one, the Danes figure. "If you have a city with a lot of cyclists, you have a city with a lot of life," said Jan Gehl, the celebrated Danish architect and urban designer, when I visited him at his office in Copenhagen. Dressed in black with rimless glasses, the burly 80-year-old has spent a career advocating for ways to make cities friendlier to pedestrians and cyclists. From London to New York to Moscow to Melbourne,

Australia, Gehl has advised civic leaders how to reshape urban surroundings to improve quality of life.

"Bicyclists have a humanizing effect, compared with cars," Gehl said. The key is to make biking as inviting as possible to city residents. "Now, I play the trombone," he said. "If I keep my instrument in a case, and I have to unpack it, and put it away, and tune it, and so on, I don't play it. But if it's ready, you're going to hear some music. It's all about making things easy to access."

Copenhagen wasn't always so bike friendly. During the 1960s, the city was a typical car-congested metropolis with pollution, noise, and stress. But the global oil crisis of the 1970s and a growing environmental movement reversed that trend, with cycling emerging as the transportation of choice. But recently, when pollsters asked Danish commuters why they prefer bikes to cars, very few mentioned either the environment or health, even though cycling reduces emissions from cars and provides riders with daily exercise. Instead, they overwhelmingly said they do it because it's more convenient.

It's convenient because the city has been designed that way. Consider the latest advantage provided by city officials. They call it the "green wave," and it basically means that, for miles at a time, cyclists in Copenhagen never have to stop for traffic lights on the city's main arteries, because the lights have been synchronized to favor bikes over cars. This allows commuters to keep up a comfortable cruising speed on the way to work. It's just one of the many cycling infrastructure investments the city has made— more than $140 million since 2005.

In the Danish city of Aalborg, Mayor Thomas Kastrup-Larsen has been another strong advocate of cycling. In fact, when I approached him for an interview, he suggested that we take a short tour of the city on bikes. I arrived at his house, and he had a pair of street bikes ready to go.

A fit-looking 45-year-old, Kastrup-Larsen wore gray slacks and black dress shoes as we pedaled away from his row house near the center of the city. He wanted to show off Aalborg's newly renovated waterfront district, which had once been an industrial eyesore. Where abandoned shipyards and factories formerly stood, there were now restaurants, walkways, benches, art galleries, and concert halls overlooking the Limfjord, the narrow body of water that separates Northern Jutland from the rest of Denmark.

"Aren't you worried that all this stylish modern architecture will threaten the city's Hans Christian Andersen–like charm?" I asked.

"Not at all," he said. "A community needs to evolve."

We turned inland toward Aalborg University and pedaled past bunkerlike brick buildings, interspersed with offices. The mayor returned to the subject of cycling, which he said would continue to be a priority in the future. "We want to make it easier for people to cycle more," he said. "And we've got a few good ideas about how to do that." Among the proposed innovations were digital signs giving distances and speeds, automatic air pumps, turn lanes inside a protective curb, and convenient stands at stoplights where cyclists could rest a foot without having to dismount.

"People in Copenhagen think they live in the only real city in Denmark," Kastrup-Larsen said, adding that Aalborg has a population of more than 200,000 and is still growing. "We have to work a little harder for success here," he said. "We're more humble and appreciate it more." That's why the waterfront renovation was such a matter of pride for him. Turning the area into a gathering place, where people could walk or bike to a restaurant or concert hall, was going to make life in Aalborg that much more enjoyable.

Burden's experience in other communities had taught him that people today still want to shop or enjoy a meal without having to drive long distances. They still value places close enough to home that they can walk, take a bus, or ride a bike to get there. Albert Lea's downtown used to be like that, people there remembered. Instead of making traffic faster, Burden told city officials, they should slow it down. Instead of making it easier to empty out the downtown area at night, they should find ways to make it easier for folks to linger on the sidewalks and enjoy themselves.

The town council decided to take a chance. It invested a total of $4.5 million. Following Burden's recommendation, the council made sidewalks wide enough for outdoor dining, restored diagonal parking in front of shops, added "bump outs" to pedestrian crossings to make them safer and more convenient, replaced traffic signals with stop signs, installed community message boards, and created amphitheater seating in an adjacent park for entertainment and events. A new bike route was also extended from a state park to downtown.

It was a gamble—revitalizing the downtown by making it more walkable and bikeable—but by all accounts, the gamble has paid off. As a direct result of the renovations, 15 new businesses have opened up downtown, according to Chad Adams, the city manager. "Before the project, we rarely, if ever, got any phone calls from people wanting to be downtown," he said. "Now I get calls every week, but we don't have any spots left." Business owners have also invested in improvements, adding another two million dollars of upgrades to the corridor.

Now residents are also returning, as Burden predicted, with pedestrian traffic up 70 percent in the downtown area. Families are coming back for farmers markets, shopping, restaurants, and special events like "Wind Down Wednesday," when the streets are closed to vehicles for music and food. In addition, real estate values have shot up by 25 percent, according to the county assessor, not only in the three renovated blocks but also on streets surrounding them, adding an additional one million dollars to the tax base.

"Oh, my gosh, it's night and day, compared to where they were eight years ago," Burden said of Albert Lea's proud new business district. "Not only did the town get what it needed to keep growing into the future, but civic leaders from around the region are now coming to see what they've accomplished. And those folks are going back home and passing the same policies to build something better in their own communities."

Designing Engagement

One of the most effective things a community can do to keep you happy is to make it easier for you to volunteer. Research has shown that volunteering is good for you, especially as you get older. Besides keeping you engaged with others and fortifying your sense of purpose, it also tends to reduce your risk of health problems and boost your well-being.

Just ask Bertha Barnes, a 79-year-old great-grandmother who came out early one morning to walk to school with kids from her neighborhood in Fort Worth, Texas. A tall African-American woman with a dusting of gray in her black hair, Barnes was wearing a blaze yellow vest over her Blue Zones Project T-shirt and comfortable shoes. Along with several other adults, she'd volunteered to be part of a "walking school bus" that was about to leave the parking lot of the East Berry Public Library and head for Christene C. Moss Elementary School a mile away.

A walking school bus is like a regular school bus—without the bus. A group of children and two or more adults follow a designated route through a neighborhood, sometimes picking up other kids at predetermined addresses along the way, and then they walk to school together. The experience, it turns out, is good for both the children and the adults. Teachers say that kids who walk to school tend to be more alert during class and better prepared to learn, while the adults report being energized by their interactions with the children.

The ultimate goal of the program is to revive a tradition that many Americans have abandoned. As recently as 1980, 60 percent of all students living within two miles of a school walked or biked to class. Today, that number has dropped to less than 15 percent, as more and more parents, concerned about traffic dangers and their kids' personal safety, have taken to driving children to school. The result: long lines of cars jamming the streets in front of schools twice a day and less fresh air and exercise for the kids.

Barnes had heard about this walking school bus from her exercise instructor at the McDonald Southeast YMCA, where she takes a Silver Sneakers class. A team member from the Blue Zones Fort Worth Project had reached out to the instructor at the beginning of the year to see if anyone there might be interested in volunteering. As organizers in other communities have discovered, senior citizens often make excellent chaperones. "People who are looking for ways to stay involved in the community can help relieve busy parents," said Tiesa Leggett, another Blue Zones Project team member. Nodding at the seniors from the YMCA, she said, "If it wasn't for them, we wouldn't have as many volunteers." Soon Barnes and several others began meeting the kids every Wednesday to walk.

At 7:30 sharp, the group filed out of the library parking lot and marched down the sidewalk along Pate Drive, with three girls near the front carrying a large cardboard cutout of an orange school bus. Taking a position midway through the line, Barnes kicked a plastic bottle out of the group's way as they proceeded through the neighborhood, which looked a little rough around the edges. Median incomes in this part of Fort Worth, I later discovered, were about half as high as those in the city as a whole.

When the group reached the first intersection, a boy named Pedro led the way across the street, holding a stop sign in his hand. Barnes noticed a little girl with an untied shoelace. "Here, let me help you with that," she said, kneeling down to work on it. It was clearly a familiar task for Barnes, who has two great-grandchildren about the same age. When she finished, the little girl raced off.

"Happiness starts with this," Barnes said.

Researchers tend to agree. According to studies by Linda P. Fried, dean of Columbia University's Mailman School of Public Health, seniors who volunteer are not only contributing to worthy causes, but they may also be improving their own mental and physical health. "Giving back to your community may slow the aging process in ways that lead to a higher quality of life in older adults," Fried wrote. More specifically, older volunteers tend to have lower mortality rates, lower rates of depression, fewer physical limitations, and higher levels of well-being. In fact, volunteering has been found to have a more positive impact on well-being than income, education level, or marriage.

"I just want to give back," Barnes said, when asked why she volunteers. "My daughter says to me, 'Oh mother, I don't know where you get all of that energy.' I say, 'You don't use it, you lose it.'"

As it turned out, one of the younger adults taking part in the walking school bus this morning was a graduate student from the University of North Texas named Abby Winstead. She was studying intergenerational volunteering for an internship in public health. "When senior adults retire, or when their kids move off, a lot of them feel like they've been removed from society, because their role isn't there anymore," she said. "But doing stuff like this shows them they can still play a part in the community. Did you see the way the older women engaged with the children? 'Have you always lived around here?' they asked, and 'Where do you live?' They're investing in children they don't even know. But the truth is that friendships don't have to be close in age. That's so cool to see."

The kids raced the last few yards to the school. Before disappearing through the door, one little girl lingered, looking back at the volunteers. She seemed slightly surprised by the spectacle of so many adults waving good-bye to her. Then she broke into a big smile and waved back, before she, too, disappeared. Volunteering engenders happiness both ways, giving and receiving.

DESIGNING A HEALTHY COMMUNITY

When the first hotel opened in Naples, Florida, in 1889, the town was a sleepy winter getaway for wealthy families from the Midwest. Today dozens of luxury hotels line the beach along the Gulf of Mexico. Multimillion-dollar mansions keep popping up along the waterfront, and golf courses stretch eastward toward the Everglades in this booming region now known as the Paradise Coast.

But for Dr. Allen Weiss, the president and CEO of NCH Health-care System, which operates two nonprofit hospitals and other facilities in Southwest Florida, that's only part of the story here.

"Sure, we've got a couple of Ritz-Carltons," he said. "I've been told we've got more retired CEOs than anywhere in the country, as well as the highest unearned per capita income in the country—or one of the highest. But 64 percent of the 46,000 children in our public schools qualify for free or reduced lunches, and 55 percent go home to non-English-speaking homes. Half of the kids coming into kindergarten have never heard English spoken before. Our community's very diverse socioeconomically and culturally, with the highs and lows literally living adjacent to each other."

As the cost of treating chronic diseases continued to rise in Naples and surrounding Collier County—in both the affluent and the lower-income neighborhoods—Dr. Weiss went before the board of his organization in 2014 with an unconventional proposal. Instead of just being a repair shop treating the sick, he said, NCH Healthcare should also invest in prevention. By making the whole community healthier, they could reduce their own costs and improve the quality of life for everyone—including the overall sense of well-being for the entire community. "Our goal was not only to help the soccer moms and executives, but also to get out into our rural communities where we've got people picking tomatoes," he said. "We wanted to help that farmworker and his family, too."

Dr. Weiss looked into various approaches to prevention, and he was attracted to the Blue Zones Project because of its focus on long-term changes to the environment. "In my own professional career as an internist, rheumatologist, and geriatrician, I knew that if you get people into a good environment, you can literally change the course of their disease," he said. "For a child with rheumatoid arthritis, the family environment is most important. For a community, the walking environment, the eating environment, and everything else are most important."

Before signing up with the Blue Zones Project team, though, Dr. Weiss wanted to see how things were going in other Blue Zones Communities. So he visited the Beach Cities in California, he dropped by Albert Lea, Minnesota, and he checked out Cedar Falls, Iowa. "We felt we had to kick the tires on our own," he said. He met with the mayor of Cedar Falls, who described the overall impact of Blue Zones Project activities on his town. "The most interesting thing he said was that the culture of the community had changed," Dr. Weiss said. "People were coming together—people who hadn't spoken to each other, who lived on opposite sides of the block. They were now taking walks twice a week or joining eating groups together, and it had just changed things."

That was exactly the kind of transformation that Dr. Weiss had in mind for Naples. So he took the Blue Zones Project proposal to his board. "I told them, we could take the money we've saved by reducing costs in our own operation and buy new X-ray equipment and computer stuff, or we could try to make the community healthier, and become the healthiest and happiest community in the country."

That was almost three years ago. Since then, the Blue Zones Project in Southwest Florida has spread out from Naples across Collier County and southern Lee County, challenging grocery stores and restaurants to offer customers healthier choices, encouraging worksites to adopt healthier practices, making suggestions to local schools to help students eat better and stay active, and enlisting churches and other organizations to help residents connect socially.

In many ways, the Naples area was already ahead of the curve in terms of providing amenities like bike lanes, sidewalks, community gardens, and farmers markets to residents, whether they were snowbirds from the north or year-round Floridians. In fact, when Gallup-Sharecare in 2016 identified the highest-ranking communities in the nation for overall well-being, the Naples area won the top spot, edging out places such as Salinas, California; Sarasota, Florida; and Fort Collins, Colorado. Of the five well-being elements that the researchers measured—purpose, social, financial, community, and physical—Naples residents scored highest in the nation in the community category, responding favorably when asked how much they liked where they live, if they felt safe, and if they had pride in their town.

"We were frankly surprised to hear that Naples scored so well—because we see all the needs in our community," Dr. Weiss said. "In the affluent neighborhoods, we still face alcoholism, obesity, depression, and mental illness, and in the rural communities, we still face lack of access to care, lack of access to good dentistry, and lack of access to healthy foods."

DE-STRESSING THE COMMUNITY

The Paradise Coast clearly had a lot going for it, but it wasn't perfect yet. In that respect, Southwest Florida had a lot in common with Blue Zones demonstration communities in the Beach Cities of California and the island communities of Oahu and Hawaii. In all of these popular locations, residents had to balance the advantages of living in a natural paradise with the pressures and stresses that came from being such a sought-after destination.

In the Beach Cities the underlying stress came from traffic and worries about real estate prices. "We live in this beautiful place, but we're all on edge," Jeff Duclos, the former mayor of Hermosa Beach, told me a few years ago. "We're stuck in the middle of this huge metropolis, Los Angeles, which is completely dysfunctional in terms of moving people around." At the same time, housing prices had gone through the roof. In Manhattan Beach, the median listing price in 2014 was just under three million dollars. More and more residents were struggling to keep up.

When Gallup-Sharecare came to the Beach Cities in 2010 to measure well-being, they discovered that people in Southern California were feeling as much stress as the people of New Orleans did after Hurricane Katrina and as much anger as residents of Detroit did after the Great Recession of 2007–2009. "I wasn't surprised that our stress numbers were higher than normal," said the local health district's chief medical officer. "But some of the highest in the country? I would never have expected that."

The situation was much the same in Hawaii, where the high cost of living was making it difficult for residents to keep up. "We live in this amazing place," said Dena Smith Ellis, a Blue Zones Project organizer. "We live outdoors a lot, so it's easy for us to keep moving naturally. And, culturally speaking, the people of Hawaii already embrace a lot of Blue Zones ways, such as putting family first, faith-based organizations, belonging, the right tribe. People are already doing these things." But the cost of living in Hawaii was ridiculous, she said. "Gas is expensive. Housing is expensive. Education is expensive. Food is outrageous. It's very challenging for middle-class families working two or three jobs."

Ellis has been helping organizations on the Big Island engage with Blue Zones Project activities. "The four communities I work in are very different," she said. "Two are blue collar, real local, lots of diversity of cultures. And the other two have some of the richest people in America. They may only live there a month or two out of the year. We're talking the one percenters." Such dramatic differences in income levels can generate stress, which undermines happiness. When Gallup-Sharecare's pollsters measured well-being on the islands, they found that Hawaiians scored in the top five states nationally in four of five categories—purpose, financial, community, and physical. But when it came to the social element—having supporting relationships and love in their lives—their rank dropped to 46.

"This was really perplexing to our team," Ellis said. "But I have a theory. In Hawaii we have a saying—aloha—which most people have heard of. Yet a lot of people outside of Hawaii don't actually know what it means. Aloha isn't just a greeting. It also encompasses connection and trust. For many native Hawaiians, that trust has been violated, so they tend to be a little guarded. If you want them to welcome you in, you have to show that you can be trusted."

The best way to do that? Get people connected socially, she said. For both Hawaii and California's Beach Cities, that turned out to be a successful pathway to de-stressing the community.

On Hawaii's Big Island, Blue Zones Project teams organized walking moais and potluck moais to bring folks together, as well as purpose workshops and volunteer initiatives at faith-based organizations. "For many people in these communities, it was a new way of approaching one another" Ellis said, not only for native Hawaiians, but also for Japanese, Filipinos, Samoans, and other ethnic groups. "Community engagement like this has provided an opportunity for cross-cultural conversations. You might have a billionaire housewife getting together with impoverished families to support a healthy food drive. It can be a great way to reverse class barriers."

In Southern California, the Blue Zones Project team also introduced walking moais and other initiatives aimed at keeping people emotionally and socially engaged. More than 2,500 people, for example, attended a series of two-hour purpose workshops in the Beach Cities, where they learned ways to identify their gifts and passions—their "reason to wake up in the morning." Participants were then encouraged to put these gifts to use in the community through volunteering.

The results were encouraging. After five years of Blue Zones Project efforts, the number of Beach Cities residents whose daily lives were classified as "thriving" rose an impressive 12 percent—up from 64.4 percent in 2010 to 72.2 percent in 2015. (To be described as "thriving," rather than "struggling" or "suffering," in the Gallup-Sharecare Well-Being Index, respondents had to rate their current lives as a 7 or higher on a 10-point scale and their future lives as an 8 or higher.) That positive assessment of their quality of life put Beach Cities residents significantly ahead of most Americans, only 54.1 percent of whom rated their lives that highly.

In part, this improved sense of well-being among people living in the Beach Cities was due to a reduction in stress levels. "We've seen a 9 percent drop in daily significant stress from where we started in 2010," said Susan Burden, former CEO of the Beach Cities Health District, which helped to sponsor the original Blue Zones Project in Southern California and has con-tinued to fund it since. That reduction in stress put local residents a full three points ahead of Californians as a whole, said Dan Witters of the Gallup-Sharecare Well-Being Index—a significant difference, he said. "It goes to show that even when demographics might be stressed or handicapped, you can move the needle if you put in place the right interventions and create the right environment for well-being."

Witters also praised the Beach Cities for boosting the number of residents who exercised at least 30 minutes a day, three days a week, from 60.5 percent in 2010 to 65.8 percent in 2015. At the same time, the number of individuals who were above normal weight dropped an impressive 15 percent to 50.8 percent, and the number of obese individuals dropped to 12.1 percent, compared with 28.1 percent nationally. Smoking was down as well, falling by more than 17 percent in the Beach Cities to only 8.9 percent of the population—less than half of the national average of 18.8 percent.

"We've seen fairly dramatic health gains here that go against trends from other parts of the country —places where not only did they not see gains, but they saw figures going the other way," Burden said of her Beach Cities home. "There's still a lot of work to do, but we're one of the few places in the country that has things in place to build a healthier community."

Following the example of these and other Blue Zones Communities across the country, the team in Southwest Florida has made real strides in finding ways to reduce stress levels among its residents. They've given special attention to building social connections and promoting healthy changes in schools, businesses, restaurants, and grocery stores. "If you want a community to be happy, you need physical well-being, you need financial security, you need meaningful work, and you need a supportive family or group around you," Dr. Weiss said. "When you have those things, you're much happier than you would be otherwise."

COMMUNITY BLUEPRINT FOR HAPPINESS

As Tolstoy wrote in *Anna Karenina*, "All happy families are alike; each unhappy family is unhappy in its own way." The same is true for cities. Certain initiatives, activities, and commitments continue to rise to the top as key methods for working on the outer ring of your Life Radius and building a community that supports the greatest happiness for all its citizens. The following list synthesizes the metrics used in the Gallup-Sharecare surveys, the recommendations of our Blue Zones Happiness Consensus Panel, and the lessons I've learned through years of visiting the world's happiest places and watching what works in our 42 Blue Zones Project Communities:

1. **Seek a healthy lifestyle.** Time and again we see evidence that good health equates to a happy life. To put it another way, obese and unhealthy people are measurably less happy than healthy people. The more that communities take steps to lower rates of disease—which includes reducing stress, known to cause low-grade chronic anxiety or depression— the more likely they are to create an environment of increased well-being.

    Lessons: Improve food choices in the community by limiting the number of fast-food stores per block. Find ways to nudge the community to drink water instead of sugary beverages. Pass a tax on soda and other sugar-sweetened drinks and invest the proceeds in local childhood obesity programs. Clean water is a strong bellwether for high community well-being, so make sure water is abundant and fluoridated. Support community noise ordinances, since evidence shows that we don't adapt to noise, and in fact excess noise increases stress. Finally, since the mentally ill account for 50 percent of a population's health care costs— and drive up a community's unhappiness proportionately— any effort to treat diseases like depression and anxiety is sure to provide manifold returns.

2. **Design a community that favors humans over cars.** Happier communities have found ways to encourage walking and biking over traveling in cars. Not only do people get more exercise that way, but also they socialize more when not in their cars. Well-designed roads and sidewalks create environments of trust and reduce vehicle emissions, and

active living street designs increase physical activity by at least 30 percent citywide.

Lessons: At the personal level, always choose walking or biking over driving when you can. Join or initiate local efforts to clean up parks, maintain sidewalks, create bike lanes, promote public transportation, and clean up unwanted graffiti—all proven ways to make it more likely that people will get out of their cars and onto their feet (or bicycles). City improvements might include narrowing traffic lanes, lowering speed limits, widening sidewalks, adding bicycling lanes, and eliminating one-way streets—all recommendations included in the Complete Streets initiative, a nonprofit movement founded in 2004 to make city transportation networks cleaner, safer, and more accessible. For more information, visit the website *smart growthamerica.org.*

3. **Limit urban sprawl.** Shorter commutes increase well-being. Concentrated population centers are less expensive to maintain, with minimized water and road services, for example. The air is cleaner, with less auto exhaust and lower emissions. When work and home are closer together—not involving a long commute through heavy traffic—a community enjoys more social interaction and a more vibrant downtown.

   Lessons: When making decisions about where to live and where to work, consider the distance and factor in the health advantages of walking or biking to work. You can learn more about the walkability of a community you're interested in by using the "walk score" site (*walkscore.com*). Urge your town or city to pass codes requiring smaller lot sizes, tax incentives for inner-city improvement, and limited public financing of services outside certain perimeters. Join with others to develop a greenbelt to enhance your community; you can use those in Portland, Oregon; Boulder, Colorado; or San Luis Obispo, California, as models.

4. **Limit smoking.** Smokers are measurably less happy than nonsmokers, and they tend to make the people around them less happy, too. Moreover, higher incidences of cancer, heart disease, and disability among smokers cost the heath care system billions of dollars annually, whether through Medicare or Medicaid or because of increased insurance premiums for treatment.

   Lessons: If you are a smoker, explore your options and find the best way to quit. Communities create the best environment to help smokers stop by denormalizing smoking: Restrict areas where smoking is allowed, impose taxes and restrictions on tobacco, and promote education campaigns to lower smoking rates. Learn from cities like San Luis Obispo and Calabasas, California, and Boulder, Colorado, which now have some of the lowest smoking rates in the country thanks to community action.

5. **Invest in beauty.** Beauty, especially natural beauty, pleases us and puts us at ease. The happiest places in America also tend to be the most beautiful. In the case of Boulder and San Luis Obispo, civic leaders banded together to preserve natural beauty; in places like Minneapolis and Portland, taxpayers made deep investments in parks and open spaces. And it pays off: Property values go up, and therefore the tax base is higher in beautiful cities.

   Lessons: Join in community efforts to protect the natural surroundings of your community, whether it means your waterways, oceanfront, mountain views, forests, or open spaces. Be wary of local growth initiatives, because they often beget a spiral of development, higher populations, and more urbanism—which can often mean more stress. Prohibit or limit outdoor advertising (no one except advertisers likes billboards). Explore and support the public purchase of desired land around the city to create more green spaces. Plant and maintain more trees along streets and in parks. Encourage your city to hire an arborist assigned to that job.

6. **Create a leadership committee.** You can't legislate or buy a happy city; it takes a community, and it takes leaders dedicated to inspiring input and action from the public sector, local businesses, and grassroots organizations.

    Lessons: A first step is to convene city officials—the mayor, the city manager, key members of the city council, along with the school superintendent, the police chief, the chamber of commerce, and directors of key health organizations—and get them to identify the policies and programs most likely to create a higher quality of life in your community. Learn more about this key action by visiting the website of the National Charrette Institute (*charrette institute.org*).

7. **Bring in expertise.** Once you have identified the ways your community needs to change in order to support the highest level of well-being, you don't have to reinvent the wheel. Turn to the experts and those who have come before you to learn more about designing streets, denormalizing tobacco, promoting healthier food, and other actions to create the best environment for happiness.

Lessons: As we have mentioned before, the cities that have been part of the Blue Zones Project over the past few years offer great models for change in the direction of happiness. Learn more about them, as well as what the Blue Zones organization can offer, on the website *bluezones.com*. Learn about how cities work (and don't) by reading Jane Jacobs's *The Death and Life of Great American Cities*. The Walkable and Livable Communities Institute (WALC; website *walklive.org*) has a lot to offer communities that want to improve their physical spaces. The Public Health Law Center at the Mitchell Hamline School of Law (*publichealthlaw center.org*) has practical suggestions for improving local policies on food and tobacco.

8. **Find ways to measure well-being.** Creating a happier, healthier community takes focus, considerable effort, and an investment from a variety of stakeholders for at least three to five years. Watching this happen in our Blue Zones demonstration communities, I've found that if you can show annual incremental improvement, people stay motivated and organizations are assured of a return on their investments. And, most important, if you can track gains in well-being and match them to policies and programs, you can better see what's working and what isn't.

    Lessons: Any community set on making changes to improve general well-being needs to commit to a measurement technique, set a starting baseline, and continue to manage to it. The gold standard is the Gallup-Sharecare Well-Being Index, which measures 55 facets of health and happiness across five distinct elements of well-being—purpose, social, financial, community, and physical. Cities can also determine their own set of metrics—body mass index, health care costs, walkability score, for example. Smaller communities that don't meet the sample criteria size are not reported in the Gallup-Sharecare Well-Being Index, so they will need to design evaluation systems that suit them and that are manageable with the information at hand. Here are the key measures I've come across in my experience:

- Clean water
- Food policies that favor fruits and vegetables and discourage fast food
- Few or no billboards
- Abundant and wide sidewalks
- Bikeability
- A robust public transport system
- High civic engagement
- High volunteer rates
- Plenty of parks
- High median housing prices
- High Gallup-Sharecare Well-Being Index scores
- Lots of dentists
- Lack of sprawl
- Laws that denormalize smoking

CHAPTER 8

❧

Designing the
Workplace

"I HAVE WHAT YOU MIGHT CALL a stressful job," said Leah Graham with characteristic humility. On any given day Graham, who works at the Fort Worth Police Department's 911 center, will answer more than 150 calls, many of which can mean life or death for the caller. After assessing the situation, the 27-year-veteran of the department dispatches police officers, firefighters, or medical technicians to the scene.

"I was on the radio with two officers on the freeway one time," she said, recalling one incident. "They were working an accident, and someone came along and hit the officers." She kept her cool and dispatched two more ambulances immediately. And she's only one of the 140 operators who work at the facility—every day any one of them can be put in a similar high-stress situation.

In an effort to reduce on-the-job stress among the call takers and dispatchers, Graham recently recruited a few dozen co-workers to join a Blue Zones Project moai—a circle of friends who share interests and agree to take regular walks together for at least

10 weeks. She figured that getting folks up and walking during their breaks would be better for their health and morale than having them sit around eating snacks. The plan caught on. Soon more than 30 additional people had signed up, including supervisors. "This is an operation that runs 24/7, and we had people from all three shifts who wanted to walk," she said. "So we broke them down into teams of four or five people and went walking whenever we could."

When lives are at stake, dispatchers are under the gun, and the stress builds with frequent staffing problems and technology issues. When an accident occurs on a busy freeway, the 911 center may be bombarded by 50 or more calls. Teamwork becomes essential, Graham said. "You need support from your co-workers. If there's any conflict between people, that adds more stress to an already stressful job."

The moais have proven helpful in that respect, she said. What began as a way to get more exercise has also strengthened relationships. "Before, some people would go on their break and sit in their car or go to the break room by themselves," she said. "But when they go walking they're interacting, talking, doing something together, and they've kind of become friends." Morale has improved.

Every workplace can feel like a pressure cooker from time to time. In fact, in a 2016 Gallup survey of job satisfaction, U.S. workers reported that what bothered them the most about their jobs was the amount of stress they felt at work. Two-thirds of those surveyed reported that they had too much on-the-job stress.

Because we spend so many of our waking hours on the job, the workplace environment has a big impact on our health and happiness. Satisfied workers take fewer sick days, are more productive, and tend to treat customers and co-workers better. They tend to get better job reviews and, over the long term, earn higher incomes. Satisfied workers also impact the bottom line for employers. According to a 2015 Gallup study, businesses with "highly engaged" employees were 21 percent more profitable on average than those with "disengaged" ones.

For much of the past decade, worker satisfaction has been in a slump, though, costing American businesses as much as $300 billion a year in lost productivity. A 2011 survey conducted by the Conference Board, an international nonprofit dedicated to improving business practices, reported that U.S. workers were the unhappiest they had been in their 22 years of tracking job satisfaction rates. Much of that, no doubt, was caused by the aftereffects of the Great Recession of 2007–2009, which undermined job security as well as satisfaction. The only people less happy than American workers during this period of slow economic recovery were those who had lost their jobs altogether.

Although the employment picture has improved in the United States since then, we still have a long way to go. That only 33 percent of all American workers say they're engaged with their jobs, according to Gallup, may sound like a depressing statistic until you realize that this is the highest level of job satisfaction in the United States in more than 20 years. What can be done to improve the situation? How can we optimize the workplace to promote greater health and happiness?

As it turns out, a lot. And many of these things don't require big investments, fancy new offices, or cappuccino machines. One of the things that matter most to employees, Gallup discovered, is free. It's having a best friend at work.

CREATING A BLUE ZONES WORKPLACE

That's one reason why Salo LLC, a Minneapolis-based staffing and consulting firm, began introducing its employees to one another a few years ago. Because so many of the company's far-flung staff were located at client worksites, rather than at Salo's headquarters, the firm had been looking for ways to strengthen connections among workers. With help from our Blue Zones Project team, Salo agreed to try a six-month experiment in 2012. They created 21 moais and assigned six to eight workers to each one based on shared interests rather than on titles or departments. The idea was for members to get to know one another through biweekly conference calls, pot-lucks, and other off-site activities.

"I was skeptical at first," said Angie Complin, who worked in business development at Salo at the time. "My moai had single people, married people, younger people, middle-aged people, even a few retired people in it. But everyone was really engaged. We learned a ton about one another, including some pretty personal things, and now I feel really close with them, even with the ones I don't see on a daily basis, almost like long-lost friends."

As an effort to boost well-being, the experiment was a big suc-cess, said Gwen Martin, a co-founder of Salo. "People were happier, more engaged and more collaborative," she said. The moais were only one part of a larger Blue Zones initiative at Salo aimed at cre-ating a healthier and happier workplace. The approach employed several dozen evidence-based nudges and defaults designed to silently get employees to eat better, burn more calories throughout the day, and, to the point of Gallup's finding, socialize more with co-workers. The company also offered free purpose workshops, life coaching, happy hours, volunteering events, and nine-minute med-itation sessions, which turned out to be surprisingly popular. "When we started, people snickered at the idea of meditating," Martin said. "But by the end, many of them were doing just that."

In fact, the range of things that Salo employees were willing to try had really evolved, she said. After the first six months of the campaign, the number of workers who were volunteering for community causes had increased by 14 percent, turnover had dropped by 9 percent, life expectancy had risen by an average of 2.6 years, and happiness levels had jumped by 47 percent! "We were really fortunate to have taken part in the Blue Zones initiative," said Martin (who later joined the Blue Zones team as our managing director).

Even before taking part in the Blue Zones initiative, Salo had adopted a number of worksite innovations, especially those designed to encourage more activity. At its main offices in downtown Minneapolis, table-desks occupied one end of the open loft–style space and a games area the other end, with table tennis and a foosball station. One whole section of the office was outfitted with standing desks, several of which even had treadmills installed. They were part of a 2007 Mayo Clinic study of active workplaces, for which 18 Salo employees spent about three hours a day walking on the treadmills while participating in conference calls or working on their computers. After six months, the study found, these employees had lost a combined total of 156 pounds and had also reduced their cholesterol and triglyceride counts.

Our team learned a lot at Salo, which became the nation's first Blue Zones–certified workplace outside of a Blue Zones Project Community. Since then, Blue Zones strategies have been adopted by more than 600 businesses across the country through our employer programs in Blue Zones Project Communities, from sprawling factories in Iowa to fruit smoothie shops in Hawaii. And in each instance, we've followed the same six-stage model to optimize the Life Radius of employees—both on the job and in their communities—focusing on a company's leadership, purpose, physical environment, social networks, policies and benefits, and well-being solutions.

Whenever a business expresses an interest in becoming a Blue Zones Project Approved worksite, we ask the following six questions, which parallel the six focal points listed above:

- Are your organization's leaders (at all levels) modeling well-being behaviors and influencing an environment that supports the well-being of others?
- Does your organization have a purpose that employees connect with, and does your organization support employees to identify and pursue their own purpose inside the context of their work?
- Does your worksite promote healthy practices and empower employees to make healthful choices through the physical layout and worksite setting?
- Is there a clearly defined engagement strategy that uses an effective mix of communications, incentives, and social events to help promote well-being improvement?
- Are your human resources policies and benefits designed to encourage well-being?
- Are there engaging solutions to support employee efforts to improve and sustain well-being?

As you can see, the Blue Zones approach is wide-ranging and comprehensive. But the potential benefits are significant. With little or no financial investment, employers can expect greater productivity from their workers, reduced absenteeism, and lower health care costs over time. In addition, Blue Zones Project Approved worksites also gain recognition from community leaders, are frequently featured in media coverage, and find it easier to extend the company brand.

To qualify for the Blue Zones designation, at least 25 percent of workers must sign a Blue Zones Personal Pledge, which requires all of them to optimize their own surroundings. This includes reviewing their homes against a checklist designed to discourage mindless eating and encourage better sleep. It also calls for them to take a free Blue Zones Purpose Workshop to identify their strengths, passions, and gifts. At the same time, employers choose from a menu of actions to promote health and happiness in the worksite, such as creating better lighting, providing stand-up desks, or redesigning furniture so people interact more. Employers must also do a policy makeover, making employee well-being a priority in the company mission statement, encouraging employees to volunteer by permitting them to take off a couple of hours a week, and allowing them to customize their workspace to reflect their personal values.

But maybe a few specific examples can tell the story even better of how a few simple changes in a workplace can make everyone happier.

When the Blue Zones team came to Redondo Beach, California, a few years ago, Russ Lesser signed up Body Glove International to become one of the first designated Blue Zones Worksites in town. Founded in 1953, the company had made a name for itself among West Coast surfers by producing the first practical wet suits from neoprene. Today it sells swimwear, activewear, dive equipment, and other accessories, as well as the latest wet suits and surfing gear.

"We used to snack on cookies and candies in the office," said Lesser, who has been president of the company for the past 27 years. "Now every morning at ten o'clock we put out a tray of fruit and apples. We also take the staff out on a pretty regular basis to walk to lunch as a team, sometimes as far away as a mile. Morale's better, health is better, absenteeism is down. So we're kind of excited about the whole concept."

At the downtown Honolulu headquarters of the HMSA, our corporate sponsor in Hawaii, management set up a farmers market on Thursdays in the street-facing alcoves to sell local produce. It was an instant success: Not only did it make it easy for employees to buy vegetables on their way home, but also it became a way for employees to connect with people in the neighborhood. They also launched a walking moai program among their 1,800 employees—reluctantly at first. "We knew we were taking a big gamble with both initiatives, said Elisa Yadao, senior vice president. "But both succeeded well beyond our expectations."

In Albert Lea, Minnesota, managers at Freeborn-Mower Cooperative Services, an electric energy company, offered workers yoga classes after work, annual biometric testing, healthy snack stations, and walking paths with signs showing the number of steps it would take to complete them. "It's about creating an environment where it's easier to make healthy choices," said Judy Jensen, who works in payroll and accounting.

Chuck Marlin started walking during his lunch break at the Lou-Rich factory in Albert Lea because he wanted to lose a little weight. Marlin, a machinist, runs a milling machine that manufactures stainless steel augers for ice makers. "Sometime around last April all of a sudden I realized I'm turning 60, and it kind of scared me," Marlin said. "I've had a few health problems, and I thought, you know, I better do something."

Lou-Rich had designated a quarter-mile-long track through the plant, and Marlin figured that walking was something he could easily do. As a bonus, he started to meet new people. "They were going everywhere, one going clockwise, one counterclockwise," he said. "Walking also gave me a chance to see what else was going on in the plant." By the end of the year, he'd lost more than 50 pounds and his back didn't ache like it used to. "I was pretty proud," he said.

Dr. Eric Hochman and his wife, Kim, run Gulfshore Concierge Medicine in Naples, Florida, and adopted Blue Zones ideas in their practice. Dr. Hochman, who is board certified in internal medicine, pediatrics, and rheumatology, began offering free exercise and yoga classes to both his staff and his patients as part of an expanded well-being program. They even experimented with holding staff meetings outside. "We went over the 10-page checklist of things the

Blue Zones said we could do and noticed that we were already doing many of them," Kim said. These included being a tobacco-free workplace and providing healthy snacks such as granola bars, fig bars, and water. But they wanted to do more, so Eric started writing about the Blue Zones in the local newspaper. "The data behind the Blue Zones is so strong that doctors' offices should make it a priority," he said.

It wasn't just a medical thing for the couple. "It was also about being connected to your family," Kim said. "It was about being connected to your friends and having social interactions. It was about having a faith-based relationship. Having a purpose. It was about finding ways to move naturally. There are direct relationships between being healthy, from the whole view, and being happy."

"It's a snowball effect," Eric said. When people are healthier, they're more active. When they're able to do things, they're happier. "I had a patient recently who was on four different kinds of medications," he said. "But then he became active and lost a lot of weight. He no longer has diabetes, his blood pressure's back to normal, his cholesterol is great—all because he embraced a lifestyle change. And it's had a big effect not only on his physical health but also on his emotional health."

OPTIMIZING YOUR WORKPLACE

But what if you don't work at a Blue Zones–affiliated business? Are there actions you can take on your own to boost your happiness on the job? There's no shortage of advice these days from consultants, psychologists, and life coaches about how to create workplace well-being, from effective meeting practices to free yoga classes. But which ideas really work? Which will yield the greatest happiness in the long run, and what can you do for yourself?

Working Too Much?

You're not imagining it. Americans are putting in more hours on the job these days than workers in other advanced nations—about 25 percent more than Europeans, according to a recent study. We're also taking fewer vacation days and retiring later in life. The question is: Are we any making ourselves any happier with all of this eager beavering?

The answer might be yes, says Adam Okulicz-Kozaryn of Rutgers University–Camden. In a paper published in the *Journal of Happiness Studies* he reported finding that, based on correlating data about working hours with surveys of life satisfaction, in general, "as the number of work hours increases, Americans become happier about life than Europeans."

How did Okulicz-Kozaryn explain this apparent paradox? One reason for our willingness to work more might be the fact that we get to keep a greater percentage of our wages than do most Europeans, who tend to be more heavily taxed, he suggested. Putting in more hours on the job pays off better for Americans. Another reason might be that European labor unions have been more successful at securing benefits for workers, including more vacation days, than their counterparts in the United States. A third reason might be that Americans are simply more obsessed with achieving success—both financial and professional—than Europeans, who put more value on spending time with family and in leisure.

There might be darker reasons, though. Americans might be working more because we feel our jobs demand it or we have no choice. A recent Gallup poll found that more than half of all U.S. workers are now putting in more than 40 hours a week, and that almost one in five are working more than 60 hours. It comes as no surprise, then, that Americans also say that they're increasingly stressed out by juggling both work and family.

There's no question that the U.S. economy has put the squeeze on family life in this country. To make ends meet, most families today need two incomes, which is why 70 percent of American children now live in households where all adults work. Back in 1960, only 20 percent of American mothers had jobs outside the home, compared with 59 percent today. And for many working women, especially single moms, tensions have only increased between work and family obligations. About a third of all professional single mothers now report working 50 or more hours a week, while many low-income single mothers hold down two or more jobs.

When Okulicz-Kozaryn published his paper online in 2011, he received many comments along these lines. "We're not crazy," Americans told him. "We'd like to have more leisure and vacations, too." But they said they couldn't afford to take time away from work because they had to pay for health care, education, and all the other benefits that are subsidized in Europe. More than a fourth of all Americans take no vacation at all. From their point of view, Okulicz-Kozaryn said, "it was better to be overworked and miserable than underworked and not have enough money to pay for necessities."

One way to fix this unhappy situation might be to update U.S. labor laws to give workers and their families more help. Of the 35 modern nations in the Organization for Economic Co-operation and Development (OECD), the United States is the only one without laws requiring paid maternity leave, paid sick days, restrictions on mandatory overtime, and other measures to make jobs more flexible and fair, including access to high-quality, affordable child care. In the end it comes down to the values of our culture and how they are expressed by our government.

The key to unlocking this puzzle goes back to the balance of three P's: pleasure, purpose, and pride. It's about creating an enjoyable work environment so that a job becomes not just a paycheck but also a calling, and so that employees look on their work and career with pride.

Let's start with purpose: Before taking a position, you should seriously ask yourself if it will allow you to use your gifts and talents in a meaningful way. Will it challenge you with just the right amount of difficulty—not so hard that it makes you give up, but not so easy that you get bored—and immerse you in that intense state of engagement that psychologist Mihaly Csikszentmihalyi calls "flow"?

Athletes describe this amazing feeling as being "in the zone," but a factory worker might also experience it while repairing a piece of complicated equipment. A surgeon might feel it while immersed in a difficult operation. A business executive might get lost in it while closing a big deal. The best jobs provide regular opportunities to have flow experiences, turning work into something you look forward to, rather than something you dread. When your goal is clear, the task is challenging and you're getting immediate feedback on how you're doing, then time simply disappears. "A typical day is full of anxiety and boredom," Csikszentmihalyi writes in *Finding Flow*. "Flow experiences provide the flashes of intense living against this dull background."

In Denmark, for example, the economic environment encourages people to choose jobs that give them a greater chance of experiencing flow. With taxes claiming a big portion of their wages and ambition being frowned upon in Danish culture, there's no personal advantage for them to seek higher paychecks or impressive titles. Which may be why so many Danes choose to pursue creative work such as furniture design, architecture, or high technology, rather than jobs that might make them more money but give them less satisfaction.

When it's done right, after all, work can feel more like sports or a game than a chore, says Jane Dutton, a professor of business administration and psychology at the University of Michigan. In other words, with the right job, you actually take pleasure in the work you are doing. Even if you haven't yet found the perfect job, she says, you can still find ways to make your current one more meaningful. Like the marketing person who was asked to do some event planning and discovered she enjoyed it so much that she made it a bigger part of her responsibilities. Or the technician who agreed to train new hires in his department and found out that not only was he good at training others but also he liked doing it. These are just two examples of what Dutton calls "job crafting," which is the art of customizing a job to fit your interests. The trick is to identify at least one thing you like doing as part of your job responsibilities and then figure out how to do it more often.

A meaningful job comes from a conviction on your part that what you do at work is important, that your talents are being put to good use, and that your work makes a meaningful difference. It also depends on the degree to which you believe in the overall mission of your employer. Is it clearly defined and something worthy of pursuit? If you find yourself grinding out work under stressful conditions more often than you'd like, it helps to know that the end result, at least, is worthwhile.

A sense of purpose is actually worth a lot, as Robert H. Frank, an economics professor at Cornell, demonstrated one day with a class of seniors. "Suppose you're weighing two offers for jobs writing advertising copy," he asked them. "One is for an American Cancer Society campaign to discourage teenage smoking, the other for a tobacco industry campaign to encourage it. If pay and other working conditions were identical, which job would you choose?" His students were ready to join the job market, remember, so the question wasn't entirely abstract for them. Almost 90 percent said they'd take the American Cancer Society job, showing that the mission of the organization made a big difference to them. "When I asked them how much more the pro-tobacco job would have to pay before they would change their minds, they demanded an average salary premium of more than 80 percent," Frank wrote in the *New York Times*.

That's why Frank tells his students to strive for success, but not to put money ahead of other goals when picking a job. If their ultimate aim is to be happy in their working life, I would add, they should also consider whether their jobs would give them regular moments of joyful emotions, a sense of satisfaction about how their lives are going, and a strong sense of purpose.

As for the third strand of happiness—pride—what matters most on the job is whether you feel a sense of accomplishment from what you do. Are your responsibilities and duties well defined? Do you have specific goals? Are you encouraged to achieve excellence? Do you get timely, regular feedback from your supervisor? Is it clear when you've completed an assignment? Are you proud of what you've accomplished?

Having a great boss is key to achieving this type of happiness. And what workers value most in supervisors is a sense that they care about workers' professional development and encourage them to use their individual strengths on the job. What else makes a great boss? The criteria haven't changed much since I described them in *Thrive*: Can you talk to your boss about your challenges and problems? Does she tell you when you're doing a good job and offer constructive suggestions when you're not? Does she meet with you regularly? Does she go out of her way to let you do your job in a way that works for you? Does she really listen to your ideas? Are you recognized for doing good work, being productive, and innovating? Do you trust your boss? Does she care about you as a person? If you're lucky enough to have a boss with these traits, you're much more likely to be happy with your job.

By contrast, workers stuck with a bad manager are among the most miserable of people in the workplace—so unhappy, in fact, that of the employees who participated recently in a Gallup poll, half reported that, at some point in their careers, they'd been forced to leave a job to get away from a horrible boss before their unhappiness followed them home and soured their family life as well.

WORKPLACE BLUEPRINT FOR HAPPINESS

Considering how much time and energy we in the United States pour into our jobs, it makes sense that to increase happiness generally, it would be a good idea to find ways to increase happiness in the workplace—the next of the concentric circles in your Life Radius. The Blue Zones Project Communities have taught us a lot, as have the countries found happiest in the world. When we asked our international panel of experts about ways to increase happiness in the workplace, their consensus answers seemed to echo much of what we had been observing. Here's what they told us:

1. **Make a best friend at work.** One of the most powerful contributors to work satisfaction and productivity is agreement with the statement "I have a best friend at work." Some studies suggest this may be because friends work better together than acquaintances, whether that is through collaborative decision-making or menial labor. It also may be that having a friend nearby just makes work more engaging and fun.

   Lessons: Develop at least one meaningful relationship among the people at work—a relationship that transcends work and becomes a true friendship. If you have someone at work with whom you sometimes collaborate, for example, you can escalate the friendship by going out together after work, by inviting that person to visit your home, and by sharing more of your personal life. If you don't have someone like this already, see if you can recruit a friend to your workplace—or join a friend by being recruited to theirs.

2. **Seek a job that fits you.** As "flow" author Mihaly Csikszentmihalyi advises, "Finding a job that engages your natural talents and gives you constant feedback is a sure way to build happiness." To do that requires self-scrutiny. Knowing your natural talents and recognizing what gives you the most sense of satisfaction and accomplishment are a big part of figuring out what job fits you—not just whether you fit a job.

   Lessons: Don't choose a career just because you think it will pay better. If possible, follow your heart rather than listening to what others tell you to do. (That may mean you take the job you want, even if it isn't what your parents had in mind for you.) If you feel stuck in your current position, take a chance on something new to see how you like it. Look for a job that feeds your passions, values, and talents, rather than simply giving you a big office or title. Put a high priority on working with people you like. Consider the concept of "good work"—a job that fits your identity, allows you to pursue excellence, and benefits society. For a good assessment, take the StrengthsFinder 2.0 test, an online assessment tool developed by Gallup that can help you identify your top five talents. For more information, visit *strengths.gallup.com*.

3. **Consider your work hours.** Here's a case where you have to know yourself: Do you find more pleasure outside of work or by doing your work? If maximizing your day-to-day

enjoyment, or pleasure outside of work, is most important to you, make a point of putting in no more than 40 hours a week on the job. But like other typical Americans, you might find more life satisfaction by working more hours. (But be sure you ask yourself why. Some researchers posit that Americans are working more because they believe they might get a raise or a promotion or make more money—not necessarily because they honestly enjoy the work.) Whatever the case, you will still need time to relax and enjoy other things. The best approach is to achieve a healthy, happy balance.

Lessons: Make sure you take a vacation every year and, if possible, take up to six weeks to maximize happiness. Go ahead and burn the midnight oil if work truly satisfies you, but be true to yourself and don't do it at the expense of your health or happiness. Allow yourself to unplug after hours, putting away your phone and signing off email, to get the most of your leisure time.

4. **Avoid long commutes.** Commuting is the least favorite activity people do on a daily basis, and it's something that eats away at happiness the more time people have to spend doing it. In fact, researchers estimate that it would take a 40 percent raise in salary to make people with long commutes (an hour each way) as satisfied with their life as those who walk to the office.

   Lessons: Find a job in your neighborhood or within an easy, fast commute (no more than 30 minutes), and you'll set yourself up for minimal angst. Better yet, set yourself up for increased happiness by choosing a job or a home location that allows you to bike or walk to work. If you must commute, take some time during your workday for a walk, so you get some exercise, even if it's not going to and from work.

5. **Set goals.** Among all the findings of our Blue Zones Happiness Consensus Project, setting goals was identified as one of the most powerful things anyone can do to achieve happiness. Setting goals gives us something to look forward to and a framework for accomplishing it. It speaks to all three strands of happiness: You work toward a purpose, you take pride in doing so, and you find pleasure in accomplishing your goals.

   Lessons: Set quarterly and annual goals for yourself—not only in the workplace but in private matters as well. Write them down or share them with someone who will support you and help you be accountable. It doesn't need to be a co-worker; it can be anyone in your life you can rely on to give you the periodic nudge to stay focused. Monitor your progress and see what you have achieved at the end of each time frame, and also plan to meet with your goals partner at least two to three times a year. Or, if you can afford it, consider a life coach—someone trained professionally to help you shape your life choices and meet your life goals. The International Coach Federation (ICF) has developed rigorous standards for teachers and programs.

CHAPTER 9

❧

Designing Your Social Network

VISIT A HOME IN COSTA RICA on a relaxing Sunday afternoon and you'll likely find relatives lingering over a sprawling lunch, small children sitting on the laps of grandparents, perhaps an uncle playing a guitar. "Where do Latin Americans get this sense of joy and cheerfulness they call pura vida?" asked Carol Graham of the Brookings Institution, who grew up in the region. "I can't tell you. But I feel it when I'm there. And every time I visit, I think, why don't I live here?"

Step into a Danish home during the long, dark winter and you'll likely find friends and family gathered around a table over good food, with candles flickering on mantels to give the room the warm sense of coziness that Danes call hygge. Described as a comforting feeling of togetherness and well-being, hygge helps Danes slow down and enjoy the moment, despite the frigid winds rattling the windows.

In Singapore, groups of Malay families depend on sharing something called the Kampong Spirit, which binds them together.

"In the past, we used to live in fishing villages called *kampongs,* where we pulled together to help each other during times of adversity or disaster or during times of celebration, like preparing for a wedding," Ahmad Nizam Abbas told me during my first visit to the island. The same thing happens today, he said. If a Malay family finds itself in need, the whole Malay community will respond with help.

Having a strong social network and a family support system are two of the most important traits of the world's happiest peoples. When people were asked by Gallup-Sharecare if they had supportive relationships and love in their lives, an impressive 59 percent of Costa Ricans reported that they did, compared with less than 10 percent of people from African nations such as Togo, Ghana, or Benin. Other research shows that happy people socialize more. In one well-known study, Martin Seligman of the University of Pennsylvania and Ed Diener of the Universities of Virginia and Utah found that good social relations—not exercise, religion, or positive events—was the strongest predictor of whether a subject would end up in the "happy" group versus the "average" group. Other studies have suggested that the connection goes both ways: Socially engaged people are the happiest, and happy people enjoy higher quality friendships.

Your social network represents the next ring in your Life Radius—and the next realm of your life worth exploring to see how well it supports your happiness. Although you may already be aware that a strong social network has a powerful impact on your well-being, you may not realize how much your friends influence you in other ways. So if your goal is greater happiness, about the most important thing you can do is to curate a social network of healthy, happy friends who care about you. This chapter may offer you some new and valuable ways to do that.

WHY MOAI?

Barbara Fredrickson teaches psychology at the University of North Carolina, where she's spent a large part of her career studying happiness. When I asked her what the average person might do right now to set up his or her life to experience more positive emotions, she didn't hesitate. Her number one suggestion: Make social connections a higher priority.

"Friends are a really good source of levity and joy," she told me. "But a lot of times, especially in the U.S., we let our friendships take a backseat to our careers or to other things, or especially to parenting." So, if we're not careful, she said, we might go for weeks or months without getting together with people whose company we enjoy. That's why it's important to make friends a priority—to make more space for them in our lives—which might require a certain degree of planning. "I really like hanging with my friends and cooking for them and so it might be setting up a dinner party," Fredrickson said. Which can turn out to be a lot of work, she added, but it's always worth it.

We recognized that fact when we put together the Blue Zones strategy to work in communities. We knew that loneliness is bad for you—as harmful to your well-being as smoking 15 cigarettes a day—and that, as you get older, loneliness actually increases your risks of high blood pressure, cardiovascular disease, and dementia. We also knew that people are happiest on days when they socialize for at least six hours. Despite that, studies by the U.S. Department of Labor show that Americans socialize an average of only 41 minutes a day. We needed to find some creative ways to bring social life back into Americans' busy lives. So we imported the concept of the moai from the Japanese island of Okinawa to address the problem.

The traditional Okinawan moai, as I said earlier, was a small group of lifelong friends who got together on a regular basis to chat, share news, give advice, and lend a helping hand in times of need. Taking the moai as our model, we helped set up similar groups in places such as the Beach Cities of Southern California. Folks would meet up once a week for 30 minutes or so to walk or have a healthy meal together. Often the members of these moais didn't even know one another when they first started meeting, but it wasn't unusual for them to develop strong bonds after only a few months of getting together and sharing their stories.

As research has shown, a few active relationships with good friends can have a bigger impact on your health and happiness than a lot of casual acquaintances. It's important that you surround yourself with the right kinds of friends, though, because their thoughts and behaviors can be contagious. According to one statistical analysis, you are 15 percent more likely to be happy if one of your close friends also is happy. By contrast, people who are negative all the time can also pass that along to you as easily as the flu.

Some of the most surprising findings along these lines came from research done by Nicholas A. Christakis, a social scientist at Harvard, and James H. Fowler, a political scientist at the University of California, San Diego. In their book, *Connected: The Surprising Power of Our Social Networks and How They Shape Our Lives,* they pointed out the many unexpected ways that you're influenced by those around you.

They discovered, for example, that your happiness may depend on how far away you live from someone in your social network. When a friend who lives within a mile of you becomes happy, they found, you are 25 percent more likely to become happy, while the happiness of a friend who lives farther away has no impact. This suggests, they wrote, that "the spread of happiness may depend as much on frequent face-to-face interactions as on deep personal connections."

Friends with bad habits, meanwhile, can be equally contagious. If someone close to you becomes obese, for example, your own chance of becoming obese can nearly triple. The same principle applies to friends who smoke, drink, or tell racist jokes. Before you know it, you can catch a harmful behavior and start sneezing conspiracy theories.

To better understand how social networks function, Christakis and Fowler took a fresh look at data from a famous epidemiological study. For almost seven decades now, researchers have been poking, prodding, examining, and questioning residents of Framingham, Massachusetts, a small town west of Boston, as part of a long-term investigation of cardiovascular disease. Today the children and grandchildren of the original 5,209 subjects are still participating in follow-up studies, which have led to important insights into links between smoking, obesity, and other factors like heart disease.

By chance, Christakis and Fowler discovered that researchers of the Framingham Study, as it was called, had kept track of friends, relatives, neighbors, and co-workers of subjects, as well as of the subjects themselves. This allowed them to construct extensive maps of social networks—who was friends with whom—and how people influenced one another. What they concluded was that happiness is "not merely a function of individual experience or choice; it is also a property of groups of people. Changes in individual happiness can ripple through social connections and create large-scale patterns in the network, giving rise to clusters of happy and unhappy individuals."

So what's the bottom line for you? Simply this: Try to set up your life so you'll spend more time with people you enjoy—those who make you healthier and happier—and less time with people who spread negativity. You might begin by stepping back and asking a few tough questions about your social world at the moment. Are your friends usually upbeat, or do they like to complain? Are they curious about the world? Is their idea of recreation watching TV or an outdoor activity? Do they listen as well as talk? Are they engaged with the world, and do they encourage your engagement? Are they tied to routine or interested in new activities? Do you feel better around them than when you're not? These are a few of the questions we developed with the University of Minnesota School of Public Health for a Blue Zones questionnaire. How you answer them might give you a few clues about who to spend more time with and who to avoid.

They might also give you ideas about the kind of friend you'd like to be yourself. Are you outgoing? Are you a good listener? Are you willing to engage in meaningful conversations? Are you upbeat and supportive? Can a friend call you on a bad day and be confident that you'll be there for him or her? Do you engage in gossip, or do you stand up for your friends when they're not there?

I think you'll discover that, when it comes to happiness and friendship, the magic works both ways. It's easier to be happy when you're surrounded by happy people—and it's easier to make friends if you're happy yourself.

ENDURING LOVE

When I heard about Virginia and Jim Johnson of Oak Park Heights, Minnesota, I knew I wanted to talk to them. In April 2015, the couple celebrated their 70th wedding anniversary. I figured that if anybody could explain the secret to a long, happy marriage, they could.

Oak Park Heights is a town of 5,000 or so residents about 25 miles east of Minneapolis, where I live. Virginia—who goes by "Jini"—and Jim live in a cozy apartment in a retirement community. When I arrived, there was a spread of homemade cookies, toffee candies, and licorice on the coffee table.

"We believe we were cut from the same cloth," Jim told me, when I asked for an insight into their marriage. "We had both grown up in small towns, only blocks from a railroad, and were raised by loving, hard-working parents, with grandparents living in the same house." As a result, he and Jini shared common values and expectations, he said. "Your basic principles and comforts are what you build a relationship on—where and how you want to live, the importance (or not) of kids and religion, how you'd like to spend your money and time. Those become the central themes and rhythms of life, and you'd best be on the same page if you want it to last."

Like many young men of his generation, Jim was shipped off to World War II in 1945—three days after marrying Jini. His unit was among those that rescued survivors of the Dachau concentration camps in Germany. When he returned, he earned a Ph.D. in engineering from Ohio State University and began a long, successful career in ceramics and nuclear energy, working for more than two decades at 3M. Jini attended the University of Cincinnati, and after graduation she devoted her time to raising their six children.

"We respect each other to the core," Jini said. "We trust each other's instincts and judgment. Sure, we've had disagreements, but never the big fights you hear about with some couples." Plus, they're huggers, she added. And kissers, too. "Not a day has gone by during the past 72 years when we haven't looked into each other's eyes and said, I love you, and meant it," she said.

At age 89 and 94 respectively, Jini and Jim were still clearly in love with each other and proud of their relationship—one that radiated a deep sense of happiness. But as I got up to leave, I couldn't help but wonder which had come first: Had their long, successful marriage made them happy? Or had they stayed married so long because they'd been happy people to begin with?

Watching What You Say on Social Media

You may not be aware of it, but messages you post on Facebook or Twitter reveal a lot about your happiness—or lack thereof. Researchers who have analyzed language posted on social media have found that they can accurately predict your happiness level, as well as your type of happiness, solely from the words that you use online.

For example, people who use words related to being active or social, such as "bike," "weekend," "coffee," "holiday," "beer," "goal," "photo," "ideas," "fabulous," and "delicious," score high for positive emotions—the strand of happiness we're calling pleasure. These are people who enjoy getting outside, partying, and hanging with their friends.

Similarly, people who use words associated with life in a corporate office, such as "customer," "event," "conference," "presentation," "meeting," and "trip" score high for life satisfaction—the strand of happiness we're calling pride. That's probably because those people are engaged and find their jobs rewarding.

People who use words representing matters of spiritual faith, such as "God," "life," "Jesus," "family," "wisdom," "blessed," "strong," "grace," and "love" score high for life meaning—the strand of happiness we're calling purpose. In their lives, thoughts and activities having to do with religion, beliefs, or principled commitments are foremost.

By contrast, as you might imagine, people whose social media posts include curse words or words expressing anger, boredom, or other negative feelings, such as "sick," "hate," "suck," "ugh," and "bored" score low for all strands of happiness.

These results may not seem surprising—you'd expect that happy people would use words about things that make them happy—but the method used to produce them is revolutionary. Instead of needing to call a few hundred people on the phone and asking them a list of questions, which is expensive and time-consuming, researchers can now tap into millions of messages posted online every day and analyze them with computer algorithms trained to identify words linked to happiness—or with some other aspect of well-being, such as health or disease. In one study, researchers using data from Twitter proved that they could predict deaths from heart disease, county by county across the United States more accurately than someone using statistics for known risk factors such as obesity, diabetes, smoking, and hypertension.

Such a tool could be invaluable for policy makers, scientists say, by giving them a way to measure the effectiveness of proposals in real time.

"Imagine that you're a governor," said Johannes Eichstaedt of the University of Pennsylvania, who was a co-author of the study on heart disease. "You want to test a policy in one county before rolling it out across the state. You could use this method to track 10,000 people—5,000 who have the changed policy and 5,000 who don't—and see if it makes a difference in their well-being."

It could also be used as an early warning system, Eichstaedt said. Researchers have already mined social media to track Lyme disease, swine flu, depression, and other common ailments. It can also be a way for you to observe your social network and find out how happy it really is.

It was the old chicken-or-the-egg puzzle, of course, and it comes up often when exploring the dynamics of long-lasting marriages, Carol Graham confirmed to me. Graham is a senior fellow at the Brookings Institution and author of *The Pursuit of Happiness: An Economy of*

Well-Being. She explained that the data on the direction of causality in marriage—whether happiness causes marital longevity or vice versa—was still unclear.

"If you compare married people to non-married people or people with friends to people without friends, you'll find that married people and people with friends have higher levels of life satisfaction," she said. In fact, a study conducted in 2004 showed that 42 percent of married couples described themselves as "very happy," compared with 17 percent of divorced people and 23 percent of people who never married.

But does that mean that marriage (or friendship) in and of itself makes you happier? Probably, she said. But the evidence isn't entirely clear.

"We know that happier people are more likely to marry each other," she said. "The same thing goes with friendships a little bit, in that happier people are more likely to seek and make friends." We also know that the bump in well-being that people feel from the fun of getting married tends to fade after about 18 months. So what the data might be telling us, she said, is that the advantage that married people hold over unmarried people in terms of their happiness level could be partly due to the fact that they were happier to begin with.

Whichever way marriage works, it clearly makes a lot of us happy. A bad match, as you might expect, causes your happiness levels to plummet, but marrying the right person, as Jini and Jim demonstrate, can lead to a long lifetime of well-being.

SOCIAL NETWORK BLUEPRINT FOR HAPPINESS

Your social network—made up of not only the friends you spend the most time with but also your partner and the family members living with you—plays an immense role in your experience of happiness. Some evidence suggests, in fact, that this is the most important of all the rings of your Life Radius in determining how happy your life will be. You may not be able to choose your family, but you can influence those relationships by bringing attention and care to them. And you can choose your partner and your friends. Do so with care, curating your social network to optimize your happiness. Here are a few of the ways of doing so that have emerged from our visits to the world's happiest places, from our experiences in Blue Zones Project Communities, and from the happiness experts we have consulted.

1. **Prioritize friends and family.** Evidence and experience prove that your social network—and your level of engagement with it—contribute significantly to your happiness and long-term well-being. Even introverts tend to be happier when they are around people than when they're alone. Make the effort to keep in touch and spend time with the people who are closest to you and whose company you most enjoy.

    Lessons: Arrange your schedule to include socializing for six to seven hours a day. In addition to your routines of work and home life, plan activities that reinforce interactions with friends and family, such as dancing, singing, and playing sports or games together. Make sure that these are active pursuits, not just passive pastimes like watching TV.

2. **Hang out with happy people.** Research on happiness concludes time and again that happiness is contagious. Our social networks have a powerful influence on us, and having positive, optimistic people around us is the top way to stay happy. It's not just a feeling, either: When we are around

happy people, we start to subconsciously mimic their body movements and facial expressions, leading us to feel happier, too.

Lessons: Curate your friend group. Limit the time you spend with people who harbor consistently negative attitudes, and put your happiest, funniest, and most trustworthy friends at the top of your contact list. You need at least three friends who are generally happy people. They should be friends with whom you can have meaningful conversations, people you can call for help on a bad day and people who can and do call on you for help, too. If you're looking for more friends with such positive attributes, try broadening your network through local clubs, teams, or even social media sites that can help you meet people.

3. **Create a moai.** A moai is a circle of friends who commit to support each other for the long run. Our work with the Blue Zones Communities has borne out the importance of this American interpretation of the Okinawan custom, which calls for groups of five to seven people who share values and interests and meet up regularly simply for the sake of getting together. We try to mix longtime friends with new acquaintances and ask them to agree to meet for at least 10 weeks, either walking together or sharing plant-based potluck dinners. If members drop out after 10 weeks, the remaining members can invite in replacements, keeping the maximum size of the group at seven. Members of the moai agree to be each other's personal board of advisers and commit to confidentiality. During each meeting—whether on a walk or at a meal—moai members each have a chance to ask the rest of the group to help them noodle through a problem, whether it's at work, with kids, or with a spouse.

Lessons: First, survey your social landscape; maybe you already have the seeds of a moai, whether it's a book club, a few fellow members of an exercise class, or a group who get together for lunch now and then. If so, start with them and introduce the more formal concept of a moai. Or, if you're new to the area, try a networking site like *meetup.com* to find people near you who share your interests.

4. **Join a club.** Research suggests that people find more success and greater happiness when they let their special talents or interests—a sense of purpose—lead the way in curating a social network. According to one study, joining a group that meets even once a month produces the same happiness gain as doubling your income.

   Lessons: Think about what your interests or talents are and find an organization that will nurture them. It could be a volunteer organization, a church mission group, or a committed self-improvement class that you attend. The idea here is to make a commitment to a sphere of people with common interests who meet on an ongoing basis. Membership in a group like this compels you to show up regularly, either because of organizational rules, or out of peer pressure, or—ideally—simply out of the pleasure you gain from the associations.

5. **Optimize your love life.** Evidence and experience both suggest that the person most likely to shape your sense of well-being is the one you choose as your partner. Those who make the search an experience in itself, guided by principles that emphasize long-lasting well-being, ultimately make the best selections. Testing a partnership by living together may not be the best idea. A study that looked at a large number

of successful and unsuccessful marriages found that living with a prospective spouse seems to make for a shorter, lower-quality marriage.

Lessons: Kiss lots of frogs. Date a wide variety of people before you choose a mate. Look for people who align with your values and interests. Look more than skin deep: While his big muscles and her pretty face may sing virtues on the surface, a sense of humor and compassion are more likely to keep you in the relationship for the long run. Avoid cohabitation.

6. **Make marriage count.** Research has shown that people who are married tend to be happier than people who are either single or divorced. Whom you marry has a lot to do with it, of course: The best marriages bring together two people who share many interests but also allow each other independence, who speak freely and listen well.

    Lessons: Marry someone similar to you who shares your interests and attitudes. If you like folk dancing, running marathons, or volunteering at church, find a mate who also likes those things. Long-term living will be more harmonious with someone on the same level of mood, extroversion, and conscientiousness. Also look for partners who make as much money as you do, or at least are inclined to share what they have. Try marriage training, too. Learning early in the relationship how to deal with conflict and listen effectively ("If I understand you correctly, you just said . . .") is the groundwork of a successful marriage.

7. **Be realistic about parenthood.** Contrary to conventional wisdom, having children does not automatically bring greater happiness. Along with its many rewards, parenthood

also brings additional stress from financial, relationship, and responsibility issues. The good news for parents is that happiness seems to rebound when children turn 18.

Lessons: Don't assume you and your partner will become happier by having children. Talk through that decision as thoroughly as you would talk through any other, such as moving to a new city or taking a new job. Recognize, in the midst of it, how the stresses are affecting your happiness. Find ways to enrich your lives as parents in the same way you do with your adult friends: Engage in active pursuits together, listen well, and do your best to create an environment of well-being for your children. While children can add stress to life, they can also contribute to all three strands of happiness in your life: pleasure, purpose, and pride.

CHAPTER 10

❧

Designing
Your Home

AS RESIDENTS OF THE WORLD'S happiest places show us, a house, an apartment, or a condo doesn't have to be huge or expensive to nurture our well-being. One of the most joyful people I ever met lived in a tin-roofed shack in rural Costa Rica, a home in which she happily raised four children and lived to celebrate her 100th birthday. What you do need for optimal happiness is a home designed to support the three P's of happiness—pleasure, purpose, and pride. And yet, as many of us have discovered, our homes can also be obstacles that get in the way of our pursuit of well-being—filled with too much stuff, too many distractions, and too many habits that foster isolation.

If you think moving into a bigger house in a fancier neighborhood will make you happy, you're likely to be disappointed, said Elizabeth Dunn, director of the Happy Lab at the University of British Columbia. "Bigger is not necessarily better when it comes to housing and happiness," she told a radio interviewer. "What really matters is whether you live in a place where you naturally bump into your neighbors often and have friendly social connections." Houses on tree-lined streets where people walk on their way to coffee shops, for example, are more likely to bring you into friendly contact with neighbors than isolated houses where you go straight from your home to your car and then fight traffic all the way to work.

Buying an expensive house doesn't guarantee happiness, either. "There does tend to be a fundamental human tendency for people to want more," Dunn said. "It's easy for you to look at what other people have and think, *Oh, I need a little bit more.*" But studies have shown that the price of a home does not necessarily correlate to how good people feel about living in it.

Many Americans assume that owning a home should be everyone's goal, but in fact homeownership may not be the key to happiness at all. "Owning a home is a dream for some people," Dunn said. "But some research shows that homeowners are not any happier than renters on average." A study at the Wharton School at the University of Pennsylvania found that homeowners spend less time than renters on leisure activities. And just to add insult to injury, surveys have shown that homeowners as a group weigh more than renters—about 12 pounds, on average. Why? For one thing, there are all the repairs and maintenance chores for homeowners to worry about, which may rob time from more pleasurable pursuits or physical activities outside the home. So despite what many people believe, Dunn said, "homeownership doesn't seem to be a ticket to lasting happiness."

But no matter whether you own or rent your house, no matter whether it's a mansion or an efficiency apartment, your home is the important next ring moving inward along your Life Radius, and it is another key realm in your life where you can nudge yourself and your family toward greater happiness. It is a question well worth asking: How can you set up your living space to improve your well-being?

A MODEL HOME

I found the best example of an optimal living space in a home just outside of the Danish city of Aarhus, where I once spent an evening a few years back. It struck me as perfectly designed to create daily comfort, togetherness, and well-being, an environment that naturally fosters closeness and connection in a family.

I met the Kristiansen family: parents Erik and Susan; as well as their teenage daughters, Esther and Hannah; and Peter, their 13-year-old son. Erik had invited me to join his family for dinner, and when we arrived that evening, we found Susan and the kids in the small kitchen, preparing various dishes. Hannah seemed to be in charge, directing her mother to marinate the salmon while she supervised her siblings as they peeled potatoes. It must have been her turn to be boss, I figured, glancing at the cooking schedule posted on an erasable board on the wall. There was hardly enough room in the kitchen for the four of them, which forced them to negotiate as they jockeyed for space.

The rest of the house was just as compact. The main living space was an all-purpose family room with a long table in the middle. A laptop computer rested on the table, along with a ledger, knitting needles, and a wool sweater in progress. Schoolbooks occupied the center of the table, beside notebooks, pens, and pencils. Floor-to-ceiling shelves flanked both sides of the room, filled with books, albums of music, and a clarinet. There was no television in sight.

We ate dinner in the kitchen, crowded around a small table lit by candles. More candles flickered on the counter, creating hygge— that sense of coziness for which the Danes are famous. As we chatted about Aarhus and its reputation for happiness, the teenagers seemed fully engaged, freely offering their opinions. None of them was checking his or her smartphone.

Digging Into Happiness

From continent to continent, gardens (in many forms) have made a recurring appearance in places that inspire happiness. At a household just outside Copenhagen, the garden was the center of social activity, with rustic picnic tables where meals were served during the warmer months and where torchlights illuminated get-togethers late into the evening. In a mountain village in Okinawa, the garden was a veritable medicine cabinet, yielding healthy supplements in the form of sweet potatoes, soybeans, turmeric, and other produce growing in neat rows just a few steps out the door.

Whether it's their aesthetic, physical, or mental benefits, gardens bring more than beauty to any home. Tending to a garden—or even just a patio plant or a pot of flowers—gets you out of doors and reminds you to reconnect with nature. In addition to the healthful dose of vitamin D you'll get from the sunshine and the exercise you'll get from digging, hoeing, planting, and weeding, research shows that gardening reduces cortisol, lowers stress, and calms nerves. In fact, some doctors, psychologists, and scientists have been exploring whether building and caring for a garden can be a form of therapy. They call it horticulture therapy, and it stimulates thought, physical activity, and awareness of our external environment.

NASA researchers have also been investigating the value of working with plants in the severe environment of outer space. As it turns out, planting and nurturing seeds in small pots provided mental health benefits, giving the astronauts who tended them a visual and tactile experience—positive sensory stimulation—that effectively counteracted feelings of monotony and isolation. The first flowers to bloom in space were zinnias, as Commander

Scott Kelly announced excitedly from the International Space Station in January 2016.

Tending plants and working with soil are ways to focus on something outside of yourself, providing a lasting sense of responsibility and purpose. You don't need a big yard, or any yard for that matter, to capture the joy of being around fresh vegetation. A few hanging plants by your doorway or herbs on your windowsill can give you something to nurture and watch grow. But if you do have the landscape for it, cultivate your own fruits and vegetables. Get the whole family or neighborhood involved in planting, watering, fertilizing, and harvesting; the social interaction gives yet another boost to well-being.

After dinner, the whole family continued their conversation in the backyard, sitting around a fire pit as the summer sky darkened. "This is the time my family usually talks about their day," Erik said. It seemed like a perfectly normal next phase of the evening, but I couldn't help considering how extraordinarily rare such moments must be for most Americans, with our busy schedules and relentless distractions.

The Kristiansens seemed to have gotten so many things right, when it came to arranging their shared living space and the family time it supported. For one thing, their all-purpose room struck me as a perfect example of what psychologist Mihaly Csikszentmihalyi calls a "flow room"—a place where people become so immersed in whatever they're doing, whether it's reading a book or playing a game or practicing a musical instrument, that time seems to melt away. Why couldn't any family create a similar space?

BRINGING IT ALL BACK HOME

Americans may find it harder to make room for flow and family time because our houses are often filled with clutter. In fact, we may have more stuff than any society in history, and according to one study, Americans spend $1.2 trillion a year on nonessential stuff. The rise of wholesalers, warehouse supermarkets, and on-demand delivery has made it easier than ever to acquire goods rapidly and without much thought to the purchase. "There are a lot of rituals and mechanisms by which stuff comes into our homes," Anthony P. Graesch of Connecticut College told an interviewer. "But we really lack regular or institutionalized ways of getting rid of stuff."

Graesch, an anthropologist, was a co-author of *Life at Home in the Twenty-First Century: 32 Families Open Their Doors,* which visually documented the many types of gear, toys, tools, and other possessions families cram into basements, garages, bedrooms, and storage units. His co-authors at UCLA reported a link between such clutter and high levels of cortisol, a stress hormone, in women. (Men didn't seem to get as stressed out by a messy house—which also annoyed the women, further upping their stress levels.) Their findings demonstrate that clutter can get in the way of greater happiness.

Graesch was so struck by the results of their study that he took measures to change his own family's home setting. For example, Graesch said, he convinced his four-year-old son to select 10 toys and donate them to a thrift store. Once he had done that, Graesch allowed his son to pick one new toy from the thrift store to bring home. It was a start, he said, but it continued to be a never ending struggle with the rest of the household. And Graesch's experience seems to be the standard here; as of 2015, kids in the United States made up 3.1 percent of the world's population of children, but U.S. families bought more than 40 percent of the toys purchased globally. But the trend of "too much" can stop here, too, as parents become more conscious consumers and show their children how to do the same.

LIVING SMALL

"I've gone from big down to small," said Graham Hill, a Canadian designer and environmentalist who champions a minimalist lifestyle on his website, LifeEdited. "And what I've realized is that a much simpler, smaller life saves me a bunch of money, gives me more freedom, more flexibility, and less to worry about."

It's no secret that North Americans have supersized practically everything during the past 50 years. "Back in the 1950s, the standard size for a Coke bottle was eight ounces," Hill said. "Now it's 20 ... That's an iconic representation of what's happened in almost every area," he reminded us in his remarks to a festival audience in Whistler, British Columbia. Indeed, in 1973 the average house in the United States measured 1,660 square feet; by 2015, that had grown to 2,687 square feet—a 62 percent increase. (The average house in the United Kingdom in 2013, by comparison, measured only 1,042 square feet.) Accompanying that expansion, as we know, is often massive debt used to purchase and fill the space with the mountains of stuff—the inclination that Graesch and others are battling.

But there's hope yet. The first step in regaining control of clutter might be getting back to basics. According to Hill, "Simpler lives are happier lives." He had that epiphany in the late 1990s, when he found himself overwhelmed by his own surfeit of stuff. With a sudden influx of cash from an Internet start-up sale, he took off on a serious spending spree. But the novelty of his giant house and the goods and gadgets that filled it quickly faded. It took Hill years to downsize, but ultimately, he achieved what he calls "a bigger, better, richer life with less."

The first step, of course, is to get rid of everything you don't need—or as Hill puts it, "to clear the arteries of our lives." That old shirt you haven't worn in years? Gone. That ratty suitcase gathering dust in the corner? Gone. Digitize your files of paperwork, books, movies, and boxes of old photographs and get rid of them. Give away all the kitchen utensils you never use. And don't bring anything new into your home that you don't absolutely love.

The next step is to think small. The objects in your life should be efficient and multipurpose. In LifeEdited's 420-square-foot demonstration apartment in New York—an extreme example of streamlined functionality—the Murphy-style bed folds into the wall, creating more space for the couch below; chairs stack to save space; and the coffee table expands to seat 10 for dinner.

Hill advocates editing our space and winnowing our belongings to focus on what matters. In an era of abundance, happiness is having just enough, says Hill. Not too much. Not too little. "It's about cutting out the extraneous so you can focus on the good stuff"—not a bad mantra for the rest of our lives, too.

BLUEPRINT FOR A HOME DESIGNED FOR HAPPINESS

How can you set up your home to favor happiness? What can you do to nudge your family into connecting more with one another, savoring the good times, and enjoying nature? You don't have to own your home in order for it to be conducive to happiness, and it doesn't need to be big and ostentatious. That's what the research tells us, and that's what all my travels have shown me as well. I've watched families and individuals in our Blue Zones Communities make changes in their own houses or apartments and seen what works the best. Based on all these factors, together with consensus opinions from our experts, here are some ideas on how to design your home for happiness.

1. **Declutter.** Just as beauty enhances your mood, messiness spoils it. A house full of clutter has a negative effect on your mood and self-esteem, research shows. The more piles of disorganized stuff around you, the more stress you feel.

   Lessons: Once a year go through your house, take a mental inventory of your closets, junk drawers, and shelves— and make a plan to purge unnecessary items. Marie Kondo, author of *The Life-Changing Magic of Tidying Up: The Japanese Art of Decluttering and Organizing,* recommends that you approach organizing your home by categories rather than rooms—surveying all books, for example, so they don't just get stockpiled in a different space. As you tidy up, hold each object in your hands and ask yourself if it sparks joy. If it doesn't, get rid of it. We hold onto so many things for nostalgia's sake, or because we think the fashion will return or we will have some future use for it. But most of those items should be triaged. As an end result, Kondo advises that you will respect and value the belongings that remain and you should, therefore, put them in a visible, accessible place.

2. **Bring in nature.** Time spent in nature is known to have mood-boosting effects, effects you can capture inside your home as well just by growing houseplants or keeping fresh flowers around. A study comparing life habits in environments with and without houseplants found that indoor plants can increase productivity, lower blood pressure, and improve well-being.

Lessons: Fill some planters with potting soil, pick out a few low-maintenance plants, and spread them throughout your home. Try golden pothos or spider plants if you want to start with greenery that's easy to maintain. If you're convinced you have a brown thumb, go to a local nursery or flower shop and ask for suggestions on the easiest plant to grow in your home. While some types of plants will grow in artificial light, sunlight is best, and it's good for you, too. So open up the shades on south-facing windows to let in the sunshine.

3. **Maximize natural light.** Several studies show that natural light improves our mood, especially on a sunny day and in the morning. Some physicians actually prescribe full-spectrum lights to help people combat seasonal affective disorder—the tendency to feel depressed in the winter, when daylight hours are shorter.

    Lessons: Install big windows and skylights throughout the house, especially in south-facing exposures. Consider investing in a full-spectrum lightbulb or light fixture for important shared spaces in your home.

4. **Create a flow room.** Flow is not just for the workplace; it doesn't require elaborate plans or commitments. You can achieve this optimal state of consciousness through at-home activities, too, like drawing, playing an instrument, or even just reading or telling a story with your family.

    Lessons: Pick one room in your house that you and your family will share as your flow room. Whether it's a living room, a sunroom, or another open space, take care to decorate it in a way that is cozy and inviting as well as aesthetically appealing so that the whole family will be drawn to spend time there. Remove all screens (television, laptops, tablets, smartphones) and clocks. Furnish it with a table large enough to seat your entire family and/or with comfortable chairs suited for reading or playing musical instruments. Line the room with shelves to store and display your favorite books, games, and other things you need for your pastimes and hobbies. Install a quality music system.

5. **Bring music into your life.** Music can lift our many various moods: Soft instrumental music can help us relax, upbeat music can help us get going in the morning, and Mozart can make workloads lighter. Research shows that "highly emotional" music can engage the reward system deep in our brains and trigger the release of dopamine, the neurotransmitter that's linked to pleasure.

   Lessons: Invest in a home-wide music system (or wireless speakers are a great option) and keep music on in the background, if you like.

6. **Limit screens.** American homes today contain an average of seven screens, including smartphones, tablets, computers, and televisions. We watch on average more than five hours of TV daily. When we surveyed more than 75,000 people using the Blue Zones True Vitality Test, we found that the happiest people watched less than an hour of TV per day, whereas in contrast, the least happy people reported watching eight hours of TV daily.

   Lessons: Do what you can to make TV screens less convenient to view in your household setup. Get down to one TV in your house. Put it in an out-of-the-way place, ideally in a cabinet you can shut when you're not watching, and not in the kitchen. Steer clear of mindless and excess eating by choosing not to watch TV while you're eating.

7. **Designate a meditation space.** Regular meditation has been shown to support health in a number of ways—from improving concentration to relieving stress. In fact, a 2014 study from Johns Hopkins found that the effects of meditation rival antidepressants for relieving anxiety. There's more to say about this in the chapter on inner self (see page 213), but setting up your home to encourage your own meditation practice is a good first step toward reaping the long-term wellness benefits.

    Lessons: Find a quiet corner that you can retreat to for a few minutes each day. Make sure you have a cushion to sit on. Surround your meditation corner with whatever icons will help you downshift—candles, religious statues such as a Buddha, for example, or other sentimental objects.

8. **Favor front porches over the deck out back.** Research shows us that the happiest Americans interact socially six hours of every day. If you're facing the street when you're relaxing instead of looking into the backyard, you're more likely to see your friends and say hello to passing strangers.

    Lessons: As much as possible, spend free time on a front porch or in some other setting where you are more likely to see neighbors and say hello.

9. **Adopt a pet.** This rule may not have to do with your house or apartment per se, but it does have to do with adding at least one other member to your household. Research shows that pet owners tend to be healthier and happier than people without pets. As any dog owner knows, being a canine's best friend means going for lots of walks. In fact, studies indicate that dog owners get more than five hours of exercise a week. In addition, pets (even cats) provide companionship. Pets

have been found to reduce stress, improve self-esteem, and win your heart in a way guaranteed to bring happiness.

Lessons: If you don't have one already, adopt a pet, preferably a dog. Rescue dogs, older and already trained, tend to be good starting points. Visit your local Society for the Prevention of Cruelty to Animals (SPCA) or other animal shelter to find the right one for you.

10. **Create a pride shrine.** To engender a shared sense of pride—the third important strand of happiness—a household will benefit from a "pride shrine," a place where pictures, objects, and other items remind everyone of things they share and can be proud of.

Lessons: Find a place in your house to celebrate family history and accomplishments. In my home, I built a display table for mementos and dedicated wall space in one hallway for family photos. Now, every time I walk by, I'm reminded of good times with loved ones and reasons for all of us to feel pride.

11. **Optimize your bedroom for sleep.** Study after study has shown that a good night's sleep improves mental well-being, while a consistent lack of sleep has been linked to obesity, memory impairment, and depression. Most people need at least seven hours a night.

Lessons: After you turn off the lights, take a look around your bedroom. Do you see glowing clocks, blinking lights, cable box displays? These can interfere with your sleep. Consider making your bedroom a no-electronics zone (no TV, computer, or cell phone). Put up light-blocking window shades or drapes to make the room dark for sleeping, and try turning down the thermostat to about 65°F to make it cool.

CHAPTER 11

♋

Designing Financial Well-Being

S O FAR WE HAVE BEEN MOVING INWARD on your Life Radius, from your community and workplace into your own home, reviewing each concentric circle for ways to design your life to optimize happiness and well-being. While your finances may seem a departure from the progression from your outer world into your living room and bedroom, in fact, the way you set up your finances may be as important to your family's health and happiness as the way you set up your house.

As research has shown, marriages and other relationships suffer when bills pile up, credit cards get maxed out, and overspending takes over. In a 2015 Gallup-Sharecare study, nearly 9 out of 10 people who were managing their finances well said their relationship with their spouse, partner, or best friend was strong, but the number of happy relationships dropped to only about 6 in 10 when finances were cited as a sore point in the household. And it didn't matter if the family was wealthy or poor. The stress of worrying about money, evidently, was toxic to happiness at all income levels.

More money wasn't the answer; what counted was managing that money well.

When your family's finances are managed in a smart way, marriages and other relationships improve, experts say. People in a household feel more secure and less distrustful when money stops being a potential source of stress and conflict. They're more likely to feel active and productive. They're also less likely to suffer from depression, diabetes, or high blood pressure, according to Gallup-Sharecare, or to engage in unhealthy behaviors like smoking. Perhaps even more interesting, Gallup-Sharecare has now established that there is an inverse correlation between financial well-being and obesity: People with better finances have lower rates of obesity. In other words, along with a good diet and regular physical activity, financial security could help keep you healthy.

It all makes good sense, and yet for many of us sound money management still seems to be out of reach. In a recent poll, fewer than 40 percent of Americans said they were currently making ends meet—and it's not simply because they didn't earn enough. It has to do with money management as much, or likely more, than it does with the size of a paycheck. How we spend our money and how we plan for the future (or fail to plan) are also part of the problem. The statistics paint a picture of a citizenry constantly running behind and constantly spending more than they can afford. Two in five American households carry credit card balances from month to month, and the average they owe exceeds $16,000. Of households with mortgages, the average borrowed is $172,000. Add to that car loans averaging $28,000 and student loans averaging $49,000 for families who choose to carry those kinds of debt. It's no wonder that about a third of U.S. households fail to pay their bills on time.

To make matters worse, more than a fourth of all American families have no savings. More than half of all households at or near retirement age have no dedicated retirement plans such as IRAs or 401Ks. For the majority of U.S. households where the head of the house is age 65 or older, Social Security remains the largest source of income. When asked about their retirement plans, more than a fourth of those surveyed by the Federal Reserve recently said their strategy was simply to keep working. Only 17 percent said they expected not to work.

So what should you do you to redesign your finances to optimize happiness? That's an easy one, says Ryan T. Howell, a psychologist at San Francisco State University who cofounded *BeyondThe Purchase.org*, a website devoted to the psychological dimensions of spending. Paying off your credit cards should be your number one goal, said Howell—and you should do it each month. Don't allow yourself to get in over your head with debt; not only is it stressful, but also it's bad for your self-esteem and may ultimately interfere with other life goals, such as getting married, having children, buying a home, or starting a business.

Howell adds that overspending is illusory: "You may get some momentary happiness, but the financial stress will overwhelm that and make you worse off." Moreover, we register a loss twice as intensely as a gain, so when the big bills hit, it can be a significant blow to our psyche. In fact, financial worry can be the most detrimental type of stress to our happiness. The takeaway is simple: Be conservative in your approach to all spending. Do your best to minimize debt and maximize savings.

Easier said than done in this economy, you might be thinking. But Howell has some ideas on ways to shape your personal habits. If you want to avoid overspending, you might consider paying for things with cash. The physical act of removing bills from your wallet and handing them over makes you more mindful of each transaction—more so than if you use plastic. You might also consider tracking your spending as you go, he said. If you make a habit of writing down what you buy, you can counteract the emotional rush of shopping—that simple burst of pleasure you feel from acquiring something new.

The 50-20-30 Rule

Taking control of your finances is a great way to boost your happiness, but setting up a budget can be a drag. So financial planners have simplified the process with what they call the 50-20-30 rule. This rule, advocated by money experts including Senator Elizabeth Warren of Massachusetts and Alexa von Tobel of the personal finance company LearnVest, recommends that you set up three buckets to manage your spending.

The first bucket is for essential living expenses such as rent, health care, groceries, car payments, and utility bills. You should spend no more than half of your take-home pay on these costs, according to the rule. Though certain living expenses are unavoidable, you do have some control over just *how much* you spend; for example, riding the bus might be a more affordable alternative to using your car for transportation.

The second bucket is for financial stability: paying down debts such as student loans, building up an emergency rainy-day fund, and saving for retirement or travel. Allocate 20 percent of your income here.

The third bucket is for personal spending, including shopping and entertainment activities, from dining out to your cable television contract and cell phone plan. You might consider the latter to be essentials, but again, there's flexibility with the amount that you spend: Make careful choices as you select the features of your phone plan and your cable network package. You should spend no more than 30 percent on this bucket.

Although everyone's situation is different, the 50-20-30 rule can be applied to any budget and lifestyle. Start with your pay stub and break it into the three percentages. That's the maximum amount you have to work with for each bucket. As you pay your bills, track which bucket the money's going into, and keep a running list of costs in each category. If you're spending too much in one area, strategize ways to trim. While living essentials take priority, there could be creative tricks to cut back, like packing a lunch for work instead of going out, unplugging electronics when they aren't in use, and buying in bulk. Minor savings can add up.

Establish a specific goal for your emergency savings fund—six months of pay is recommended—and set up an automatic withdrawal to help you meet that goal within three to five years. If possible, leave room for charitable giving in your savings bucket. Most people underestimate the amount of satisfaction they get from being generous. And be sure to take advantage of retirement funds at work by contributing to 401Ks and other IRA plans.

The very act of monitoring your spending will help you manage your money better. Write in a notebook, create your own spreadsheet, or try an online system or app like *mint.com.* Experts say that sticking to a program of regularly recording your spending tends to promote more thoughtful purchasing patterns and limit impulse buys. Budgeting can also bring the pure satisfaction of setting and meeting goals. When you know what you have to spend, you are less likely to overspend and thus avoid more debt—a sure way to preclude stress. On the flip side, managing your money will give you more freedom to spend on the things that make you happiest, such as traveling or hanging out with friends.

What you purchase with your money also makes a difference, according to Howell. As a growing body of research has shown, people who spend their resources on experiences rather than stuff—taking a family vacation, say, rather than buying a new riding lawn mower—end up making themselves happier. That's because life experiences such as dance classes, scuba diving training, or music lessons enable you to learn new skills, feel a sense of accomplishment, and interact with others, giving you long-lasting memories—all the deeper, less tangible life experiences that we recognize as essential to happiness. Material purchases such as a new dress or a fancy smartphone, on the other hand, rarely live up to your happiness expectations. That doesn't mean you should max out your credit cards on a big vacation, though. "You can't go into debt to buy a memory," Howell said. The stress you'll feel owing money will overwhelm any happiness you get from your experience.

The important thing to remember when spending your money on experiences is to choose ones that feel right for you, Howell suggested. "I'm a big sports fan. I like to go to baseball games. My wife and daughter do, too. It's an expression of our identity as baseball fans." But if they were to decide one afternoon to go to the opera instead, simply because that's what other people do—or maybe to impress their friends—they probably wouldn't enjoy it. "You have to be true to who you are," he said.

Another proven way to boost your sense of well-being, say the experts, is to spend your money on others rather than on yourself. According to research by Lara Aknin of Simon Fraser University in Canada (and by others), many people get more pleasure out of buying a small gift for charity than purchasing one for themselves. In a 2013 experiment conducted in both Canada and South Africa, one group was told they could purchase a goody bag of chocolates or juice for a sick child in a local hospital, while a second group was told they could buy one for themselves. In both countries, those choosing the gift for the child got a significant boost of happiness, while those buying for themselves did not. This result backed up another study by the same scientists in which residents of 136 countries were asked if they had donated money to charity within the past month. In just over half of the countries, including both rich ones and poor ones, people who had done so reported being happier—so much happier that it would have taken a doubling of their household income to match it.

Although it's hard to live without it, money isn't the key to greater happiness, experts say. If you're the kind of person who constantly compares your success to that of others, then you might look down on yourself if you live in a neighborhood where everyone is wealthier than you. People tend to compare themselves to those around them, and nobody wants to be the poorest in the neighborhood.

The happiness value of acquiring more money is also tricky, says Ed Diener. As you move up the ladder of wealth, it takes more money to keep you happy. Although a $10,000 windfall might impress someone who makes $100,000 a year, it might not seem like much to someone earning $1 million a year. "In commonsense terms, people will respond to increases in income in response to percentage rises in income, not to increases in specific amounts of raw income," he explained. In other words: The richer you are, the bigger the raise you need to be happy.

In the recommendations at the end of this chapter, you'll find practical ideas for setting up your finances for greater well-being, from enrolling in an automatic savings plan to setting up a "giving account" to benefit others. But the bottom line, according to researchers around the world, is that seeking to maximize your income may not be the ultimate answer in your quest for the happiest life. What you gain in terms of pulling in a bigger paycheck might well be offset by a lack of joyful emotions in your life. Friends and family are better than your bank account at giving you happiness. So it might be smarter to plan your finances in a way that maximizes social relationships. Or, as Diener puts it, the key to greater well-being is to have money but not to want it too much.

BLUEPRINT FOR DESIGNING FINANCES FOR HAPPINESS

Many people fall into the trap of believing that more money or more, bigger, and more expensive possessions will make them happier. Research findings and the Blue Zones Happiness Consensus Project suggest otherwise. Granted, a general sense of well-being does need a certain baseline of financial security, and some of the happiest places in the world do tend to have a high per capita income level. But not all of them. In some of the happiest places we have visited, people eat food from their gardens or live in small apartments, proving that you don't have to have a lot of money to optimize your financial life. Look at it this way: We register a loss twice as intensely as we do a gain. In other words, losing $100 is twice as painful as winning $100 feels good. So for the sake of your happiness, better to be financially secure than to position yourself to play the odds to get rich. Here, based on what we have observed and what our Blue Zones Happiness Consensus Project has told us, are some ways to set up your financial life to favor happiness.

1. **Enroll in an automatic savings or investment plan.** Slow, steady savings can bring you a sense of purpose and pride as you see them grow. Invest for the long run. According to Warren Buffett, if you're looking at an investment with at least a 10-year time horizon, the best and most dependable is a low-cost fund that mimics the S&P 500 Index or the whole stock market.

   Lessons: Make long-term savings happen without even thinking about it. Set up automatic transfers of a percentage of your paycheck into a savings or retirement account.

2. **Consider insurance.** Peace of mind is the most important goal as you redesign your finances. While most insurance

policies are not great financial investments, they can provide that.

    Lessons: Investigate life insurance and other possibilities. Make sure you have at least catastrophic health care coverage and term life insurance to cover your loved ones.

3. **Reconsider your credit card.** Research shows that the pain of paying is reduced when we use credit cards, which are less transparent than cash, so we tend to spend more money. Studies have also shown that compared with credit card users, shoppers who pay cash feel increased emotional attachment with the purchase and are likely to treat the new item as more valuable.

    Lessons: Credit cards can be a convenient way to carry money, and if you pay off your monthly balance and take advantage of reward programs, they can make good financial sense. But unpaid monthly balances are often subject to usurious interest rates. If you can't pay your monthly credit card bills, destroy those cards and use a debit card or cash instead. You'll be much more aware and careful about how you spend your money, and you will lift the burden of mounting debt.

4. **Rent instead of own.** For those people who find it hard to save, buying a house and taking on a mortgage can actually be a decent forced savings plan: As long as you can keep up the payments, you are investing in real property with lasting value. But owning a home is not the best plan for everyone. When you consider the monthly mortgage payment, property taxes, household insurance, upkeep expenses, utilities, and the opportunity cost of money—that is, how much you would have made putting that money in the stock market

instead of in a house— renting can often add up to being the more cost-effective way to live.

Lessons: Assess your situation in terms of both time and money. Compare the costs and benefits of either owning or renting in the area where you live or are moving. If you plan to live in a place fewer than five years, renting is more likely the better alternative.

5. **Pay down (or off) your mortgage.** Some people include a long-term mortgage as part of their financial plan, since the payments are often tax-deductible. But paying off a mortgage can provide long-term financial security and free your monthly budget for other expenses, investments, or retirement savings.

   Lessons: Consider the options: Which provides you with more peace of mind, paying down a mortgage slowly and using it as a tax-deductible way of investing or, if you can swing it, paying off your mortgage and owning your house outright. No one knows what the equity markets will do in the future. Owning your house outright may be your best investment in terms of life satisfaction.

6. **Gift experiences, not things.** Studies show that those who spend money on experiences, experience greater well-being than those who purchase material possessions. New things glisten, but the thrill of their novelty fades, while experiences become a part of our identity. The memories they make gain luster and add to our happiness over time. And when the experience involves others, it can deepen connections by bringing you together in the moment and into a shared story that you will remember for years to come.

Lessons: Rethink your definition of gifts—both those given to loved ones and, honestly, those you provide yourself. Consider offering experiences instead of physical objects, for example, cooking classes, a weekend vacation, concert tickets, and a dinner out on the town.

7. **Make financially savvy friends (or mates).** Our social circle influences us in so many ways, which is one of the reasons curating your circle of friends is an important step in maximizing your happiness. If your best friend's favorite social activity is shopping, and she's always buying the latest fashion, newest car, or coolest gadget, you're more likely to follow suit.

    Lessons: To gain the financial security that can be the foundation for happiness, make friends with people who are financially secure. This especially applies to your choice of a spouse: Seek a partner whose sense of values and money management match yours. If you want to shape your life according to the principles we've learned over the years of our Blue Zones Project, find friends who look for bargains, cook at home, invest successfully, and make their own fun instead of buying it.

CHAPTER 12

❧

Designing Your Inner Life

TRYING TO MAKE YOURSELF HAPPY almost always fails. In fact, the harder you try, the more you fail. The more stuff you buy, the faster the newness wears off. The more you pin your hopes on making yourself more attractive, the more you're disappointed when age catches up with you. The more you chase happiness, the more it seems to elude you.

What does lead to greater happiness is making changes to your surroundings—to your home, workplace, community, and ultimately your nation. The more you design your home to favor good habits, the better your family will feel simply by living in it. The more friends you make at work, the more you'll look forward to getting the job done. The more your community nudges you out from behind the steering wheel and onto your feet, the better you'll feel. The more trust you put in your government, the more secure you'll feel. The challenge is to reshape your life so that you're constantly being nudged into well-being.

But can this approach work when it comes to your inner self? Can you reshape the prism through which you look at your life, to see the proverbial glass half full rather than half empty? Can you take steps to increase your sense of pleasure, purpose, and pride in your life, braiding them together to make for more happiness overall? And can you make these alterations last?

The answer is yes.

One of the most effective things you can do to nudge yourself in the direction of greater happiness is to reconsider your purpose in life—to take stock of your personal gifts and talents and to ask yourself, honestly, if you're using them as much as you could. That may not be so easy if, like many people, your life feels busier than ever, whether you're chasing after a toddler, juggling child care with a demanding job, putting in extra hours to finish a project, going back to school to learn a new skill, working two jobs to make ends meet, managing an illness, or caring for an elderly parent. When you find yourself racing from one task to the next from the moment you get up in the morning to the hour you fall into bed, there's precious little time to reflect on the meaning of it all.

But every now and then, you may catch yourself staring into the mirror, wondering if this is the life you really wanted—if this is what you were meant to do? At such a moment, ask yourself about your personal sense of purpose—your plan de vida, as the Costa Ricans call it—your reason for living.

"Each of us is on a lifelong quest to find our purpose, whether we are consciously pursuing the quest or are vaguely aware that something is missing," Richard Leider writes in his book *The Power of Purpose*. "If we do not discover our purpose, then a large portion of each day is spent doing something we might not truly care about and would rather not be doing."

Leider is an expert in the power of purpose. Along with his colleague Barbara Hoese, he's held "purpose workshops" in Blue

Zones Project Communities across the country since 2009 to help residents define their personal strengths, passions, and values, and to find ways to put them to better use. We're all good at something, he reminds us. But too often we fail to give ourselves enough credit for the talents we possess.

"If you want to uncover your life purpose, you must think of yourself in a new way," Leider writes. "What gifts do you bring to serving others?" Perhaps you have a knack for numbers. Or a sense of humor. Maybe you play a musical instrument. Or you sing in the choir. Perhaps you're good at inspiring people. Or you're a natural teacher. Maybe you're the kind of person friends count on. Or you're a great mom or dad. Perhaps you're an athlete, or a dancer, or a teacher, or a coach. The first step in finding your purpose is to recognize what your greatest gift might be.

At the purpose workshops Leider holds, he often invites his audiences to identify their gifts by taking part in a 15-minute exercise with "calling cards." These cards resemble playing cards, except that each has a phrase describing a talent, such as "seeing the big picture" or "bringing out potential." After handing out decks of 52 cards to everyone in the audience, he instructs people to select five cards that describe their personal gifts. Then he asks each person to tell the others in the audience how they've used their number one gift to accomplish something that they care about.

"All of a sudden, when they see how they're using their talents on things they love to do, the energy and the heat goes up in the room," Leider said. "The whole place lights up, and they see their purpose as a real living, breathing thing." What would it be like to feel that energy all the time, he asks. Think of all the good things you could accomplish.

"Having a purpose that provides real power requires a goal outside ourselves," Leider writes. "Only when our focus—our purpose—is larger than ourselves can meaning be deeply savored and long lasting, not just a goal completed and then forgotten."

That's the bottom line with purpose: Whether your goal is to be a better parent or write the Great American Novel, if you take time to recognize what makes you feel alive—and stop thinking of life as a never ending to-do list—you can accomplish something truly memorable.

POSITIVE PSYCHOLOGY

Most of the happiness strategies that are popular today fall under the banner of the new field of study and treatment called "positive psychology." Until relatively recently, the subject of happiness had been largely ignored by traditional psychologists, who focused mainly on treating mental illness. As a result, new models of behavior had to be formulated, because "it turns out that the skills of happiness, the skills of the pleasant life, the skills of engagement, the skills of meaning, are different from the skills of relieving misery," said the University of Pennsylvania's Martin Seligman, one of the founders of the positive psychology movement.

Researchers are taking a scientific approach to questions such as "Where does happiness really come from?" and "What can we do to reliably increase it?" Through carefully designed experiments, they've tested a wide range of activities, or "interventions" as they call them, to determine which have measurable impacts on elements of happiness such as pleasurable emotions, engagement, and meaning. Could such interventions be effective, they want to know, in building well-being over the long term?

Quite a few of these happiness-building interventions have ancient pedigrees, with roots in Buddhist or Greek philosophy. They involve such familiar practices as expressing gratitude to someone you haven't adequately thanked, or savoring the pleasure of a crisp autumn morning in the woods. They advocate committing random acts of kindness, setting up a media-free zone during dinner to encourage conversation, and establishing a set of practical goals to help you better manage your time—many of the practices we have been finding to be important as we visit the world's happiest places and watch our Blue Zones Communities evolve.

Another leading researcher in the field of positive psychology, Sonja Lyubomirsky of the University of California, Riverside, wrote a popular book a few years ago called *The How of Happiness*. In it she advocated such happiness-boosting practices as keeping a gratitude journal or doing something kind for a stranger—activities that have been empirically shown to increase positive emotions, a sense of purpose, and overall satisfaction with life. But I wanted to know how exactly that worked in the long term.

"It's relatively easy to become happier for the short duration, just as it's a piece of cake to quit smoking for a day or temporarily keep a tidy desk," Lyubomirsky writes. "The challenge lies in *sustaining* the new level of happiness." This is a central theme of Lyubomirsky's research, which challenges you to take happiness building more seriously. "Consider how much time and commitment many people devote to physical exercise, whether it's going to the gym, jogging, kickboxing, or yoga," she writes. According to her research, if you want greater happiness, you need to be similarly dedicated.

Described recently as the "queen of happiness" by one of her peers, Lyubomirsky was still a promising young researcher back in January 1999, when she was invited by Martin Seligman and Mihaly Csikszentmihalyi of Claremont Graduate University to join a dozen or so other academics in the coastal resort of Akumal, Mexico, to brainstorm about the emerging field of positive psychology. Today she's a professor at the University of California, Riverside.

I met Lyubomirsky about a decade ago and was struck by how easily she engaged in conversation about her research with nonexperts. Tall and slender, with a disarming wit, she combined a wide knowledge of the latest research—much of which she'd done herself—with a gift for knowing what interested people. When she spoke to a group, people leaned in. So I was glad for the opportunity to call her again for an interview. The first thing I asked was for an update on the latest research—the top things we now know can make us happier.

"There are probably hundreds of things we can do," she replied. "But I'd say one was anything having to do with the positive thinking basket." By that she meant being optimistic about the future and looking on the bright side when coping with difficulties. Being appreciative and expressing gratitude were two good ways to engage in such thinking, she said. But it was also important not to dwell on negative thoughts.

There were other baskets she spoke of, representing other parts of your life where you can make a difference in your level of happiness. One had to do with relationships. "Lots of research has shown that the happiest people have good relationships," Lyubomirsky said, whether they involved intimate friends, fellow workers, or even pets. A third basket related to goals: "There's no happiness without them. People who are happy have meaningful life goals, and it's important to choose them wisely and be absorbed in pursuit of those goals."

What these recommendations all had in common was Lyubomirsky's conviction that greater happiness was within your grasp if you were willing to put in the time and effort to adjust your thinking and behavior. A great deal of research had gone into studying the traits and habits of happy people, she said. You could be more like them with enough practice.

At the heart of her approach was a provocative idea about what determines your happiness—an idea depicted on the cover of her first book as a delicious pie. (For the hardback version, it was a cherry pie; for the paperback, a meringue-covered one.) In both cases, the pie had been cut to remove a sizable chunk. That piece, somewhere around 40 percent of the whole, is, as Lyubomirsky writes, "within our ability to control." The pie raised a number of questions that I was hoping Lyubomirsky would explain.

"So where did that estimated 40 percent come from?" I asked.

"The question we were asking was what is the primary determinant of happiness?" she said. Her research team looked first at genetics. As studies had shown, identical twins (who share the same genetic makeup) are more similar in their happiness than are fraternal twins (who don't), which suggests that our personal capacity for happiness is at least partly influenced by genetics. In fact, scientists have estimated that as much as 50 percent of the differences in happiness among people can be explained by genetics.

"What about the other estimated 50 percent?" I asked. "What determines that?"

"Well, about 10 percent of the differences between people are due to life circumstances—whether you're married; what your age, religion, and health are; what your ethnicity is," Lyubomirsky said. "Those things do affect your happiness. But on average, if we put everyone in the same situation, the differences in their happiness would be reduced by only 10 percent."

"Which leaves somewhere around 40 percent," I said.

"Exactly. My colleagues and I argue that the remaining 40 percent is what we can affect through our behaviors, how we think and act every day," she said. Although these percentages were just estimates—it might be better to think about "a large portion of the pie" rather than a specific number, she said—this was still good news. It meant that a significant amount of your happiness wasn't locked in by genetics or life circumstances but rather could be improved through your behavior. The more you acted and thought like the happiest people—those who spent time with family and friends, acted generously toward others, maintained optimistic outlooks, lived in the moment, remained physically active, and pursued worthy goals—the happier you could become. That big piece of the pie, in other words—that slice of your happiness—represented a golden opportunity for you to take control of your own well-being.

The challenge, Lyubomirsky cautions, is that if you repeat the same happiness-boosting strategies too often, they begin to feel routine. They lose their ability to lift your spirits, in the same way that a raise or a new title at work eventually loses luster and novelty. Or, as Martin Seligman colorfully put it, "It's like French vanilla ice cream. The first taste is 100 percent. By the time you're down to the sixth taste, it's gone."

If you want to keep the experience fresh, you need to know which happiness-boosting activities to try and how often, Lyubomirsky advises. For example, you might plan to meditate before a visit from your in-laws, or cultivate optimism on mornings when you wake up gloomy, or avoid dwelling on negative thoughts after an email from your boss. Find out which interventions work for you, she said. It's also important to keeping varying your happiness activities, just as people trying to keep off the pounds benefit from new and different weight-loss routines. "As long as the positive experiences are varied, we don't get used to them," she writes. "Work on several happiness activities at once, so if one is not going so well, you can relish another."

Although the emotional lift from such experiences may be short-lived, Lyubomirsky says, there's encouraging evidence that such feel-good activities may eventually add up to long-lasting changes. For one thing, people who enjoy positive emotions on a regular basis may develop greater resilience in responding to setbacks than others. While unhappy individuals tend to see the world in a way that reinforces their unhappiness, happy people tend to react to events in more positive ways that make it easier for them to weather life's ups and downs.

As Barbara Fredrickson, another leading happiness expert, has said, positive emotions such as joy and gratitude aren't just fleeting experiences that make you feel good; they're also experiences that broaden your awareness and build personal resources that last. Fredrickson, a professor of psychology at the University of North Carolina (UNC), describes this as an upward spiral. The big question, then, becomes how to make it easier for people to put themselves in situations and surroundings where they will experience the right kind of positive emotions—the ones that add up to greater long-term happiness. Could we nudge people into positive behaviors as effectively as walkable neighborhoods nudge them into being more active or automatic savings accounts nudge them into being more successful with their retirement funds? Could we find lasting ways to stack the deck in favor of the three strands of happiness that the Blue Zones Project focuses on—pleasure, purpose, and pride? If so, we might have strategies to address both sides of the same coin.

That's what I decided to ask Fredrickson myself.

THE UPWARD SPIRAL

In his book *Authentic Happiness* psychologist Martin Seligman describes the moment nearly two decades ago when he discovered Barbara Fredrickson's groundbreaking research on positive emotions. At the time, he was chairing a selection committee for a major prize, and Fredrickson, who was then teaching at the University of Michigan, had been nominated. "When I first read her papers, I ran up the stairs two at a time and said excitedly to Mandy, 'This is life-changing!' At least for a grouch like me."

What Seligman was so eager to share with his wife, Mandy, was Fredrickson's theory that happiness-related emotions such as joy, pride, and love had an unrecognized evolutionary function. Not only were they pleasant to experience, she argued, but also they helped you to grow—by opening your mind and heart to new connections. Positive emotions didn't just feel good, that is. They were also good for you.

Her theory went something like this: The evolutionary function of negative emotions was easy to see. When triggered by a threat, feelings such as anger or fear prepared you to fight or to flee. But the evolutionary advantages of positive emotions were subtler. They may not initiate some survival tactic, but feelings such as amusement or love expanded your awareness so you could see the forest for the trees. And that broader perspective helped you to make discoveries, acquire knowledge, form alliances, and pick up skills that might increase your chances of survival in the future. She called her idea the "broaden-and-build" theory.

When Seligman read her papers and supporting research, he realized that, even for a grump like him, feeling good might serve a useful function. She "utterly convinced me that it was worth trying hard to put more positive emotions into my life," he wrote. Not surprisingly, Fredrickson won the Templeton Positive Psychology Prize that year.

I remember being impressed the first time I heard about her research, too, because it just made sense to me that emotions related to happiness could lead to other good things, such as better relationships, better decision-making, better health, and even longer life. The other experts I'd talked to, such as Sonja Lyubomirsky, had already pointed to a wealth of studies showing that happiness contributed to higher incomes, greater productivity, higher quality work, longer marriages, more friends, stronger immune systems, lower stress levels, less pain, and greater longevity. Fredrickson's theory seemed to explain why.

I'd also seen for myself in Blue Zones Project Communities that the joy and satisfaction that people experience after volunteering, socializing, or just taking a walk in the park often create an appetite for more generosity, community-building, and healthy exercise in a kind of virtuous cycle. I began to see more clearly how the work being done by positive psychologists like Fredrickson dovetailed with the many different activities we were promoting in cities and towns across the nation to increase well-being.

So I was eager to learn more about the nuts and bolts of Fredrickson's research, figuring that a conversation with her about the inner workings of happiness would be like peering under the hood of a NASCAR race car with a master mechanic. I caught up with her on the phone in September 2016 at the UNC campus in Chapel Hill as she was getting ready for a meeting.

"Can you tell me a little more about your work on the evolutionary rationale for positive emotions?" I asked.

"That's the broaden-and-build theory," she said. "The backdrop of that is that negative emotions narrow our thinking to address a threat in a way that helped our ancestors get out of life-and-death situations. But positive emotions aren't organized around threats. They're organized around opportunities."

Positive emotions don't grab our attention as much as negative ones, she said, because missing an opportunity isn't going to kill you. It's just a missed opportunity. But feelings such as joy, gratitude, serenity, interest, hope, pride, amusement, inspiration, awe, and love—the 10 positive emotions she focused on in her research—do serve a valuable function by broadening our awareness, and experiments have shown it. "Researchers actually have evidence from brain imaging studies that our peripheral vision expands to take in more information," Fredrickson said.

In one experiment, for example, researchers decided to monitor activity in two areas of the brain, one that responds to human faces and another that recognizes places. Before beginning the main part of the experiment, the researchers showed pictures known to induce positive feelings (such as images of playful kittens) to some of the subjects, but to other subjects they showed pictures known to induce negative feelings (such as images of crying children). To a third group, they showed pictures known to induce neutral feelings (such as images of furniture). Next they showed the subjects another set of images with faces in the center surrounded by pictures of houses and asked them to say if the faces were male or female, ignoring the houses. Subjects who had been shown the unpleasant pictures had less activity in the part of their brains devoted to places, while those who had been shown the pleasant pictures had more activity. This confirmed the idea that negative feelings narrowed fields of view to focus on the faces, while positive ones expanded views to include the houses.

"Positive emotions make us more exploratory," Fredrickson said. They've also been shown to make us more creative, more open to new relationships, more sympathetic to people from other cultures, and more flexible in solving problems, such as making management decisions, diagnosing medical conditions, or conducting negotiations. People who experience happy emotions—even ones as fleeting as imagining a joyful memory or receiving a small kindness—tend to be more optimistic, resilient, accepting, and purpose-driven, as well. Meditation appears to compound these effects, as if it offers a super-dose of happiness resilience when practiced over time. In one study, subjects who completed a three-month course in which they meditated about 90 minutes a week later described life as measurably more satisfying and fulfilling, she said.

"So, positive emotions might not help you in a moment of danger," I said, "but over time they could help you acquire other useful skills."

"Exactly," Fredrickson said. "That's the 'build' part. The more people have these moments of awareness, which accumulate and compound, the more they're building resources, and, in a way, becoming a better version of themselves—more resilient, more socially integrated, more knowledgeable." Although positive experiences tend to be short-lived, lasting only seconds or minutes, she said, they were like nutrients for your psychological well-being, helping to grow resources. That's the "broaden" part.

"But how long do these resources last?" I asked. "I mean, if you ask someone to perform meditation for three months and they accumulate resources because of the positive emotions they feel, how long will they actually last?"

"Well, I think there can be a long-lasting effect if the practice becomes part of your day-to-day habits," she said. "We have one study that showed that such resources were largely maintained 15 months later, especially if people continued to meditate. But it didn't necessarily hinge on that. I think the meditation just put people on this positive trajectory of growth, and then that became a sort of self-sustaining upward spiral of growth." People who enjoyed regular emotional boosts from everyday activities such as helping others, playing, learning, or praying, in other words, developed a greater aptitude for generosity, socializing, and mindfulness, which encouraged them to seek out more opportunities for pleasant emotions in that upward spiral.

But pleasant feelings are fragile, Fredrickson warned. Moments of joy, serenity, or inspiration can be easily quashed by worries, doubts, and demands. As a result of their urgency, negative emotions such as fear or anxiety packed a bigger punch than positive ones such as amusement or awe. So people who wanted to experience an upward spiral of positive experiences could start by organizing their days to include at least three "heartfelt" positive feelings for every "heart-wrenching" negative one. That appears to be the difference between people who are flourishing and those who aren't, she said.

For most of us, achieving that three-to-one ratio of positive to negative emotions might be a challenge. One national survey found that more than 80 percent of the participants did not meet the criteria for flourishing mental health. (Separately, Fredrickson found that the average ratio of positive to negative emotions was about two-to-one.) Which means that, for most of us, the broaden-and-build spiral might never take place unless we adopt healthier emotional habits.

The strategies Fredrickson proposed to accomplish that were largely the same ones Seligman and Lyubomirsky advocated. They included such techniques as savoring the moment, counting your blessings, practicing kindness, living with passion, and imagining your best future. The key, she said, was doing whatever you chose to do with an open heart, avoiding the common mistake of turning positive experiences into repetitive chores.

At the same time, Fredrickson said, you could also improve your daily ratio of good feelings by reducing the number of negative ones. "Do you ever get so wrapped up in your own head that you fail to fully appreciate the beauty of nature that surrounds you, your children's laughter, or the good smells coming from the kitchen as your partner cooks you dinner?" she asks in her book *Positivity*. "Gratuitous negativity can hold you hostage, as if you had cinder blocks tied to your ankles and a black hood pulled over your face."

"So how do you actually achieve that ideal ratio?" I asked. "How do you set up your life so you're more likely to have these positive emotions?" I had my own ideas about the answers. In Blue Zones areas, pockets where people live the longest, they survived not because they maintained better habits or were more diligent about dieting or exercising, but because they were nudged into it every day by their cultural and physical environments. And I suspected that the same thing was happening in places around the world where people tended to be happier than the rest of us, like Denmark. I mentioned these Blue Zones to Fredrickson and asked if there wasn't some way for us to learn from their examples, to shape our environments so they nudged us into having more positive experiences?

"Yeah, I think you're onto something," she said. "Living in these Blue Zones, like you described, you know, interacting with nature, having social engagement—those are some really reliable ways to increase your positive emotions. Those environments are ways to ensure that you have a ready supply of positive emotional experiences to help you to grow."

Too often, she said, we neglect to put enjoyable items on our to-do lists. We don't prioritize positivity. But everyone should, whether it's by taking a walk in nature, calling a friend, or getting ready to host a dinner party. We're better at regulating our emotions by changing our situations, Fredrickson agreed.

"But how can you do that without relying on willpower?" I asked. "What if you don't want to have to remember to meditate or to be nice to your neighbor?"

"Well, you can't just wish yourself into feeling positive emotions," she said. That actually boomerangs. But you can use one of several quite specific levers that turn on your positivity, such as spending more time with people who are energizing and less with those who are draining. "The main thing is to allow yourself to do these things more often, instead of just being wistful about it and saying 'Oh, yeah, I really enjoy that, but I never get to do it,'" she said.

I wasn't hoping for another to-do list, but I admit that Fredrickson had demonstrated during her two decades of research that good feelings such as joy, amusement, and love weren't just reflections of happiness. They actually drove it. From Hawaii to Florida, our teams were doing their best to boost overall happiness by creating surroundings that nudged people into joining walking groups where they could get to know their neighbors, or volunteering for a good cause, or riding their bikes to work, or taking a cooking class. When people worked such things into their lives, they increased their chances of feeling engagement, generosity, amusement, and pride, which made them more outgoing, empathetic, fit, and confident, and thus more likely to go walking, volunteering, biking, or cooking again. Which meant they were getting happier. We were creating our own upward spiral.

"We normally think of healthy behaviors as eating right, being physically active, not smoking, and so on," Fredrickson said. "But I think that the big unnamed one is having positive connections with others, having positive experiences in one's day, either at work or in your leisure time, or in nature."

At that point in our conversation, she must have looked at the clock because she realized that she was running late for her meeting. So I thanked her for the interview and said that I hoped we could talk again soon. I was looking forward to learning more about the power of positive emotions to launch that upward spiral of growth and happiness.

"You explained it really well," I quipped. "You should be a professor."

"Yeah, I've heard that would be a good fit," she quipped back.

Both Fredrickson and Lyubomirsky have great, evidence-backed ideas, but as they themselves will admit, the impacts of their interventions tend to be modest and short-lived. They lift your spirits for a while, but the glow soon fades as the stresses of daily life resume. To build well-being over the long term, the positive psychologists say, you must commit to a disciplined program of interventions every day. You must make positive thinking a regular habit, just as people trying to lose weight must exercise regularly and eat healthy foods every day.

To me, that's a fatal drawback, since changes that require personal willpower almost always fail in the long run. I prefer strategies that make changes to our surroundings, if possible—changes that constantly nudge us into doing the right things so we don't have to remember them on our own.

The Quiet Blockbuster Treatment

We know that good health and long-term happiness are inextricably intertwined. And yet, for many people, one particular illness undermines that goal more than any other—the syndrome we call depression. This insidious disorder is more common than you might think. Last year, more than 16 million American adults suffered episodes of depression, roughly one in 15 people. (Worldwide the number affected has been estimated at 350 million.) And the impact is terrible. Studies have shown that depressed individuals are 40 percent more likely to die in any given year and 50 percent more likely to develop heart disease, stroke, lung disease, or arthritis. Their needs also drive about 50 percent of hospitalization costs and 50 percent of social services.

Depression affects individuals in different ways. Its symptoms may include feeling sad, anxious, or empty for most of the day; having difficulty concentrating, remembering details, or making decisions; feeling fatigued or lacking energy; experiencing insomnia, early-morning wakefulness, or oversleeping; feeling guilty, worthless, or helpless; overeating or losing one's appetite; losing interest in activities that were once pleasurable, including sex; feeling restless or irritable; feeling hopeless or pessimistic; experiencing persistent aches or pains, headaches, cramps, or digestive problems; and having thoughts of suicide.

As you can imagine, trying to cope with debilitating symptoms like these often leads to difficulties between spouses or to trouble at work. By one estimate, American businesses lose about $44 billion a year in productivity and other costs because of depression among workers. To make matters worse, people with depression often experience problems with alcohol, drugs, smoking, or eating disorders; they may have nightmares or suffer panic attacks. And yet, despite all of these hardships, surprisingly few depressed people seek help—or else they wait years to do so.

That's too bad, because therapists have now developed a number of effective treatments for depression, from psychother- apy for relatively mild cases to antidepressant drugs for more severe cases, or sometimes a combination of both. One common treatment for depression is called cognitive behavioral therapy (CBT), which focuses on identifying self-defeating patterns of thoughts, such as low self-esteem or negative self-perceptions. Over the course of several months, therapists teach depressed individuals techniques to counter such thoughts by identifying them and testing them against reality. These individuals may also be asked to do "homework," such as keeping a journal to record thoughts and feelings, keeping a sleep diary, or setting up an exercise schedule. In many cases, such therapy can be as effective as medication. CBT, research shows, can resolve up to half of all depression cases. If a drug could prove that effective, it would be a billion-dollar blockbuster. Not only that, as Lord Richard Layard of the London School of Economics has estimated, if society would invest in evidence-based therapies like CBT for those who have both mental and physical health problems, the therapy would pay for itself with benefits. With fewer depressed people, we'd likely have less crime, less absenteeism, more productivity, and a lower drag on social services—returns that benefit everyone. So, why aren't we capitalizing on this opportunity?

In a groundbreaking effort to extend mental health services to more people who need them, in 2005 the United Kingdom launched a bold initiative called Improving Access to Psychological Therapies (IAPT), which more than doubled the national budget for treating depression and anxiety. Based on the work of psychologist David

Clark, the initiative was championed by Richard Layard, who argued that IAPT would pay for itself by helping depressed individuals return to work, thus reducing unemployment and disability costs.

In 2006, as a test of the concept, IAPT selected two communities in England as demonstration sites and sent a small army of therapists into the town of Doncaster in Yorkshire and the borough of Newham in London. Over the course of a year, about 1,900 people were treated, of whom more than half were described as recovered by the end of treatment. In addition, 5 percent of the unemployed patients were working again by the end of the year. Since then, the program has been rolled out across the United Kingdom, with about 600,000 people a year being treated for depression or anxiety—an amazing achievement in mental health outreach. On top of that, the program was estimated to have saved the health care system more than £1,000 per patient, which covers the cost of treatment.

As in any big rollout, the IAPT team had to iron out a few kinks in the program, as therapists struggled with high caseloads and patients complained about wait times. But for Richard Layard the bottom line was clear. "The biggest cause of our misery is mental illness," he said. "Someone who is mentally ill should have the same access to care as someone who is physically ill. The best investment for the happiness dollar is to treat mental illness."

TAMING THE MONKEY BRAIN

Soon after graduating from college, at an age when most young adults embark upon a useful and productive professional life, I struck off on my bike to see the world. I spent eight years organizing and executing three transglobal expeditions. With an ever changing crew of friends, I rode from Alaska to Argentina, around the world through the Soviet Union, and across the length and breadth of Africa. All told, I pedaled roughly 50,000 miles, rolling along like a modern centaur loaded down with a hundred pounds of supplies and equipment in four bulging saddlebag panniers.

Along the way, my friends and I suffered from malaria, giardiasis, dysentery, and intestinal worms, among other discomforts. We got lost in the Sahara, pedaled 32 days across a largely roadless Congo, where we bartered Bic pens for bananas, and got attacked with clubs in South Africa. In eastern Siberia, we pushed our bikes through a 400-mile bog. I could go on, but you get the point: We endured some serious hardships. But nothing was harder than what happened to me after my bike trips were finished, as I sat cross-legged in a temple in northern California, in near total silence, for 10 days. I can still feel the effects of that experience today, more than 15 years later.

At the time, I was coming off a tough romantic breakup that had left me emotionally devastated. I wasn't sleeping well. I felt tired all day. And nothing felt appealing. Moreover, I got into a loop of thinking that the world had conspired to make me sad, and that I'd always be miserable. At least, I couldn't conceive of being happy again.

I read a news story about a type of guided meditation called Vipassana—a technique that promised access to internal wisdom and the ability to see the world in a calmer, more balanced way. Its name meant "insight" or "to see clearly," and it was Buddhism's oldest form of meditation. Once you saw clearly, it suggested, it would be hard to "unsee."

I'd heard that Vipassana had been used in a program to soften hardened criminals at Seattle's King County Jail. A two-year follow-up study had shown that those who completed just 10 days of meditation were about 20 percent less likely to become repeat offenders. The report also showed that Vipassana was effective in reducing alcohol and substance abuse, reducing psychopathological symptoms, and increasing positive behaviors. If it could reframe a criminal's brain, I wondered, could it also short circuit a depressed brain? It was worth a try.

After my application was accepted, I flew from my home in Minneapolis to Fresno, California, where I took a taxi to a retreat at the foot of Yosemite National Park. There on several acres of rolling grounds were a half dozen barracklike accommodations, a dining hall, and a large airy temple. One hundred of us, 50 men and 50 women, had gathered for the 10-day retreat. I saw no yogis or gurus or monks in saffron robes. Instead, the center was run mostly by volunteers in ordinary clothes.

Early on during the first day, one of these volunteers, a trim middle-aged German with a buzz cut, wire-rim glasses, and unusually precise diction greeted us briefly and then launched into a litany of rules. For the next 10 days, he told us, we'd be completely silent. Except for emergencies and an optional five-minute daily conversation with the teacher, we'd talk to no one.

He asked us to take a simple pledge that approximated the one that Buddhist monks take. We agreed not to leave the grounds or to communicate with the outside world. We vowed not to kill any living being, including insects, and to abstain from sexual activity, telling lies, stealing, and all intoxicants. Further, he asked that we do no writing, reading, or engaging in any other form of communication. He also asked that if we belonged to a religion, we put it "on the shelf" during our stay. Other than taking contemplative walks on the grounds, he asked that we avoid exercise. And then he got serious.

"The first day is not hard, but the second day is," he said. "Most of you will cry on the third day and will want to leave. You'll likely cry again on the eighth day. If you don't think you can live with these rules and stay here silent for 10 days, now's the time to leave." After that, we were committed.

I spent the next 10 days moving between the meditation temple, a simple mess hall that served vegetarian meals, and the spartan, barracklike quarters that I shared with six other guys. My room-mates included an aging rock star who'd done too many drugs, an artist, a massage therapist, a laser scientist, and a couple of rock climbers from Yosemite who'd joined the program to sharpen their concentration skills.

Up in the meditation temple, a shaft of light angled down through a skylight as we spent long hours in silence. For the first three days, we focused only on our breath, breathing through the nose, mouth closed. I found it amazingly difficult. My back hurt, my legs cramped, my knees ached. My mind played an endless loop of loss and regret, and I made desperate plans to escape. I couldn't focus for more than 15 seconds at a time.

By day three, I found my mind had slowed down enough for my emotions to catch up with my thoughts. As the instructor predicted, my eyes welled with tears. At times during the day, the people to my left and right also were weeping.

We spent days four and five focusing our attention on a square inch between our upper lip and nostrils. This, too, was exceedingly difficult. The snot chute, as I liked to think of it, provided scant stimulation for my rampaging mind. Near the end of day five, our instructor introduced us to the actual technique of Vipassana. He guided us to move our focus from our upper lip to the very top of our head. After a moment or two, I felt my scalp tingling with a low-voltage sensation. I discovered that I could move that sensation downward, over my face, down my neck, along my right arm, then my left arm, and so on. The feeling was electric. I did this for the next two hours.

Vipassana, like most meditation techniques, has a few basic tenants. First, it assumes that at our core we are all basically good and that if we stop long enough to listen to our inner voice, we'll make better decisions about our relationships, our jobs, our health, and our spiritual lives.

Second, it assumes that we don't really control our thoughts, but rather that they operate on their own, like digestion or breathing.

Third, it assumes that, left to their own devices, especially in our busy, hyperconnected world, our thoughts rampage out of control. (If I told you to stop reading this now, and think of nothing, you probably couldn't do it. Instead, your thoughts would gravitate to memories, plans, sex fantasies, or getting on to the exciting next page of this book.) Many people who meditate liken this darting of our thoughts to a wild monkey—hence the term they use to describe the normal state of our minds, the "monkey brain."

Fourth, Vipassana assumes that it's possible to slow down the mind, so that our thoughts scroll by slowly—slowly enough to observe them and even feel emotions associated with them. A gesture of kindness, a job well done, a moment of selflessness all tend to occasion the kind of positive feeling that we might miss if our minds are pinballing from one thought to the next. By the same token, a boast or a mean word tend to engender palpable negative feelings. If we conditioned ourselves to feel these emotions, Vipassana teaches, we wouldn't need the Koran or the Ten Commandments to tell us right from wrong.

Fifth, Vipassana assumes that the way to slow down the mind is to focus on something outside the mind (breath, skin sensations, a mantra) and let thoughts emerge as they will. When they do, we can observe the thought—the memory, the worry, or the plan—and let it pass out of our minds. When we choose not to indulge the thought, it loses energy and fades. In other words, if we put the monkey in a cage, it eventually will go sit down.

Once the mind has slowed down, the gaps between our thoughts become wide enough to let our basically good, inner voice percolate up to our conscious mind. And herein lies Vipassana's power: Since wisdom is knowledge plus experience, it gives us the ability to sense what we really feel about what we have done in our lives. The past is past and the future is uncertain, so all that is sure is the present. If we can slow down our minds for long enough, and fully experience the present, we have a chance to actually observe our thoughts and control them rather than letting them control us.

Sometimes old memories bubble up. In the process of observing them, we may experience how they make us feel. For instance, I remembered once when my father noticed a dent in the family car. He assumed that someone had hit the car and driven away. Actually I had dented the car. But since my father hadn't asked me directly about it, I figured, why volunteer the information? During Vipassana, I not only remembered that incident but also experienced the sneaky-sick feeling that accompanied my lie, however small. And I recalled other versions of being less-than-honest, with all of their attendant feelings. I now possessed the wisdom and resolve not to do such things again.

I came out of the 10-day Vipassana session completely zoning—seeing amoebas floating across my field of vision. I was in a euphoric stupor and could barely speak. I packed my bags and headed to the airport. On the way, I stopped at a Denny's for lunch. But the din and confusion of so many people talking at the same time overwhelmed me. I had to leave.

In the days that followed, I found that I could concentrate better than I ever could before. Although that sensation wore off after a couple of weeks, the visceral feeling of being able to tell right from wrong stuck with me, and the insights I discovered during my 10 days of sitting became part of my psychological hardwiring. Even now, 15 years later, I can still focus my mind, observe my thoughts, and fine-tune my behavior and reaction to others. And I'm not the only one who has found this helpful. Several scientific studies have shown Vipassana to be an effective way of reducing impulsiveness and managing stress.

But the ultimate value of the experience was a certain rewiring of my brain. It reshaped the lens through with I looked at the world. Just reducing the noise in my head gave me permanent insights I've never forgotten. It clarified my purpose, which remains clear to this day, and endowed me with a lasting downshift tool, there whenever I need it.

Not long ago, I met a human rights lawyer named Amandine who has devoted many years to helping the people of Afghanistan. In 2004 she was working for the U.N. in Kabul as a civic education officer when three of her colleagues were kidnapped. She was evacuated from the country. Suffering from post-traumatic stress disorder, Amandine sought relief from her inner turmoil in India, where she took up yoga and Vipassana meditation. Then in 2011, she returned to Kabul with a renewed sense of purpose. Her new mission: to promote peace and nonviolence through yoga and meditation and through working with refugees, displaced persons, prisoners, students, and other Afghans.

I asked her if she thought that Vipassana had permanently changed her.

"Yes!" she said. "It was a life-changing experience. My life is less of a roller coaster now, and I am more in tune with people, more compassionate, more empathetic." Speaking in wonderfully French-accented English, she said Vipassana had taught her to see her thoughts as clouds passing in the sky, which had given her control over her troubled emotions.

"Meditation for me was the trick to give a banana to my monkey and tame it, so it wouldn't jump every second in my life," she said. "I found an inner peace that I'd never discovered before."

That sounded good to me.

BLUEPRINT FOR INNER SELF HAPPINESS

Some people assume that you're stuck with the personality you're born with. Some people were lucky enough to be born cheerful, and others are destined to be grouches all their lives. Cognitive psychologists are telling us otherwise, as are the experiences we've been watching as we work with communities committed to the Blue Zones Project. There are ways that you can fine-tune your happiness quotient internally: recognizing your gifts and talents and putting them to use to benefit others, surrounding yourself with good friends, losing yourself in pursuit of challenging goals, and avoiding gratuitous negativity in your thoughts—these are all key steps in the process. Combining what we've learned with what the experts are telling us, here's a short list of things you can do to set up your inner self for long-term happiness:

1. **Know your purpose.** As we've discovered in the happiest places, and in research from the experts, being invested in something greater than ourselves is fundamental to a richer, happier life.

    Lessons: Take time to reflect on what makes you feel alive. Richard Leider recommends taking a personal inventory, and he teaches a simple formula to help you get clarity: Gifts (what you have to offer) + Passion (what really excites you) + Values (what you find most important) = your Calling, or $G + P + V = C$. When you find where your greatest abilities, passion, and values intersect, you're on purpose. Here's another exercise to try:

    - Imagine you had $10 million in the bank.
    - Write down five things you'd do.

- Pick one of the five and set a three-year goal to achieve it.
- Write down what you'd have to accomplish in each of the three years leading up to the goal.
- List three things you can do right now in support of achieving it.

2. **Learn the art of likability.** Smiling, trusting, and giving others your time have been shown by research to create happiness. Being open and approachable also can help break down stereotypes about strangers—you never know whom you might connect with or who might become a friend. Research shows that people are often overly pessimistic about the risks of getting to know others, but now that you know everything you've got to gain, try making the first move and initiate conversation.

   Lessons: If you were born likable, you're set. If not, make the effort to learn social skills, such as being a good listener, greeting people by name, and using positive body language such as keeping eye contact and keeping arms uncrossed. Welcome the ideas of others and encourage them more. Offer at least three positive comments to each of your friends and loved ones, on average, for every negative. Try talking to relative strangers on your commute. Ask questions and really listen to the answers. Act extroverted, even if you're an introvert.

3. **Focus on others.** Giving of both money and time generally boosts well-being more than people expect. Volunteers tend to weigh less, to feel healthier, to have less chance of suffering a heart attack, and to score higher in every happiness domain.

   Lessons: Take the focus off yourself. Make a list of things that will help make others happy and devote time to it.

Donate money to or volunteer for a local church or charity on a regular basis. Start by signing up to serve once a month, preferably in a way that makes the best use of your particular skills, and your involvement will likely increase as you enjoy the benefits of giving. Practice random acts of kindness, too, such as bringing coffee to a co-worker, calling friends to tell them you're thinking about them, or helping a neighbor carry groceries into the house.

4. **Get out of your comfort zone.** Each of us has a "comfort zone"—a behavioral and psychological construct in which our activities and thinking fit a routine pattern. Our comfort zone is a healthy adaptation that helps us operate efficiently and minimize stress and risk—that's why we're hardwired to seek comfort. But being able to break outside of your comfort zone is essential to transitioning and growing; putting yourself into slightly uncomfortable situations can push you to achieve goals you might never have expected. Taking risks, despite fear of failure, can push you to peak performance and to be more creative—both of which can have lasting impacts on how we frame our lives.

    Lessons: Try new things, even if you know you might not be the best—or even good—at them. You may be the worst skater on the ice, and you may fall, but you're more likely to remember the experience. Embrace failure. Let your social network, your workplace, and your community nudge you into new possibilities—but also learn when you should say "no thanks."

5. **Learn meditation.** Studies show that meditation has positive effects on emotions, physiology, stress, cognitive abilities, and health. It helps slow the mind, making it more likely that

you'll clearly see the important things in life. Plus, it's like learning to ride a bike: Once you've learned, you never forget how to do it, and you can come back again and again to reap these benefits through your lifetime.

Lessons: If you're like me, you're sick of seeing the recommendation to meditate. But it works, and just learning how to do it right once can stick with you for the long run. I recommend everyone try Vipassana once in their lives (just Google Vipassana to learn more), but a good teacher or even a tape can be useful. Download recordings from Jack Kornfield, Jon Kabat-Zinn, or Tara Brach to start, or check out a local class or session open to the public. Each instructor has his or her own style, so keep switching it up until you find someone you like.

6. **Keep the faith.** In most countries, religious people are happier than nonreligious people. A 2015 study by the London School of Economics and Erasmus University Medical Center in the Netherlands found that participants who went to services in a church, mosque, or synagogue regularly experienced a more significant mental health boost than those who engaged only in other social activities.

    Lessons: If you're religious, attend services regularly. If you're not, take the time to visit a half dozen places of worship to see if any resonate. If organized religion just isn't your thing, look for groups in your area with whom you might share and practice your spiritual beliefs. Whatever you believe in, engaging regularly in a spiritual practice can influence your life in a deep, sustained, and positive way.

The Power 9 of Happiness

Something to do, someone to love, something to give,
and something to look forward to.

I 'D LIKE TO THINK I've offered you the world's best information to create a blueprint for your best life. But now you might be asking how to remember it all and put it to work. My answer—something I call the Happiness Power 9.

When I wrote *The Blue Zones: Lessons for Living Longer From the People Who've Lived the Longest,* I identified the nine common denominators of the world's longevity hot spots and summed them up in a tidy pyramid I dubbed the *Power 9*—you saw it earlier in the book, on page 26. This visual aid seemed to stick in people's minds. So now I'm going to do my best to sum up all we've learned about happiness in the same sort of compact graphic.

I have learned through the years of observing the work going on in our Blue Zones Project demonstration communities, when a community takes steps toward health and longevity, the people living there grow happier as well.

So that is why, as part of the background to this book, we convened the Blue Zones Happiness Consensus Panel. One of their tasks was to identify effective and feasible strategies that individuals could use to improve long-term happiness. The panel came up with more than 120 suggestions, and when asked to rank these suggestions for effectiveness, many of the themes that rose to the top of their list—no surprise—were the very ones we had identified as key characteristics of the happiest places we had visited: investing in family and friends, finding and practicing your faith, living near nature. Some of the other ideas, less enduring but still effective, included being active every day, focusing on the happiness of others, continuing to learn, being generous, being nice to people, and volunteering.

Separately, my team did an academic literature review to find all of the evidence-based techniques to increase daily positive affect (pleasure), life goals (purpose), and life satisfaction (pride)—our three P's. We reviewed those strategies through a lens of sustainability, asking which would authentically make a lasting difference. I don't believe that asking you to change your behavior does you much of a service: Most people forget, run out of discipline, or get bored after just a few months. So the question I asked was, which of these evidence-based techniques would have staying power and make a lasting difference in people's lives.

Putting all this together—the years of work with Blue Zones Communities, the visits over the years to places deemed the happiest in the world, the results of our Happiness Consensus Panel, and the top research results I could find—here is the Happiness Power 9, the best ways to permanently shape your surroundings for happiness:

Lesson One

Love Someone. Commit to someone compatible with you who shares your interests and values and whose company you enjoy. Research shows that you're more likely to be happy if you're married or in a committed relationship. Loners are mostly unhappy. That said, picking the *right* partner can determine 90 percent of your personal happiness or lack thereof.

Lesson Two

Inner Circle. Create a circle of at least three friends with whom you can have meaningful conversations, who you can call on a bad day for help, and who are generally happy. Your mother told you you're known by the company you keep. Now researchers will tell you that you actually begin to *become* the company you keep—obesity, substance abuse, smoking, and even unhappiness are all contagious. In fact, for every new happy friend that enters your social network, your own happiness increases by about 15 percent.

Lesson Three

Engage. Get out of your house. Identify your interests and then join a club, a team, or a civic organization that matches them. Volunteer. If you are religious, show up regularly for services. Try things that make you feel uncertain or uncomfortable. Curious people invest in activities that make them stretch to reach higher psychological peaks, and happiness is a by-product of being fully engaged. Our expert panel found that just making an effort and *doing something* is often more important for happiness than *what* you do.

Lesson Four

Learn Likability. Some people are just born likable, others—like me—have to learn it. Cultivate generosity and empathy; be interested and interesting, learn social skills. Happiness and unhappiness are contagious, and they both start with *you*. We tend to like people who care about us, who really listen to us, who can tell a good story, and who are generous with their time and resources. These types of people make us happy and, not coincidentally, they look for these qualities in us. Act extroverted, even if you're an introvert. Give at least three positive comments for each negative comment you speak.

Lesson Five

Move Naturally. A daily dose of physical activity is a potent cocktail of happiness. It boosts mood, releases endorphins, increases energy, enhances sleep, lowers chances of obesity and chronic disease, tends to be a pro-social activity, and is likely to make you more attractive. If you're among the tiny percentage of people who have the time, discipline, and desire to "exercise" 30 minutes a day, you're covered. Otherwise, find opportunities to move that are woven into the routine and habits of your life, such as walking or cycling to work. If you sit at a desk for work, consider a stand-up desk, even one with a treadmill, or set a timer so you take a quick walking break every half hour.

Lesson Six

Look Forward. Focus on meaningful things, set goals, and monitor progress. Research indicates that people who set goals and monitor them are happier in the long run. This may be because they're more likely to get what they want out of life (though research shows they mis-predict more than half of the time). Or it may be because the process itself is enjoyable. Either way, you win.

Lesson Seven
Sleep Seven Plus. Establish routines that promote at least seven and a half hours of sleep nightly. The Cornell Sleep Lab, which followed the sleeping habits of Americans for decades, found that most people need between seven and a half and nine hours of sleep nightly. Gallup found if you're sleeping less than six hours per night, you're about 30 percent less happy than you would be if you had slept enough. Cutting sleep is almost always a bad idea; you are less productive and less creative, you have less energy, and you will likely lose time in the long run because sleep-deprived people live shorter lives.

Lesson Eight
Shape Surroundings. Set up your home, workplace, finances, social network, and inner life to favor happiness. Trying to change our behavior to favor happiness almost never works in the long run, but science shows that you can shape your surroundings so you're most likely to be happy. Throughout this book, I've offered a number of ways that you can reshape each of the concentric circles of your Life Radius. I'm sure you (and your friends and loved ones) can find more.

Lesson Nine
Right Community. Of all the things people can do to try to increase their happiness, the most effective and lasting one is to choose to live in a community that supports well-being. For many people, that means getting involved in efforts to reshape the community where they already live—improving schools, making streets walkable, and

creating better access to healthy foods. We've watched people living in areas caught in a downward spiral turn around and get healthier and happier thanks to changes initiated once their communities became part of a Blue Zones Project. For others, the best answer may be simply to move. We've seen this with immigrants who moved from less happy countries to happier places such as Canada and adopted the happiness levels of their new country or community within a year.

It's taken me years of observing, interviewing, traveling, and consulting to bring these principles down to the Power 9 of Happiness. It may seem like a simple and obvious list, but I can assure you, it's a list the world agrees on.

There's an even bigger lesson:

You can't do it on your own. To use the cliché, it takes a village. Or a neighborhood, or a community, or a city, or a state, or a nation. You can redirect your life toward greater happiness and well-being only when the world you live in supports you. Once your environment nudges you toward healthier choices, you will become happier.

Think of dieting as an analogy. That's where this realization started in my own mind.

We all know what we need to do to lose weight. Change the daily menu to include more fruits and vegetables and less sugar, fat, and processed foods. Don't eat more when we've had enough. Get more exercise. Easy, right? So why don't we do it? Because when you put it that way, it's a long to-do list that puts the burden directly onto you, your willpower, and your staying power. We're all human. We might stick with it for a day, a week, or even a month, but eventually we slide back. We grab the easy snack food, get lunch at a drive-through, use our free time for lounging, drive a few blocks rather than walk. Our world is set up to make all those things so easy for us!

And that's the point. If the world you wake up to every day were designed to support healthier choices, you wouldn't need that extra oomph of willpower. If your grocery store featured the finest produce, if your friends dropped by every afternoon to take a walk together, if your neighborhood had easy-access sidewalks and bike lanes, if your workplace were a mile away from home, think how much easier it would be to make the choices I've outlined in this book that we all know lead to greater well-being!

And that's why I began our discussion in this book at the outermost ring of everyone's Life Radius: at the level of the nation and the community. It's taken me years of visiting communities, both in the United States and around the world, to recognize that the happiest places are the ones where community leaders have committed to making changes for the better of all. I'm thinking of Costa Rica, where a culture of peace, tolerance, and pleasure prevails; of Denmark, where young people are encouraged to take time to discover their calling; and of Singapore, where everyone enjoys working hard and takes pride in doing so. And, likewise, I'm thinking of the successes we have seen in the U.S. communities that have joined our Blue Zones Project—Albert Lea, Minnesota; the Beach Cities of California; Fort Worth, Texas. All of these nations or communities have been shaped by brave and visionary leaders who pushed for changes to nudge their citizens into choices that made their lives happier.

What does this mean for you? Engage in local or regional efforts to make changes in your own landscape. And in the meantime, keep the Happiness Power 9 in mind for yourself and your loved ones. Share these ideas with your family, your close circle of friends, your neighbors, your mates at work. Choose one lesson and see what you can do to reshape the environment you share with them, to add a few nudges toward greater well-being. The broader the reach of the message, the more likely change will occur—and the happier your world will be.

APPENDIX

❧

The Blue Zones Happiness Consensus Project

CONSENSUS RESULTS

Using the Delphi technique, our international panel of experts winnowed a master list of more than 120 strategies for promoting happiness into the top ten policy recommendations and the top ten personal recommendations to improve well-being. Over a period of months, they ranked the leading happiness-boosting ideas for effectiveness and feasibility, debated the results, and re-ranked them to arrive at the following:

TOP TEN POLICY RECOMMENDATIONS
(Starting with highest effect and feasibility)

1. Promote volunteering and national service
2. Measure national well-being

3. Focus on the least happy people
4. Combat discrimination
5. Allow freedom to make life decisions
6. Invest in education
7. Teach life skills in school
8. Support families
9. Prioritize prevention in health care
10. Provide free health care

TOP TEN PRACTICES
(*Starting with highest effect and feasibility*)

1. Prioritize friends and family
2. Get involved—in a club, a team, or a civic or religious organization
3. Learn the art of likability
4. Get at least 30 minutes of physical exercise daily
5. Focus on the happiness of others
6. Make a best friend at work
7. Monitor your health
8. Live together, but choose the right spouse
9. Savor life—in the moment or in anticipation of positive future events
10. Set meaningful goals and monitor progress

Expert Profiles and Recommendations

Dan Ariely
Duke University
Durham, North Carolina

Ariely is the James B. Duke Professor of Psychology and Behavioral Economics at Duke University and a founding member of the Center for Advanced Hindsight. He is the author of the best-selling books *Predictably Irrational, The Upside of Irrationality*, and *The Honest Truth about Dishonesty*.

"I do research in behavioral economics and try to describe it in plain language," Ariely writes. "I became engrossed with the idea that we repeatedly and predictably make the wrong decisions in many aspects of our lives and that research could help change some of these patterns."

Recommendation highlights
Public policies: When asked for recommendations about policies that would yield long-term happiness, Ariely said, "If I was the government, I would require some kind of civic service for young people, even if only for three months or six months. It would become like a melting pot, because everybody would have to participate. It would get people to try new things. To volunteer. To view themselves as part of the collective in a deeper way. That's one of the things we're missing. An understanding of our society. Caring about the society at large. Feeling that we're connected to it."

In Israel, where Ariely grew up, he found that the army was a great way to overcome stereotypes. "Having a woman commander in the army telling you exactly what to do is a wonderful thing—particularly for young men to start their lives by having to do push-ups or whatever when a woman commander tells them to is a happiness-creating realization of the world."

Personal practices: Ariely makes two suggestions about ways to boost personal happiness: "1) Have more control over our lives and 2) Know that lack of control results in learned helplessness, reduction in the quality of the immune system, and lots of difficulties, whereas a sense of control, which we can gain in all kinds of ways, is incredibly important." We have control over what we eat, what we buy, how we work, how we manage time with our kids, and so on. The important thing, according to Ariely, is to become aware of our control over these things and to try to gain more control.

Ariely's second point is that we don't always know what will actually make us happy. Ariely explains, "You could say, *Oh, a vacation on the beach makes me happy. Or writing a book would make me happy. Or doing some carpentry, or getting some exercise, or finding some drinking buddies.*" But we don't really know if it will make us happy or not. We don't really have much insight into our own happiness. Thus, his second recommendation is: "Experiment more. Think of it as first-person science."

Mak B. Arvin

Trent University
Peterborough, Ontario, Canada

Arvin is a professor of economics at Trent University, where he has been a faculty member for more than 30 years, and the editor in chief of the *International Journal of Happiness and Development* and the *International Journal of Education Economics and Development*. "In my research, I look at questions involving the consequences of happiness, and also how some different variables could impact on happiness," Arvin said. In addition to the economics of happiness, his research interests include applied microeconomics, applied macroeconomics, and the economics of foreign aid.

Recommendation highlights

Policies and practices: In response to the Blue Zones Happiness Consensus Project, Arvin notes that with respect to both government policies and personal practices, happiness depends on putting into place measures to improve the following interrelated broad factors: 1) physical and mental health and medical care; 2) basic needs (food, shelter, and clothing); 3) empowerment and opportunity; 4) knowledge; 5) family connections (marriage and children); 6) connections with friends, colleagues, and communities (neighborhoods, religious congregations, sports teams, trade unions); and 7) success. Individuals should remember that happiness is not a goal but a byproduct of other activities, Arvin suggests.

Leonardo Becchetti

University of Rome Tor Vergata
Rome, Italy

Becchetti is a professor of economics at the University of Rome Tor Vergata, a public research university in Rome. He is the author of more than 360 works, including 11 edited books and 86 (published or forthcoming) publications in international journals, and he contributes to a blog titled Sustainable Happiness. He has more than 10,000 followers on Twitter (@leonardobecchet).

Recommendation highlights
Policies and practices: In his recommendations to the Blue Zones Happiness Consensus Project, Becchetti points out that unemployment, income inequality, and behaviors such as drinking and gambling have harmful effects on life satisfaction. He endorses a greater emphasis on education, a sense of purpose, gratitude, and social relations.

Robert A. Cummins
Deakin University
Melbourne, Australia

Before he was appointed emeritus professor in 2014, Cummins held a personal chair in psychology at Deakin University. He is a fellow of the Australian Psychological Society and of the International Society for Quality of Life Studies. His special research interest is quality of life, and he is regarded as an international authority in this field. Cummins is the originator of the concept that subjective well-being is under homeostatic control—not unlike how the body maintains its temperature in a steady state. He was the first to demonstrate that each person has a "set-point" for his or her level of subjective well-being and that the dominant composition of subjective well-being is "homeostatically protected mood." Cummins is especially focused on applying this knowledge to understanding the life quality for people who are disabled.

Cummins has published more than 300 books, monographs, chapters, papers, tests, and reports. In 2015, he released a report entitled "What Makes Us Happy," which presented the results of 15 years of research into personal well-being conducted out of Deakin University, using more than 60,000 responses to the Australian Unity Wellbeing Index survey. The Index evaluates life satisfaction across a range of areas—standard of living, health, achievement (purpose) in life, personal relationships, safety, community connection, and future security. Together these metrics are believed to provide a measure of mood happiness.

Recommendation highlights
Public policies: In nations where citizens are exposed to systemic violence or poverty, eliminating these threats to happiness is a clear priority, Cummins says. In developed economies where such threats are no longer systemic, governments should consider public policies that reduce inequality and provide citizens with enough income, support relationships, provide free education at all levels, and reduce unemployment.

Personal practices: The secret to happiness, Cummins suggests, depends on three factors he describes as the Golden Triangle of Happiness: 1) good personal relationships; 2) financial security; and 3) a sense of purpose in life. When these three elements are present, Cummins reported that normal positive levels of mood happiness will almost certainly be found, regardless of age, income, or health status.

Ed Diener

University of Virginia and University of Utah
Charlottesville, Virginia, and Salt Lake City, Utah

Diener is a professor of psychology at the University of Utah and the University of Virginia. He is also Alumni Distinguished Professor of Psychology (Emeritus) at the University of Illinois, where he has been a faculty member since 1974. Since 1999, as a senior scientist, Diener has advised Gallup on research in psychological well-being. His current research focuses on the theories and measurement of well-being, as well as temperament and personality influences on well-being, income and well-being, and cultural influences on well-being. He also studies how employee well-being enhances organizational performance. Diener is the past president of the International Society for Quality of Life Studies, the International Positive Psychology Association, and the Society for Personality and Social Psychology.

As a pioneer in happiness research, Diener is perhaps best known for defining and using the term "subjective well-being," which he calls an umbrella term. "Subjective well-being is the scientific name for how people evaluate their lives," Diener writes. According to this approach, people can evaluate their lives in terms of a global judgment (such as life satisfaction or feelings of fulfillment), in terms of evaluating the domains of their lives (such as marriage or work), or in terms of their ongoing emotional feelings about what is happening to them (feeling pleasant emotions, which arise from positive evaluations of one's experiences, and low levels of unpleasant feelings, which arise from negative evaluations of one's experiences)." The key, Diener explains, is that each person is making his or her own evaluation of life, rather than experts, philosophers, or others. Ask yourself: Is my life going well, according to the standards that I choose to use?

Recommendation highlights

Policies and practices: To promote well-being, Diener suggests that governments should 1) Consider higher unemployment benefits; 2) Consider ways to support marriage; 3) Provide more generous health care coverage; 4) Implement measures to reduce air pollution; 5) Consider polices to provide cleaner water, access to green space, less suburban sprawl, and shorter commutes; 6) Support neighborhoods designed to increase social interaction; 7) Provide mental health programs; 8) Support antibullying measures; 9) Support antidiscrimination measures; 10) Implement tougher smoking laws; and 11) Support more generous parental leave.

Johannes C. Eichstaedt
University of Pennsylvania
Philadelphia, Pennsylvania

Eichstaedt is a dean's scholar and Ph.D. candidate in psychology at the University of Pennsylvania. A former physicist, he co-founded and led the World Well-Being Project in 2011, which now pioneers methods to measure the psychological states of large populations using social media, text mining, and machine learning. Eichstaedt's work has shown that geographic variation in heart disease in the United States can be predicted using Twitter—a finding that drew media attention from around the world and was featured in such publications as *The New Yorker* and the *Washington Post*. In 2014, the American Association for the Advancement of Science elected Eichstaedt an Emerging Leader in Science & Society. He is currently working with governments and international organizations to measure population well-being and health in cheaper and less obtrusive means, via social media. Eichstaedt received an M.S. in the physical sciences with a concentration in particle physics from the University of Chicago and two master's degrees in psychology from the University of Pennsylvania. His major extracurricular passion is taking long-distance, ultralight backpacking expeditions around the world; to date, he has Arctic, Siberian, and many Himalayan traverses under his belt. Eichstaedt actively practices tai chi and qigong and has spent time in monasteries over the years to dive deeper into the practice.

Recommendation highlights
Public policies: Eichstaedt suggests that governments should consider measuring societal well-being in response to public policies; encourage nonprofits, philanthropic organizations, and time off for workers to volunteer in their communities; provide more generous parental leave and a professional child care system; and invest more in early education.

Personal practices: In an ideal world, according to Eichstaedt, kids would have the chance to spend a year doing public service after high school. This would strengthen young people's sense of purpose by letting them explore different activities and values of their own to find something that aligns with world values. To encourage people to connect with others, he recommends mentoring, doing things for others, and training in relationship skills.

Bruno Frey
University of Basel
Basel, Switzerland

Frey is a permanent visiting professor of political economy at the University of Basel as well as the co-founder of the Centre for Research in Economics and Well-Being there.

He is also research director of the Centre for Research in Economics, Management and the Arts, Switzerland. Additionally, Frey is an honorary editor of *Kyklos*, where he served as managing editor from 1969 to 2015. Previously, Frey was a professor of economics at the University of Zurich, a distinguished professor of behavioral science at the Warwick Business School at the University of Warwick, and senior professor of economics at Zeppelin University in Friedrichshafen, Germany. He seeks to extend economics beyond standard neoclassics by including insights from other disciplines, including political science, psychology, and sociology.

In 2015, Frey was ranked third among "important economists" in Switzerland, fifth in the same category in Germany by the newspaper *Frankfurter Allgemeine Zeitung*, and first with respect to "life achievement" in the ranking produced by the German business newspaper *Handelsblatt*.

Recommendation highlights

Public policies: When asked by the Blue Zones Happiness Consensus Project about government policies to promote well-being, Frey responded: "I think governments should not try to maximize happiness," meaning he believes that governments should be reluctant to interfere with the lives of individuals. It would be better, Frey suggests, to give people a way to find their own happiness. How to do that? Give people a sound education, Frey says. Make sure everybody who wants to work can get a job. Maintain a democratic society through political participation. Protect individual rights. Decentralize political decision-making. Give people honest government. "You cannot force people to trust," Frey adds. "Government must behave in a good way. It must keep to the rule of law."

Personal practices: As for enhancing happiness at the individual level, Frey suggests seeking and maintaining good relationships with relatives, friends, and acquaintances. "Such relationships are more important than we think," he says. "Now I try to meet my friends more often."

Carol Graham
Brookings Institution
Washington, D.C.

Graham is Leo Pasvolsky Senior Fellow at the Brookings Institution and College Park Professor at the University of Maryland. She has also served as a vice president at Brookings and as special adviser to the deputy managing director of the International Monetary Fund. She has been a consultant at the Inter-American Development Bank, the World Bank, the United Nations Development Program, and the Harvard Institute for International Development, helping to design safety net programs in Latin America, Africa, and Eastern Europe. Graham has testified in Congress several times and has appeared on NBC News, National Public Radio, and CNN among other media networks. Her writing has been published in the *Wall Street Journal,* the *Christian Science Monitor,* the *Financial Times,* and the *Washington Post,* and her research has been reviewed in *The New Yorker,* the *New York Times,* and *Science,* among other publications. In 2013, Graham received a distinguished research fellow award from the International Society for Quality of Life Studies.

Graham is the author of numerous books and academic articles on poverty, inequality, and well-being, including *Happiness for All? Unequal Hopes and Lives in Pursuit of the American Dream, Happiness Around the World: The Paradox of Happy Peasants and Miserable Millionaires,* and *The Pursuit of Happiness: An Economy of Well-Being.* Her work explores the causes and consequences of happiness, as well as the promise and potential hazards of injecting the "economics of happiness" into public policy making.

Recommendation highlights

Public policies: In Graham's opinion, governments should not be in the business of "providing" happiness. "[Happiness] is a multi-dimensional concept that could be manipulated by politicians—and already is in some countries that have created happiness 'ministries,' such as the UAE in Venezuela," she cautioned. Graham does, however, note that governments can play an important role in measuring well-being, in all of its dimensions, and in making those results available to the public. She believes such information would help individuals understand the trends and patterns underlying happiness outcomes in their own societies (and beyond), and that in turn, they may be able to adapt lifestyles and behaviors in a way that enhances their own well-being.

Personal practices: "People who seek happiness are the least likely to find it," Graham warns. For this, she gives two main reasons: 1) At least some percentage of human happiness is determined by individual character traits, as demonstrated in both psychological and genetics research. The former—psychological research—focuses on positive and negative affect, and the latter—genetic research—focuses on alleles in genes that carry more serotonin. Reason 2) The happiest people are those whose lives "incorporate a range of purposes that go beyond personal enhancement and include volunteering, time with friends/family, and meaningful work." In other words, Graham says, "These people do not seek happiness; they live it."

David Halpern
Chief Executive, The Behavioural Insights Team
London, England

Halpern has led the Behavioural Insights Team (BIT), known as the "nudge unit," since its inception in 2010. Partly owned by the British government, the BIT was created to use behavioral science to "make public services more cost-effective and easier for citizens to use." The BIT puts ideas through tests and trials before making its recommendations.

One of the team's best known experiments was to see if social pressure could be used to persuade people to pay their taxes. The team sent letters to British taxpayers reading: *The vast majority of people in your local area pay their tax on time and people with a tax debt like yours have paid by now.* The experiment raised the rate of tax repayment by five percentage points.

Before joining the BIT, Halpern was the founding director of the London-based Institute for Government and served as the chief analyst at the Prime Minister's Strategy Unit. Before entering government, Halpern held tenure at Cambridge, as well as posts at Oxford and Harvard. Halpern has written several books on subjects relating to behavioral insights and well-being, including *Social Capital, The Hidden Wealth of Nations,* and *Inside the Nudge Unit: How Small Changes Can Make a Big Difference.*

Recommendation highlights

Public policies: Halpern suggests a number of government policies to increase happiness: 1) Create standard measures to track the well-being of populations in a format that enables people to compare their local areas with other regions so they can make better choices for themselves; 2) Increase support for volunteering and giving, including allowing workers to spend at least one day a year doing volunteer work; 3) Provide greater support for professionals treating mental illnesses; 4) Provide lessons in parenting skills; 5) Take measures to reduce unemployment and job insecurity; 6) Implement taxes on gambling; 7) Incentivize individuals to build up rainy-day savings; 8) Increase minimum wages; 9) Provide access to green space; and 10) Reduce corruption and abuse of power.

Personal practices: For individuals, Halpern recommends the "Big Five" to promote greater happiness: 1) Connect with others (listen and engage); 2) Find ways to stay active, including exercise, dancing, singing; 3) Embrace curiosity; 4) Engage in activities that challenge you; and 5) Give of both money and time.

Bruce Headey
University of Melbourne
Melbourne, Australia

Headey is a principal research fellow at the Melbourne Institute of Applied Economic and Social Research. Formerly the director of the Centre for Public Policy, he is a specialist in welfare and distributional issues and at the forefront of international research into the efficacy of social welfare policies in western Europe and North America. Headey has published extensively in Australia on the subject of social welfare policies and related issues that concern life satisfaction, subjective well-being, and income inequality. He co-led a major research project on political agenda setting in Victoria and has carried out a number of inquiries on housing and human services for the Australian and Victorian governments.

Recommendation highlights

Public policies: Headey cautions, "I have seen little convincing evaluation evidence that any government policy change which was specifically intended to enhance life satisfaction actually did so." Headey notes that although there are lots of studies finding relationships between something governments can affect (e.g., air pollution), these relationships, in his words, "do not necessarily show that when the government intervenes to make an apparently desirable change, people are happier rather than just quickly reverting to baseline." Headey adds, however, that he believes we do know enough about the effects of unemployment on life satisfaction to say that reducing it should be a high priority—even if it means more inflation or has other adverse side effects.

Personal practices: Headey recommends that individuals give high priority to pro-social and family values. He further suggests that you 1) Make contributions of time and effort that benefit the community and family members; 2) Exercise regularly; 3) Participate with people you like in social activities, such as social events, sports, and cards; 4) If you are religious, go to church, mosque, or whatever; 5) Find a job that you believe contributes something worthwhile as well as providing income for you; and 6) Sustain good long-term relationships with a partner and family, which Headey says is most critical to happiness.

How to pull it all off? Headey recommends that you try to recognize what makes you happy and then repeat those things. If you don't, the effects of happiness-inducing activities will wear off.

John Helliwell
University of British Columbia
Vancouver, Canada

Recognized as one of the world's leading happiness researchers, Helliwell is a senior fellow of the Canadian Institute for Advanced Research and co-director of the institute's program on Social Interactions, Identity, and Well-Being. He is also Professor Emeritus of Economics at the University of British Columbia, a member of the National Statistics Council, and a Research Associate of the National Bureau of Economic Research. His books include *The Science of Well-Being, Well-Being for Public Policy, International Differences in Well-Being* (edited with Ed Diener and Daniel Kahneman), and the *World Happiness Report* (edited with Richard Layard and Jeffrey Sachs).

Recommendation highlights

Public policies: Happier societies are marked by adequate real per capita incomes, healthy life expectancy, social support, freedom to make key life decisions, generosity, and absence of corruption, according to Helliwell. He says, "Other research has shown that trust in all aspects of life is important, stretching well beyond the absence of corruption in business and government. Furthermore, people are happier in societies where they have a sense of purpose to their lives and where there is less inequality in happiness."

Helliwell emphasizes that citizens will be happier if they are productively engaged in the design and delivery of public services—such as education, policing, health care, and public administration—rather than subject to rigid top-down structures. "Effective governments are those that are respected and 'owned,' rather than simply tolerated or fought, by their citizens," he writes.

Personal practices: Helliwell writes that perhaps the best way to enhance individual happiness is by indirection. Focus on things that will help to make others happy, he says. Rethink daily activities, on and off the job, to increase positive social contacts and connections. "Smiling, trusting, giving of time to shared activities for the benefit of others are all strategies that have been shown by research to create happiness," Helliwell explains. He cautions not to let smartphones interfere with personal relations. Helliwell also recommends spending more time with family and friends, and treating strangers, workmates, customers, and fellow students as friends. To that end, he adds, "Remember the Golden Rule: Treat others as you would hope to have them treat each other and you."

Lord Richard Layard

London School of Economics and Political Science
London, England

Layard is a co-director of the Wellbeing Programme at the Centre for Economic Performance, an interdisciplinary research center at the London School of Economics and Politics. A labor economist, Layard has worked for most of his life on how to reduce unemployment and inequality. He is one of the first economists to work on happiness, and his current main interest is how better mental health could improve social and economic life.

In 1985, Layard founded the Employment Institute, which has played a major role in pushing the idea of welfare-to-work. He was Chairman of the European Commission's Macroeconomic Policy Group during the 1980s. From 1991 to 1997, Layard was a part-time economic adviser to the Russian government, and from 1997 to 2001, he served as part-time consultant to the British government on welfare-to-work and vocational education. In 2000, Layard was made a member of the House of Lords, and he is currently a member of its Economic Affairs Committee.

In 2005, the British government accepted Layard's proposals on psychological therapy, and since then he has, as an adviser, been heavily involved in implementing the government program Improving Access to Psychological Therapies (IAPT). In 2010 the program was extended to cover children.

Recommendation highlights

Policies and practices: To promote well-being, Layard recommends that governments offer "evidence-based psychological therapy to all the one-sixth of the population with depression or anxiety disorders." He points to the IAPT program in England as a good model of that. Started in 2008, the IAPT now treats half a million adults annually. All outcomes are monitored, and 50 percent of participants recover in the period of treatment (the average duration is seven sessions). An editorial in the journal *Nature* called the initiative "world-beating." Layard writes, "The same principles should be applied to children and young people, and [that is] being done in England." Layard also recommended teaching life skills in schools and parenting classes to adults.

Richard Lucas

Michigan State University
East Lansing, Michigan

Lucas is a professor of psychology at Michigan State University. As director of the MSU Personality and Well-Being Lab, he explores the causes, consequences, and measurement of subjective well-being. Specifically, Lucas focuses on three interrelated questions about positive emotional experiences. First, he investigates the associations between personality traits and well-being, particularly the relation between extraversion and positive affect. He uses the results of these studies to develop theories about the functions of emotions and the mechanisms underlying personality traits. Second, Lucas investigates more general questions regarding the causes and consequences of positive emotional well-being. For example, he has examined the extent to which factors such as age, sex, marital status, and unemployment are associated with well-being, and the extent to which people can adapt to major life events. And finally, in all of these projects, Lucas pays careful attention to measurement issues, focusing on the quality of the measures that we use to assess personality and well-being. He has also been involved in efforts to improve research practices in psychology and other sciences, including promoting replication in studies.

Recommendation highlights

Public policies: Lucas suggests that the most effective public policies might be those that target finances and health, in particular, policies that address poverty or stress related to health problems.

Personal practices: For individuals, Lucas emphasizes the importance of 1) Maintaining a strong romantic relationship; 2) Maintaining a number of close, supportive nonromantic relationships; 3) Finding some occupation/hobby/activity that is engaging and provides a sense of purpose; 4) Having enough money to meet basic needs; 5) Having enough money to avoid worrying about money; 6) Having enough money to increase the opportunity for enjoyment; and 7) Being able to avoid major health problems.

The Blue Zones of Happiness

Sonja Lyubomirsky
University of California, Riverside
Riverside, California

Lyubomirsky is a professor of psychology at the University of California, Riverside, and the author of the books *The How of Happiness: A New Approach to Getting the Life You Want* and *The Myths of Happiness: What Should Make You Happy but Doesn't, What Shouldn't Make You Happy, but Does*. She received her B.A. from Harvard University and her Ph.D. in social psychology from Stanford University. Lyubomirsky and her research have received many honors, including the 2002 Templeton Positive Psychology Prize and a multiyear grant from the National Institute of Mental Health.

The majority of Lyubomirsky's research career has been devoted to studying human happiness. Her current research addresses three critical questions: 1) What makes people happy? 2) Is happiness a good thing? and 3) How can we make people happier still?

Kristin Layous
California State University, East Bay
Hayward, California

Layous is an assistant professor of psychology at California State University, East Bay, in Hayward, California. Her doctoral adviser at the University of California, Riverside was Lyubomirsky. Layous says that, broadly, her interest is in using psychology to improve people's lives. She is currently investigating the complex nature of gratitude—how it may be simultaneously uplifting and slightly uncomfortable. Layous is also exploring how positive activities can mitigate maladaptive habits such as rumination.

Layous and Lyubomirsky submitted their recommendations together to the Blue Zones Consensus on Happiness.

Recommendation highlights
Public policies: Layous and Lyubomirsky suggest that governments should support policies that ensure at least a minimum standard of living for citizens. Specifically, their recommendations to governments to promote social interaction include: 1) Sponsor low-cost social events such as state fairs and festivals to promote social interaction; 2) Create publicly accessible green spaces such as parks to promote interaction between citizens and nature; 3) Protect religious freedom to promote social activities as well as spiritual and religious ones; 4) Make health care and mental health care accessible to citizens; 5) Sponsor low-cost public gyms, races, and better education in schools about keeping active; 6) Subsidize healthy foods (or tax unhealthy foods); and 7) Teach healthy diets in schools.

Layous and Lyubomirsky further recommend that governments should: 8) Encourage volunteering through tax breaks and help support websites that connect people with volunteer organizations; 9) Make education affordable and effective for people of all socioeconomic statuses; 10) Change the time that schools start to promote better sleep and encourage policies to make workweek hours and payment more flexible; 11) To decrease stress, make cities safer, adopt policies that help people have a livable income, make social support systems stronger, improve education, better prepare for emergency situations, strengthen family relationships, and strengthen laws against abusers; and 12) Consider funding for schools to teach emotion regulation and happiness strategies.

Personal practices: According to Layous and Lyubomirsky, individuals who want to experience greater happiness should try the following practices: 1) Consider writing gratitude letters; 2) Count blessings; 3) Practice savoring; 4) Share personal positive experiences with a partner on a regular basis; 5) Perform kind or pro-social acts (including spending on others); 6) Try to make someone else happier; 7) Live this month like it's your last (to help you appreciate the people and surroundings that make your life enjoyable); 8) Write about an intensely positive experience; 9) Write a forgiveness letter; 10) Practice loving-kindness meditation; 11) Visualize your best possible self; 12) Identify signature strengths and then use them; 13) Set goals and monitor them; 14) Laugh and use humor on a regular basis; 15) Engage in physical exercise on a regular basis; 16) Act extroverted (even if you aren't); 17) Seek activities with the right balance of challenge and skill to increase "flow" experiences; 18) Practice religion and spirituality (if fitting); 19) Maintain an attitude of self-compassion; 20) Prioritize close and fulfilling social relationships; 21) Regularly go out in nature; 22) Establish routines that promote adequate sleep (such as limiting screen time before bed); 23) Spend money on experiences rather than material possessions; and 24) Engage in activities that promote feelings of competence, connectedness, and autonomy.

Andrew Oswald

University of Warwick
Coventry, England

Oswald is a professor of economics and behavioural science at the University of Warwick. His research is principally in applied economics and quantitative social science and currently includes the empirical study of job satisfaction, human happiness, unemployment, labor productivity, and the influence of diet on psychological well-being. Oswald serves on the board of editors of *Science* magazine and is the principal adviser on economics and business research at the Leverhulme Trust. He was formerly Research Director at the IZA Institute in Bonn in Germany and Pro-Dean (Research) at Warwick Business School.

Oswald previously held posts as an associate, Institute of Economics and Statistics, at Oxford and as senior research fellow, Centre for Economic Performance, at the London School of Economics, with spells as lecturer, Princeton University; DeWalt Ankeny Professor of Economics, Dartmouth College; Jacob Wertheim Fellow, Harvard

University; visiting fellow, Cornell University; visiting fellow, University of Zurich; and visiting fellow, Yale University.

Oswald has a long-standing interest in labor markets and continues his research on job satisfaction and stress in the workplace. He pursues such questions as: To what extent does economic progress improve psychological well-being? Some of this is joint research with the psychologist Professor Gordon D. A. Brown. He is also interested in status, especially in work settings, and in understanding how the state of the mind affects physical health and longevity. He co-wrote *The Wage Curve* and *Pay Determination and Industrial Prosperity*.

Recommendation highlights

Public policies: Oswald suggests high levels of unemployment benefits and cleaning up the air to promote greater happiness at the community and national levels.

Personal practices: "If we are looking for simple and implementable strategies," says Oswald, "I would advise people to alter their diet—in particular, to eat more fruit and vegetables."

Ruut Veenhoven
Erasmus University
Rotterdam, Netherlands

A leading happiness expert, Veenhoven was co-director of the Blue Zones Happiness Consensus Project. He is director of the World Database of Happiness as well as emeritus professor of Social Conditions for Human Happiness at Erasmus University in Rotterdam and extraordinary professor at North-West University Vaal Triangle Campus in Vanderbijlpark, South Africa. Veenhoven was also a founding editor of the *Journal of Happiness Studies* (JOHS).

Veenhoven's current research is on subjective quality of life. He is the author of the books *Conditions of Happiness* and *Happiness in Nations* as well as numerous research papers, including "The Four Qualities of Life," and "Greater Happiness for a Greater Number: Is That Possible and Desirable?" Veenhoven has also written published work on the topics of abortion, love, marriage, and parenthood.

Recommendation highlights

Public policies: To promote well-being, Veenhoven suggests that policy should 1) Provide a predictable institutional environment, including rule of law and good governance; 2) Support stable economic growth; 3) Provide basic social security (health care, old age pensions, unemployment benefits)—and he adds that such lavish levels as are provided in Scandinavian countries are not required; 4) Maximize freedom—economic, political, and private freedom; 5) Support equal rights rather than equal incomes; 6) Support ongoing modernization, including globalization; 7) Support autonomy development in education; 8) Invest in mental health care; 9) Professionalize the life-coaching business; and 10) Invest in happiness research.

Personal practices: For individuals, Veenhoven suggests that you 1) Keep active, whether paid or unpaid; 2) Invest in intimate ties, marriage, in particular—loners are mostly unhappy, he says; 3) Be generous: give and help; 4) Live healthy and, in particular, get sufficient sleep; 5) When looking for a more satisfying way of life, monitor how you feel during daily activities using (electronic) diary techniques, especially those that involve comparison with similar people. If you're not too happy in your current life situation, Veenhoven says, "Dare to change. Though this involves the risk of going from the frying pan into the fire, it mostly works out positively." If you're unhappy and you do not know why, Veenhoven encourages you to seek professional advice/therapy. He adds that such help is effective most of the time; 6) Buy your house rather than rent. Homeownership adds to happiness, according to Veenhoven; 7) Reduce commuting time; and 8) Save money and stay out of debt.

Heinz Welsch
University of Oldenburg
Oldenburg, Germany

Welsch is a professor of economics at the University of Oldenburg. He was previously a senior research fellow at the University of Cologne and a research fellow at the University of Bonn. He has written about the relationships between reported subjective well-being and environmental quality, especially air pollution. He has also written about the costs of social conflict in terms of national happiness, as well as about income distribution, unemployment, and financial crises.

In response to the Blue Zones Happiness Consensus Project, Welsch notes that his suggestions are "confined to those branches of happiness research to which I have made original contributions. The suggestions are informed by empirical evidence from those branches of the literature. Some of that evidence is confined to Western, economically developed nations; transferability to developing nations is not necessarily straightforward."

Recommendation highlights
Public policies: Welsch suggests that governments should 1) Combat excessive inequality of incomes and wealth by means of progressive income taxes, property taxes, and inheritance taxes; 2) Enact policies that minimize unemployment, in particular long-term unemployment, even if associated with increased inflation. He explains that being unemployed negatively affects individual well-being far beyond the effects of the associated losses in income. Long-term unemployment is particularly detrimental to well-being, and there exists little hedonic adaptation to unemployment; 3) Enact regulation that minimizes systemic instability of financial markets and the risk of major

financial crises. Welsch notes that in those countries that the financial crisis of 2008–2009 affected most strongly, well-being dropped to a degree comparable to the effect of major personal life events (such as divorce); and 4) Both governments and society should concentrate more on environmental aims and less on monetary or materialistic ones. The literature suggests that "green variables" have large direct effects on human well-being, Welsch notes, whereas greater consumption of things in Western society cannot be expected to make us much happier.

Personal practices: Welsch recommends that individuals focus on activities that are intrinsically rewarding (such as spending time with friends and family, or participating in pro-environmental or pro-social behavior) rather than those that promise external rewards (such as the acquisition of wealth, or materialistic consumption). People fail to correctly anticipate the consequences of their choices for their own individual well-being. The satisfaction people expect to get from extrinsically motivated choices tends to be overrated, relative to the satisfaction they get from intrinsically motivated choices, he says.

Dan Witters
Gallup-Sharecare
Omaha, Nebraska

Witters is research director of the Gallup-Sharecare Well-Being Index. This daily assessment of U.S. residents' well-being provides near-real–time measurement and insights needed to improve health, increase daily productivity, enhance basic needs, and lower health care costs. A researcher at Gallup for more than 25 years, Witters presents regularly at well-being–related conferences and summits around the country. His insights from this work appear regularly on Gallup.com and in the media. Witters's recommendations for the Blue Zones Happiness Consensus Project are based on the Gallup-Sharecare Well-Being Index.

Recommendation highlights
Public policies: To promote broader well-being, Witters suggests: 1) Providing a strong, sustained voice of commitment to well-being. One of the biggest mistakes that leaders can make is to treat well-being as nothing more than a benefits program or, in his words, "some sort of fringe, flavor-of-the-month initiative"; 2) Verbalizing a consistent and uniform definition of what is meant by well-being. Leaders of communities and organizations need to be on the same page about what well-being *is;* 3) Leading by example, setting the agenda, and using the bully pulpit. This doesn't just mean appearing at local events or showing up in the company fitness center, Witters says. It also means establishing hard policies in city or state workplaces that directly influence the foods employees consume, how they are incentivized for good health, the opportunities and encouragement they receive for building financial security, and what is expected of

their conduct at home and in their communities; 4) Ensuring that residents believe their well-being is authentically cared about; 5) Scientifically evaluating the effectiveness of programs as a function of change in well-being over time. Among the biggest misses observed inside of communities that execute well-being interventions is to actually *test* whether they are working. Witters suggests that leaders should be asking *What percentage of residents are participating in programs that stand to benefit them? How does their well-being change over time?* Keep funding the programs that are doing some good, he urges. Drop the programs that aren't; 6) Increasing investment in learning. Cities that offer their residents rich opportunities to learn new and interesting things commonly have low obesity and low smoking rates; 7) Providing easy access to fresh fruits and vegetables. Cities with high well-being often have farmers markets that are readily accessible to the public, grocery stores that prioritize high-quality produce, and restaurants that default to fruits or vegetables instead of fries with their entrées; 8) Making sure there are safe places to exercise. Nearly all cities with high well-being provide their residents with safe places to exercise, something workplaces can emulate; and 9) Getting people to the dentist. People who go to the dentist at least once a year have considerably higher well-being than those who don't, which is one reason why a common feature of the U.S. cities with top well-being is good oral health.

Personal practices: For individual well-being, Witters recommends that you 1) Manage your money well and live within your means; 2) Have a vocation in life that is well aligned with your natural aptitudes; 3) Set and reach goals on an ongoing basis; 4) Make time for trips or vacations with family or friends; 5) Use your strengths to do what you do best every day; 6) Feel safe and secure in your community; 7) Learn something new or interesting every day; 8) Have someone in your life who encourages you to be healthy; 9) Maintain a healthy diet; 10) Get to the dentist at least once per year; and 11) Do something to help improve the city or area where you live.

Acknowledgments

S UCCESS, AS THE SAYING GOES, has many mothers. In the case of Blue Zones, it has a father too. Peter Miller first recognized the potential of Blue Zones in 2004 when he assigned me a cover story for *National Geographic* magazine. Since then, his editorial genius has shaped three best-selling books, along with this one. Without him, the blue spark of the idea to reverse engineer well-being might have been extinguished early.

To the editorial team, Susan Hitchcock and Anne Smyth, researcher Lia Miller, National Geographic Partners editorial director Susan Goldberg, communication virtuosos Ann Day and Kathleen Carter Zrelak, and especially National Geographic Books publisher and editorial director Lisa Thomas, who has commissioned every Blue Zones book and orchestrated their success, I am deeply grateful.

Ruut Veenhoven, the consummately kind and avuncular curator of the World Database of Happiness, has generously provided me data-backed insights for more than a decade. He, along with University of Minnesota epidemiologist Dr. Toben Nelson, helped design and execute the Blue Zones Happiness Consensus—a 10-month effort. The consensus idea was born over breakfast in Minneapolis with the late, great Dr. Robert Kane of the University of Minnesota's School of Public Health. I'd also like to thank Aislinn Pluta for her help with happiness research.

To the University of Pennsylvania's wunderkind, Johannes Eichstaedt, who is pioneering the mining of social media data to understand the human psyche, I give my thanks. Since I met him at a UN World Happiness Summit in 2012 he has generously offered expertise on everything from statistical analysis to how to buy liquor in Dubai.

Gallup's senior scientist Dan Witters, who possesses an uncanny gift for mining and communicating complex survey analyses, generously created the National Geographic Gallup Special Index to identify America's happiest place. Also for this book, he did a deep dive into more than two million surveys to distill the true drivers of happiness in America. I also want to thank CEO Jim Clifton, Jim Harter, and Kristopher Hodgins of Gallup for their generosity and expertise.

Of the dozens of academic experts who've contributed to this book, I'd like to especially recognize Ed Diener, John Helliwell, Richard Layard, Sonja Lyubomirsky, David Chan, Dan Ariely, and Carol Graham.

The Blue Zones of Happiness

National Geographic photographer David McLain, my collaborator on a dozen stories, helped conceive the original story and bring it to life visually.

In Denmark, journalist Anders Weber has been a guide, translator, and consummate interpreter for nearly a decade of research there. I'd also like to thank Peter Gundelach, an early academic expert on Danish happiness, and the crew in Ledreborg, Silvia and Jock Munro, Martin Krusbaek, Martin Ritter, Joseph de Bourbon-Parme, Kris Kent, Karim Aoussar, Frederik Bligaard, and especially my mentor and Life Virtuoso, Remar Sutton. They've all provided valuable insights and guidance on the Danish lifestyle.

In Costa Rica, my longtime fixer Jorge Vindas, the king of "can-do," completely coordinated my Costa Rica research. He wrangled interviews with everyone from presidents and Nobel Prize laureates to transvestite hookers. Also, to Luis Rosero-Bixby and Alvaro Salas for their health care expertise, geneticist David Rehkopf, former presidents Óscar Arias and José María Figueres, and current president Luis Guillermo Solís, I wish to express my thanks. Special thanks to Dr. Fernando Morales, who rescued me from a vicious lung infection that might have put an early end to this book.

In Singapore, I especially want to thank Sharon and Hilda Chaung. In their quiet and uber-efficient Singaporean way, they fulfilled every manner of strange requests. Thanks also to Kumar, Donald Low, and Janadas Devan. And to the late Lee Kuan Yew and his son, current Prime Minister Lee Hsien Loong, I'd like to express my gratitude for the rare access they gave me. I'd also like to thank Jok Kwang for showing me the country behind bars, and Jennie Chua, Singapore's Grand Dame.

In Boulder, Patrick von Keyserling helped orchestrate my visit and Christina Allen shared her keen insider views.

At the Blue Zones headquarters I'd like to thank Aislinn Leonard, Gemma Miltich, Amelia Clabots, Tony Buettner, Nick Buettner, Ben Leedle, and Sam Skemp. I'd also like to give a special shout-out to Samantha Thomas and Dan Burden for lending their vast city design expertise to the effort. My colleagues at Sharecare who help me deploy the lessons in this book to American cities include Jeff Arnold, Ken Goulet, Alfred Lumsdaine, Michael Acker, Jennifer Sanning, Jennifer Furler, and Shannon Sanders. And to the unsinkable Mayor Betsy Price of Fort Worth; Susan Burden, former CEO of the Beach Cities Health District; Barclay Berdan, CEO of Texas Health Resources; Mike Gold and Elisa Yadao of the Hawaii Medical Service Association; Allen Weiss, CEO of NCH Healthcare System; Mark Ganz, CEO of Cambia Health Solutions; Kim Miller, CEO of Beaver Dam Community Hospitals; Michelle Briggs, CEO of Avedis Foundation in Shawnee, Oklahoma; and Randy Kehr, Ellen Kehr, and Chad Adams, who are still keeping Albert Lea, Minnesota a Blue Zone community, I'd like to express my gratitude.

Finally, I'd like to thank my father, Roger, for instilling my curiosity, and my mother, Dolly, for nurturing it.

Selected Sources

Part 1: Blueprint for a Happier Life

Diener, E., S. Oishi, and R. Lucas. "Advances and Open Questions in the Science of Subjective Well-Being." Submitted to *Psychological Bulletin* (2017).

———. "National Accounts of Subjective Well-Being." *American Psychologist* (April 2015).

Dolan, Paul. *Happiness by Design: Finding Pleasure and Purpose in Everyday Life.* Allen Lane, 2014.

Graham, Carol, and Julia Ruiz Pozuelo. "Is Happiness Just a Matter of Waiting for the Right Age?" *Brookings Institution* 7 (November 2015).

Howell, R., M. Kern, and S. Lyubomirsky. "Health Benefits: Meta-Analytically Determining the Impact of Well-Being on Objective Health Outcomes." *Health Psychology Review* (March 2007): 83–136.

Newman, David B., Louis Tay, and Ed Diener. "Leisure and Subjective Well-Being: A Model of Psychological Mechanisms as Mediating Factors." *Journal of Happiness Studies* 15, no. 3 (2013): 555–78.

Part 2: The World's Happiest Places

Bearak, Max. "Denmark Says You Are 'Ethically Obligated' to Eat Less Beef." *Washington Post,* April 28, 2016.

Bixby, L. "Assessing the Impact of Health Sector Reform in Costa Rica through a Quasi-Experimental Study." *American Journal of Public Health* (2004).

Chan, D. "Find Your Own Meaning in Life." *The Straits Times*, June 11, 2016. bsi.smu .edu.sg/news/2016/06/11/find-your-own-meaning-life.

Graham, Carol, and Juliane Wiese. "The New (Latin) American Dream, Part 1." Brookings Institution, July 21, 2015.

"Hell Is Other People, for Swedes." *The Economist* 27 (February 2016).

Helliwell, J., R. Layard, and J. Sachs, eds. *World Happiness Report 2015.* Sustainable Development Solutions Network, 2015.

———. *World Happiness Report 2016, Update (Vol. I).* Sustainable Development Solutions Network, 2016.

———. *World Happiness Report 2017*. Sustainable Development Solutions Network, 2017.

"How's Life in Denmark." OECD Better Life Initiative, October 2015.

Neslen, Arthur. "Copenhagen Set to Divest from Fossil Fuels." *The Guardian,* January 29, 2016.

"On Global Warming, World Seeks Viking Leadership." CBS News, April 20, 2016.

Ordóñez, J., S. Andrews, and P. DeGennaro. "The Republic of Costa Rica: A Case Study on the Process of Democracy Building." International Development Research Centre, Canada (2008).

Quality of Life in European Cities. European Commission, January 2016.

Rosero-Bixby, Luis. "Socioeconomic Development, Health Interventions, and Mortality Decline in Costa Rica." Scandinavian Journal of *Social Medicine Supplementum* 46 (1991): 33–42.

———. "Studies of the Costa Rican Model I: Peace, Health, and Development in Costa Rica." *NHV-Report* 5 (December 1991).

Rosero-Bixby, Luis, William H. Dow, and David H. Rehkopf. "The Nicoya Region of Costa Rica: A High Longevity Island for Elderly Males." *Vienna Yearbook of Population Research* 11 (2013): 109–36.

Rosero-Bixby, Luis, and William H. Dow. "Exploring Why Costa Rica Outperforms the United States in Life Expectancy: A Tale of Two Inequality Gradients." *Proceedings of the National Academy of Sciences* 113, no. 5 (2015).

Stutzer, A., and F. Frey. "Recent Developments in the Economics of Happiness: A Selective Overview." Institute for the Study of Labor (IZA), 2012.

Wiking, Meik, ed. *The Happy Danes: Exploring the Reasons Behind the High Levels of Happiness in Denmark*. The Happiness Research Institute, 2014.

Part 3: Happier by Design

Aknin, L., et al. "Prosocial Spending and Well-Being: Cross-Cultural Evidence for a Psychological Universal." *Journal of Personality and Social Psychology* (2013), 635–52.

Arnold, J., A. Graesch, and E. Ragazzini. *Life at Home in the Twenty-First Century: 32 Families Open Their Doors*. Cotsen Institute of Archaeology Press, 2012.

Blanchflower, David, Andrew Oswald, and Sarah Stewart-Brown. "Is Psychological Well-Being Linked to the Consumption of Fruit and Vegetables?" NBER Working Paper No. 18469 (October 2012).

Bradberry, T. "13 Habits of Exceptionally Likeable People." *Forbes* (January 27, 2015), Forbes.com.

Chancellor, J., et al. "Everyday Prosociality in the Workplace: The Reinforcing Benefits of Giving, Getting, and Glimpsing." *Emotion* (in press).

Christakis, Nicholas A., and James H. Fowler. *Connected: The Surprising Power of Our Social Networks and How They Shape Our Lives*. Little, Brown, 2009.

Cohn, Michael A., et al. "Happiness Unpacked: Positive Emotions Increase Life Satisfaction by Building Resilience." *Emotion* (June 2009), 361–68.

Croezen, S., et al. "Social Participation and Depression in Old Age: A Fixed-Effects Analysis in 10 European Countries." *American Journal of Epidemiology* 182, no. 2 (May 2015): 168–76.

Csikszentmihalyi, Mihaly. *Finding Flow: The Psychology of Engagement with Everyday Life.* BasicBooks, 1997.

Diener, Ed, and Robert Biswas-Diener. *Happiness: Unlocking the Mysteries of Psychological Wealth.* Wiley-Blackwell, 2008.

Diener, E., J. De Neve, L. Tay, and C. Xuereb. "The Objective Benefits of Subjective Well-Being." *World Happiness Report, 2013.* Sustainable Development Solutions Network, 2013.

Diener, E., and M. Chan. "Happy People Live Longer: Subjective Well-Being Contributes to Health and Longevity." *Applied Psychology: Health and Well-Being* (2001): 1–43.

Dunn, E., D. Gilbert, and T. Wilson. "If Money Doesn't Make You Happy, Then You Probably Aren't Spending It Right." *Journal of Consumer Psychology* (2011): 115–125.

Edwards, M., and L. Abadie. "Zinnias from Space! NASA Studies the Multiple Benefits of Gardening." NASA (April 25, 2016), www.nasa.gov/content.

Eichstaedt, J. "Status Update: Stressed, Angry, At Risk? Using Powerful New Tools, Scientists Are Mining Social Media to Assess Mental and Physical Health from Afar." *Scientific American Mind* (2016): 63–67.

Meyer, William B. "Book Review: *Happiness and Place: Why Life Is Better Outside of the City* by Adam Okulicz-Kozaryn." *LSE Review of Books* 18 (December 2015).

von Tobel, Alexa. "5 Financial Rules to Live By." Presentation, TEDx, New York, N.Y., April 2012.

Index

"Dan Buettner has gathered some of the top scientists in the world to study so-called blue zones. He wrote the book about these remarkable places where it's been proven people tend to live longer."—**NBC News**

"Buettner would like to draw a big blue circle around the entire USA." —**USA Today**

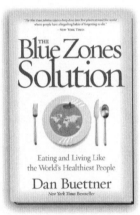

"... The Blue Zones Solution *takes a deep dive into five places around the world where people have a beguiling habit of forgetting to die.*"—**New York Times**

"*The Cheater's Guide to Living to 100: 4 super-simple secrets to living longer, healthier and happier—from longevity expert Dan Buettner and centenarians around the world.*"—**Parade**

"*In addition to sharing his extraordinary accounts of the happiest people on the planet, Buettner details how to incorporate these powerful characteristics into our daily routine so that we, too, can thrive.*"—**Psychology Today**

"*[Buettner] also recommends 'land-mining your home with photos and memorabilia, so you're constantly reminded of your history.' Adorning a hallway or a highly trafficked room with sentimental objects is a good way to start.*"—**Real Simple**